Learning MICROSOFT WORD 2013

Other Titles by the Same Authors

- PageMaker 7
- 3D Max
- Computer Fundamentals
- Java 7
- Internet & E-mail
- HTML 5
- JavaScript with HTML 5
- Visual Basic 6
- SQL
- Web Designing
- Multimedia
- Networking
- PC Hardware
- Desk Top Publishing
- C
- C++
- Windows XP
- Windows Vista
- Windows 7
- Windows XP, Vista, Office 2007 & Internet & E-mail
- MS Office XP
- MS Access 2013
- MS Excel 2013
- MS Word 2013
- MS Office 2013
- MS Access 2007
- MS Excel 2007
- MS Word 2007
- MS Office 2007
- Tally 9.0 with ERP
- Dreamweaver CS4
- CorelDRAW X4
- Photoshop CS4
- Flash CS4
- Illustrator CS4
- Microsoft Access 2010
- Microsoft Excel 2010
- Microsoft Word 2010
- Microsoft Office 2010
- AutoCAD 2010
- Dreamweaver CS5
- CorelDraw X5
- Flash CS5
- Illustrator CS5
- Photoshop CS5
- ASP.Net 4.0
- C# 4.0
- ASP.Net and C#.Net
- Tally 9.0 (Hindi)
- Internet & E-mail (Hindi)
- Desk Top Publishing (Hindi)

Learning MICROSOFT WORD 2013

Ramesh Bangia
B.Sc., Dip. Comp. Sc.
Formerly Managing Editor, Software Today
Formerly Incharge Computer Centre, Hindustan Copper Ltd., New Delhi

KHANNA BOOK PUBLISHING CO. (P) LTD.
::: Publisher of Engineering and Computer Books::

Head Ofice : 4C/4344, Ansari Road, Darya Ganj, New Delhi-110002
Phone : 011-23244447/48 **Fax** : 011-23244447
Regd. Ofice : 1694-95, Nai Sarak, Delhi-110006
Phone : 011-23283211 **Fax** : 011-23256658
E-Mail : contact@khannabooks.com
Website : www.khannabooks.com, www.khannapublishers.com

Learning MICROSOFT WORD 2013
Ramesh Bangia

ISBN : 978-93-82609-35-3
First Edition : 2014

Published by:
KHANNA BOOK PUBLISHING CO. (P) LTD.
4C/4344, Ansari Road, Darya Ganj, New Delhi-110 002
Phone: 011-23244447-48 **Fax:** 011-23244447
E-mail: contact@khannabooks.com
Website: www.khannabooks.com, www.khannapublishers.com

Regd. Off: 1694-95, 1st Floor, Nai Sarak, Delhi-110006 (India)
Phone: 011-23283211 Telefax: 011-23256658

Printed in India by:
S.P.S. Printers & Binders, Delhi

PREFACE

Learning of a software is both easy and difficult. It depends upto what level you are planning to learn. If you are learning only for the working use, then it is very easy. But, when you try to go deep into it, then you realise how difficult it is to master it.

Microsoft Word 2013 is such a vast subject that it will take a lot of time to understand it fully. This book has been written in mind to make you aware of the options available in the software and how they can be used. It is like telling the child about the steps and stairs. You are the one who is to climb the stair. This book will just guide you how to use the stairs.

I am indeed debited to my publishers Khanna Book Publishing Co. Pvt. Ltd. for their suggestions and encouragement given in producing this book.

I would like to thank my family specially my wife Sadhna, kids Mayank and Samarth, for without their criticism this book would not have seen the day.

Suggestions for improvement of the book are indeed welcome.

Ramesh Bangia

CONTENTS

CHAPTER 1

Introduction to Microsoft Office 2013

Introduction

Microsoft Office 2013 comes in twelve different editions, including three editions for retail outlets, two editions for volume licensing channel, five subscription-based editions available through Microsoft Office 365 program, the web application edition known as Office Web Apps and the Office RT edition made for tablets and mobile devices. Office Web Apps are available free of charge on the web although enterprises may obtain for on-premises installation for a price.

What is Microsoft Office?

There are software and software. But, when you come to using the computer and a single software which can do everything for you, the choice mostly is Microsoft Office. This is not a software but a combination of software which can perform various aspects of your office routines. It can be writing letters, maintaining accounts, keeping databases, making a presentation, etc. This Microsoft Office has a solution for everything.

Microsoft Office 2013 (formerly Office 15) is a version of Microsoft Office, a productivity suite for Microsoft Windows. It is the successor of Microsoft Office 2013 and includes extended file format support, user interface updates and support for touch among its new features. Office 2013 is suitable for IA-32 and x64 systems and requires Windows 7, Windows Server 2008 R2 or later version of either. A version of Office 2013 comes included on Windows RT devices.

Development on this version of Microsoft Office was started in 2013 and ended on October 11, 2012 when Microsoft Office 2013 was released to manufacturing. Microsoft released Office 2013 to general availability on 29 January 2013. This version includes new features such as integration support for online services (including SkyDrive, Outlook.com, Hotmail, Skype, Yammer and Flickr), improved format support for Office Open XML (OOXML), OpenDocument (ODF) and Portable Document Format (PDF) and support for multi-touch interfaces.

Microsoft Office applications may be obtained individually; this includes Microsoft Visio, Microsoft Project and Microsoft SharePoint Designer which are not included in any of the twelve editions.

Let us take a look at the various constituents which are there in Microsoft Office 2013.

Microsoft Office Word 2013

A word processing software which allows you to write letters, edit them and print them after formatting it according to your needs. It has all the possible options of a word processor in the form of font style and size; indents; line spacing; margins; spell checking and grammar checkers to name a few.

Microsoft Office Excel 2013

This spreadsheet program allows you to manipulate and present your data in almost any way you choose. It allows you to work on a tabular pad consisting of columns and rows where you can perform all your mathematical, financial and statistical calculations. These calculations can be as simple as totalling a row or column of values or as complex as figuring the rate of return on an investment under varying circumstances. It also allows you to make a graphical representation of all your data in the form of 2-dimensional or 3-dimensional graph or pie chart.

Microsoft Office Access 2013

A software to take care of most of your database requirements. It allows you to store and organize information in sets of tables, which can be displayed in the form of columns and rows to look like a table or an index card. What's more it allows you to perform calculations and find for you simple statistics like totals and averages. It allows you to sort the data in any form and extract the required information based on the key given by you.

Lineup of Microsoft Office 2013 icons, from left to right: Word, Excel, PowerPoint, Outlook, Access, OneNote, Publisher, Lync and InfoPath. Absent in this lineup: Visio, Project, SharePoint Designer and SkyDrive Pro

Microsoft Office PowerPoint 2013

Want to make a presentation in a hurry! This is an ideal program of the same. Make sophisticated slide shows and professional looking electronic presentations. It also allows you to add charts, tables and pictures for make the presentation look alive.

Microsoft Office Outlook 2013

It is an electronic tool for managing appointments, addresses, e-mail, and notes. With lots of stress being given to the e-mail these days, it is an ideal software for sending and receiving e-mail.

Microsoft Office Publisher 2013

It is Microsoft's answer to the various other publishing software available in the market like PageMaker. It allows you to create invitations, design business-cards, and letter-heads, make your own calenders, produce newsletter, etc.

Microsoft Office OneNote 2013

It is used to gather information during meetings, brainstorming sessions, interviews, and more. The notes you create can include text, drawings, images, and audio recordings. OneNote uses a freeform page layout, so you can place and move information wherever you want.

Microsoft Office InfoPath Designer 2013/InfoPath Filler 2013

Microsoft Office InfoPath is a software application for designing, distributing, filling and submitting electronic forms containing structured data. According to one of its inventors, a key architectural design decision was "to adhere to the XML paradigm of separating the data in a document from the formatting." Thus the product features a WYSIWYG form design area in which the various controls (dropdowns, text boxes, etc.) are bound to data fields represented separately as a hierarchical tree view of folders and data fields.

Microsoft Office Lync 2013

Microsoft Lync (formerly Microsoft Office Communicator) and Microsoft Lync for Mac are instant messaging clients used with Microsoft Lync Server or Lync Online available with Microsoft Office 365 and Live@Edu. They are replacements for Windows Messenger which was used with Microsoft Exchange Server.

Both Microsoft Lync and Microsoft Lync for Mac are enterprise software; unlike Windows Live Messenger, they have a different feature set that is targeted toward corporate environments.

Microsoft Office SkyDrivePro 2013

SkyDrive (officially Microsoft SkyDrive, previously Windows Live SkyDrive and Windows Live Folders) is a file hosting service that allows users to upload and sync files to a cloud storage and then access them from a Web browser or their local device. It is part of the Windows Live range of online services and allows users to keep the files private, share them with contacts, or make the files public. Publicly shared files do not require a Microsoft account to access.

The service offers 7 GB of free storage for new users. Additional storage is available for purchase. Users who signed up to SkyDrive prior to April 22, 2012 could opt-in for a limited time offer of 25 GB of free storage upgrade. The service is built using HTML5 technologies, and files up to 300 MB can be uploaded via drag and drop into the web browser, or up to 2 GB via the SkyDrive desktop application for Microsoft Windows and OS X.

Starting Above Software

You can start any of the above mentioned software by one of the following methods:

From Start Button

Click at Start button to access the various commands. Click on All Programs to get the various programs. From here click at the program called Microsoft Office 2013 group and then the required program

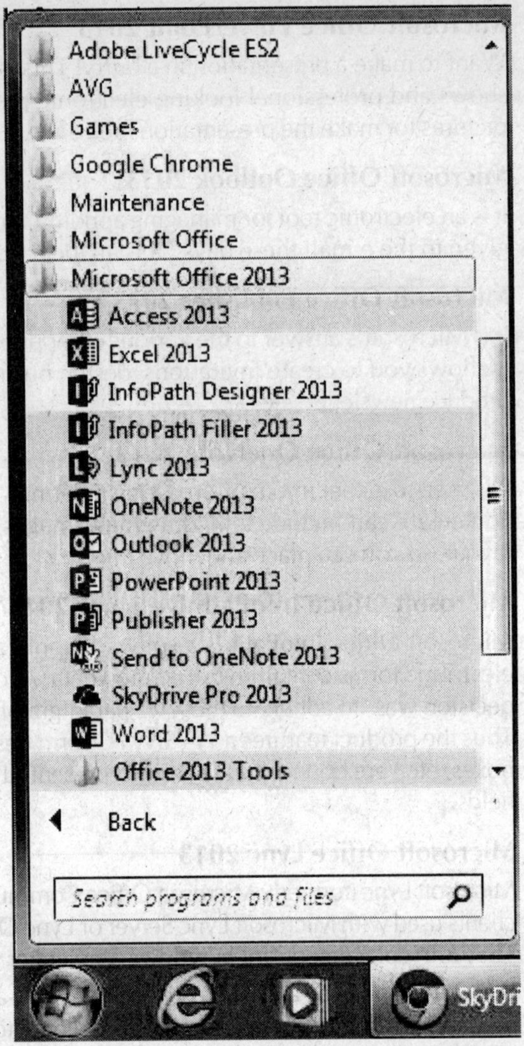

From Icon or Shortcut

You can choose to have an icon of the software on your desktop. This icon can be created by using the feature of Creating Shortcut.

Working with Various Constituents of Microsoft Office 2013

Let me give you here the tips for working under various constituents of Office 2013.

Microsoft Word 2013

As you know that Word is used for creating a document. So in simple terms, follow the following procedure to create a document.

1. Open Word 2013.
2. Click at Blank Document.
3. A new blank slate for writing would be opened for you.
4. Type the text as you would otherwise too.
5. Do not bother about any formatting or spelling.
6. Save the document at this stage to avoid loosing the text, if the lights go out.
7. Now format the text of the document according to your needs, i.e., Bold, Italics, etc.
8. If required, change the alignment of the text or part of it.
9. Save again.
10. Close the document from Info button.
11. Now open the same document again.
12. Spell check the whole document, correcting the wrong words.
13. Your document is ready.
14. Print it on the attached printer.
15. See the result of your effort.

If you follow these steps for creating a document in Word 2013, I am sure that you would never fail.

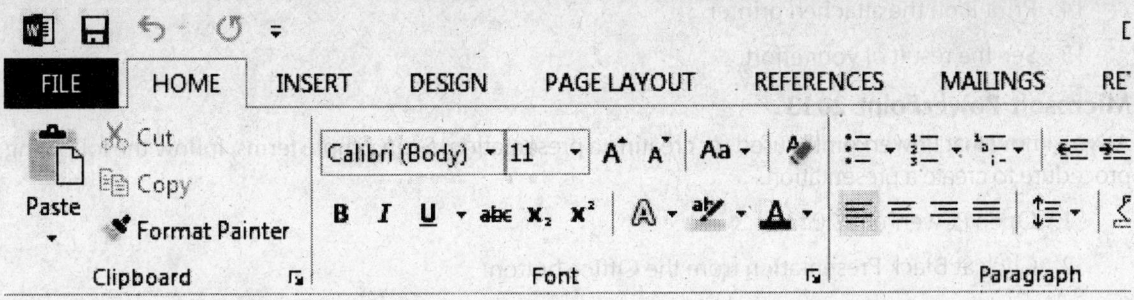

Microsoft Excel 2013

As you know that Excel is used for creating a spreadsheet. So in simple terms, follow the following procedure to create a spreadsheet.

1. Open Excel 2013.
2. Click at Blank Worksheet.
3. A new blank spreadsheet would be opened for you.
4. Type the number, text, formula, as the case may be.
5. Do not bother about any formatting at this stage.
6. Save the document at this stage to avoid loosing the typing, if the lights go out.
7. Now format the spreadsheet according to your needs, i.e., Bold, Italics, etc.
8. If required, change the alignment of the cells.
9. Save again.
10. Close the spreadsheet from Info button.
11. Now open the same spreadsheet again.
12. Spell check the whole spreadsheet, correcting the wrong words.
13. Your spreadsheet is ready.

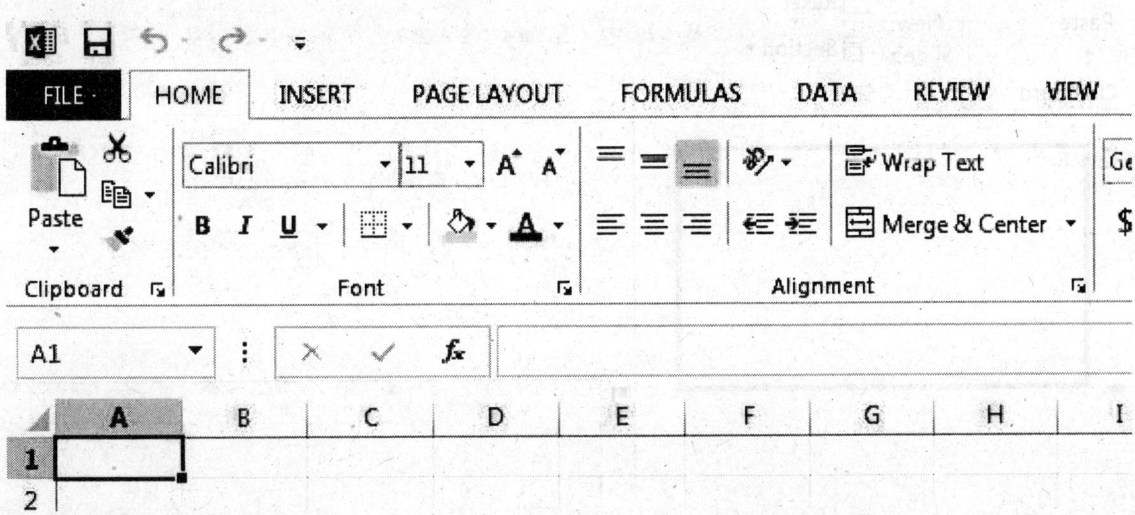

14. Print it on the attached printer.
15. See the result of your effort.

Microsoft PowerPoint 2013

As you know that PowerPoint is used for creating a presentation. So in simple terms, follow the following procedure to create a presentation.

1. Open PowerPoint 2013.
2. Click at Black Presentation from the Office button.
3. A new blank presentation would be opened for you.
4. Select the type of slide you want to create.
5. Type the text and other details, as the case may be.
6. Save the slide/presentation.
7. Now format the slide according to your needs, i.e., Bold, Italics, etc.
8. If required, change the alignment of the text within presentation.
9. Save again.
10. Add a new slide, if the need be.
11. Close the slide from Info button.
12. Now open the same presentation again.
13. Create a slide show of the slides.
14. Run the slide show to see the effect.

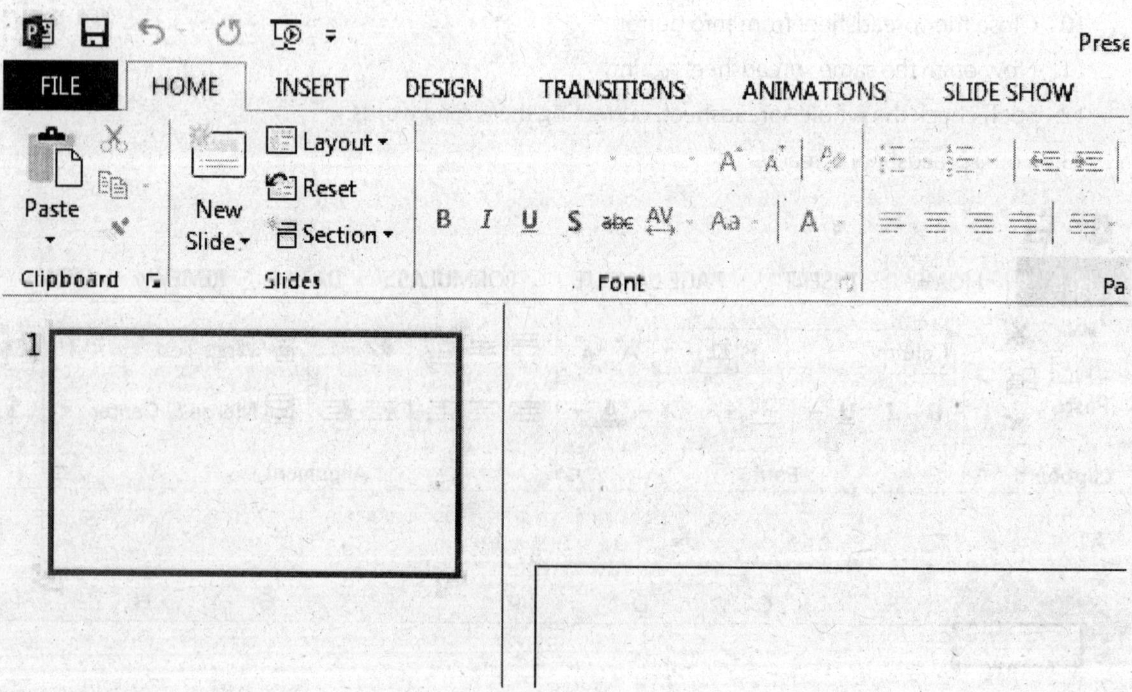

In similar way, you can run the other software of Microsoft Office 2013.

Using the Mouse

Since most of the activities in Microsoft Office are done using the mouse, it is very important to have the complete knowledge of working of mouse while using the constituents of Microsoft Office.

To click

Position the pointer on a menu, a button, or an icon and click the left mouse once.

To double-click

Position the pointer on an item and click the left mouse button twice in quick succession.

To select

1. Position the pointer on the first item to select.
2. Click and hold down the mouse button.
3. Move the mouse pointer across the items to select.
4. Release the mouse button.

To drag

1. Position the pointer on an item.
2. Click and hold down the left mouse button.
3. Move the mouse.
4. Release the mouse button.

To scroll

Drag the scroll button in the scroll bar up or down.

Or

Click a scroll arrow at either end of the scroll bar.

To choose from a menu

1. Click a menu name.
2. Click an item on a menu.

   Or

   If the item is followed by an arrow, position the mouse pointer on the item to open the submenu and then click an item on the submenu.

To move a window

Position the pointer on the window's title bar and press and hold the mouse button as your drag the window.

To resize a window

Position the pointer on the window's corner and, when you see the diagonal pointer, drag to resize the window.

To minimize a window

Click the Minimize button.

To restore a minimized window

Click the button for the window on the taskbar.

To maximize a window

Click the Maximize button.

To switch windows

Click any visible part of the window

Or

Click the button for the window on the taskbar.

To close a window

1. Click the Close button on the window

   Or

   Right click the button for the window on the taskbar and choose Close from the shortcut menu.

Remember

1. Menus in Office programs might be collapsed to show only frequently used items. To view the complete menu, click the More icon at the bottom of the menu or pause with the pointer on any menu option.
2. Menu items that are grayed out are not currently available.
3. To display a tooltip, which is a description of a toolbar button, position the pointer on the button and pause for a moment without clicking.
4. To minimize all windows, you can rightclick the taskbar and then click Minimize All Windows from the shortcut menu.
5. If one window fills the screen, you might have to click its Restore button to return it to a partial-screen window. You will then be able to see and click other windows.

Common Keyboard Commands

Ctrl + N	Open a new document
Ctrl + O	Opens a existing document
Ctrl + S	Saves the current document
Ctrl + W	Close the current document
Ctrl + P	Prints the current document
Ctrl + C	Copies the highlighted matter to store it in clipboard
Ctrl + X	Cuts the highlighted matter to store it in clipboard
Ctrl + V	Pastes the matter available on the clipboard
F1	Call for help
Shift + F1	Use the What's This? Button
Ctrl + F6	Switch between open documents
Ctrl + Z	Undo an action
Ctrl + Y	Redo an action

CHAPTER 2

Introduction to Microsoft Word 2013

Introduction

Microsoft Word 2013 is a word processing software which allows you to write letters, edit them and print them after formatting it according to your needs. It has all the possible options of a word processor in the form of font style and size; indents; line spacing; margins; spell checking and grammar checkers to name a few.

What's New in Microsoft Office Word 2013

Do more with your docs: Pop in an online video, open a PDF and edit the content, align pictures and diagrams with minimal fuss. The new Read Mode is clean and distraction-free—and it works great on tablets. Teaming-up is better too, with direct connections to your online spaces and streamlined review features like Simple Markup and comments.

Tip To get started creating your first Word document, see Basic tasks in Word 2013.

Enjoy the read

Get absorbed in Word documents right from your screen with a new clean, comfortable reading view.

New Read Mode

Enjoy reading with a view that displays your documents in easy-to-read columns on the screen.

Editing tools are removed to minimize distractions, but you still have access to the tools that are always handy for reading such as Define, Translate, and Search on Web.

Object zoom

Double-tap with your finger or double-click with your mouse to zoom in and make tables, charts and images in your document fill the screen. Focus on and take in the information, then tap or click again outside the object to zoom out and continue reading.

Resume reading

Reopen a document and keep reading right where you left off. Word remembers where you were—even when you reopen an online document from a different computer!

Online video

Insert online videos you can watch right in Word, without having to leave the document, so you can stay focused on the content.

Expand and collapse

Collapse or expand parts of a document with just a tap or click. Put summaries in headings and leave it to readers to open the section and read the details if they want.

Work together

Work with others with streamlined collaboration tools.

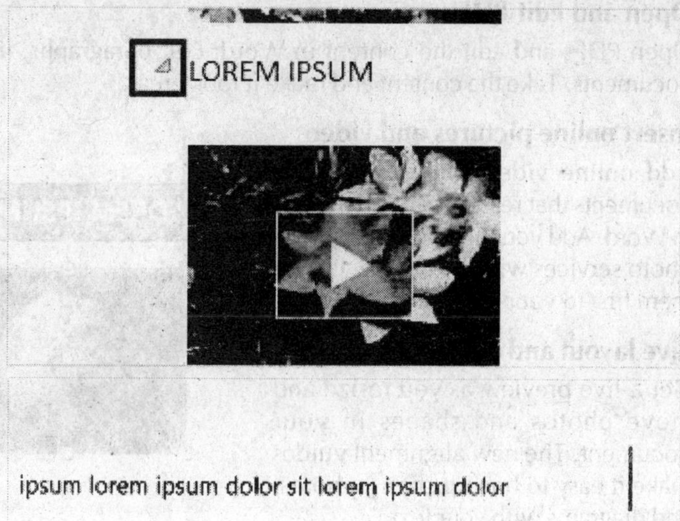

Save and share files in the cloud

The cloud is like file storage in the sky. You can get to it anytime you're online. Now it's easy to share a document using SharePoint or SkyDrive. From there you can access and share your Word docs, Excel spreadsheets, and other Office files. You can even work together with your colleagues on the same file at the same time.

Simple markup

A new revision view, Simple Markup, provides a clean, uncomplicated view of your document, but you still see indicators where tracked changes have been made.

Reply to comments and mark them as done

Comments now have a reply button. You can debate and easily track comments right next to the relevant text. And when a comment is addressed and no longer requires attention, you can mark it as done. It will be greyed out to keep out of your way, but the conversation will still be there if you need to revisit it later.

Add polish and style

With Word 2013 you can create more beautiful and engaging documents, and you can work with more media types—like online videos and pictures. You can even open PDFs.

Start with a template

When you open Word 2013, you're offered a choice of great new templates to help get you started along with a list your recently viewed documents so you can get back to where you left off in no time.

If you'd rather not use a template, click the Blank document.

Open and edit PDFs

Open PDFs and edit the content in Word. Edit paragraphs, lists, and tables just like familiar Word documents. Take the content and make it look great.

Insert online pictures and video

Add online videos directly to your documents that readers can watch right in Word. Add your pictures from online photo services without having to save them first to your computer.

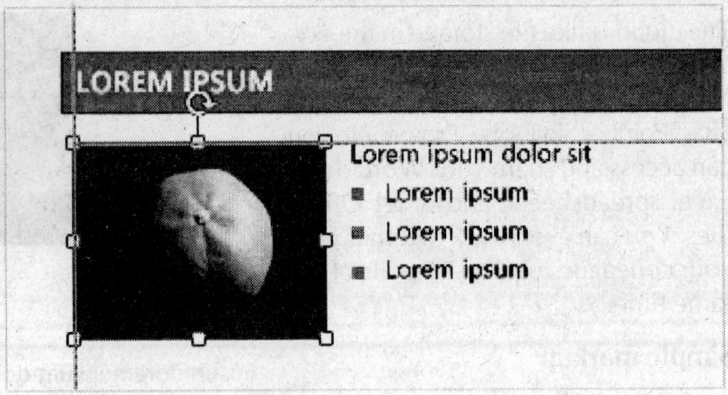

Live layout and alignment guides

Get a live preview as you resize and move photos and shapes in your document. The new alignment guides make it easy to line up charts, photos, and diagrams with your text

Opening Screen of Microsoft Word Screen

Gone are the days of Menu, for example, File menu, Edit menu, etc. Now everything is there on the screen. You have to just click it and presto, you have the command available to you. But, first have a look at the opening screen, which is shown next. There are some main Tabs, which are basic substitutions for the menus. They are: File, Home, Insert, Design, Page Layout, References, Mailings, Review, and View. Let us see what each one of them contains.

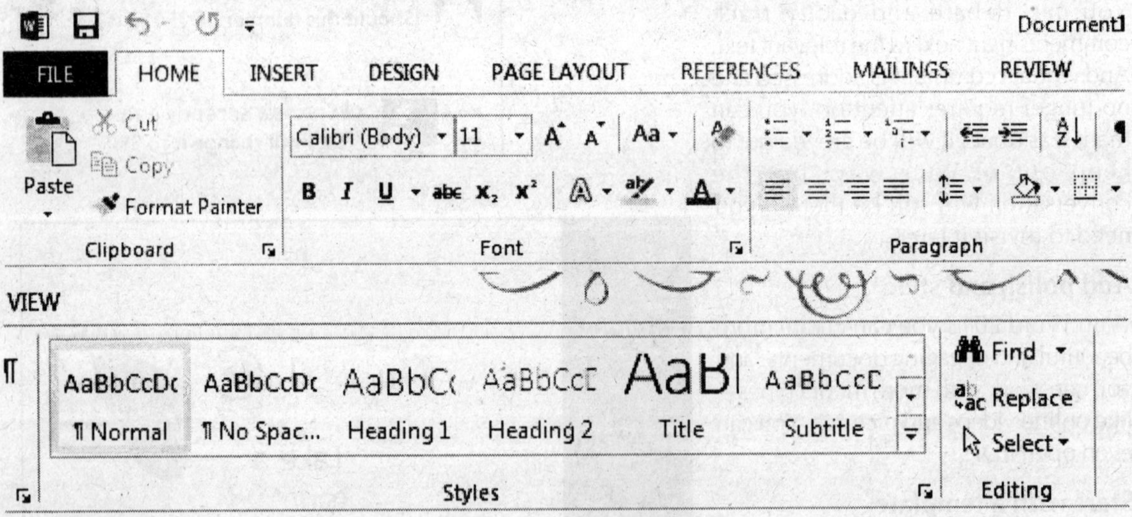

Home Panel

It has the various options of changing the style and type of text. Among the various important features are: Clipboard, Font, Paragraph, Styles, and Editing. Let us look at them one by one.

Clipboard

Most important commands here are: Cut, Copy, Paste and Format Painter.

The Format Painer is used for copying formattting from one place and applying it to another. Paste includes options like, Paste Special and Paste as Hyperlink.

Font

Various options of the font dialog box are all here. You can choose Font, Font size, Grow font, Lower font, Clear formatting in the first row. The second row contains options for Bold, Italics, Underline, Strikethrough, Subscript, Superscript, Change case, Text highlighting, and Text colour. The underlining option contains options for different type of lines which can be chosen for underlining and then choosing the colour of the same too. In Change case you have the option of changing the case to Sentence case, lowercase, UPPERCASE, Captalize Each Word and tOGGLE cASE. Text highlighting and colours have various options too.

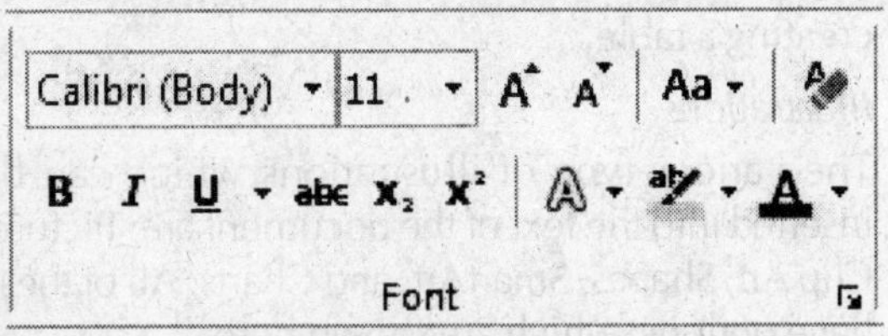

Paragraph

It has options for paragraph styling. The first row contains options for Bullets, Numbering, Multilevel numbering, Shifting text to left, Shifting text to right, Sort, Show/hide non printing characters. In the second row you have the options of making paragraph, Left aligned, Centrally aligned, Right aligned, Box aligned, Line spacing, Shading, and Bottom border. Bullets have different options. Numering can be done in different styles too. So can be done in the case of Multilevel numbering.

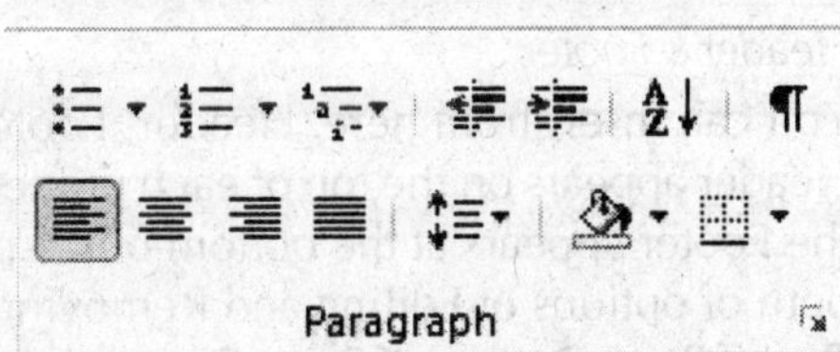

Styles

It displays the various styles which you have created. Just click at the one you want to apply to your text and it will be done. You can also Change Styles and create your own style from it.

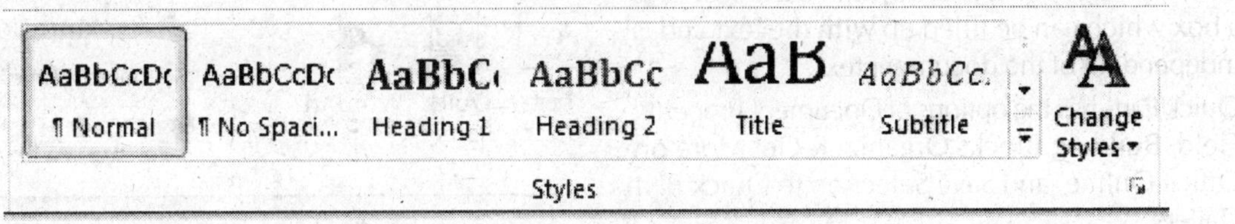

Editing

It has various other editing options, like, Find, Replace, and Select. Find allows you to find a particular word in the text. Replace allows you to find the word and replace it with another one. Select allows you to select text, select objects or the text with similar formatting.

The next panel is Insert.

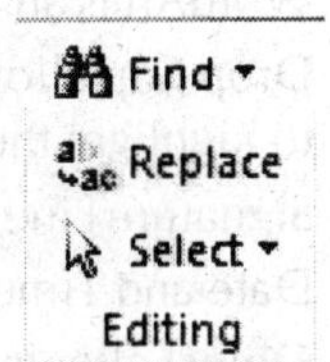

Insert Panel

It has options like: Pages, Tables, Illustrations, Links, Header & Footer, Text, and Symbols.

Pages

It has options of Cover Page, Blank Page, Page Break. Blank page inserts a blank page in the text. Page break puts a page break in the text.

Tables

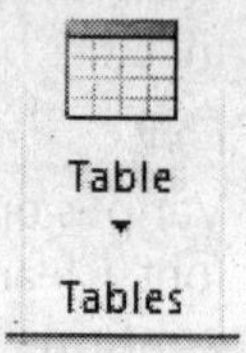

Inserts table format in the text. If you click at the arrow, you will see the options shown here, which not only describe the type of table you are choosing but also draws the table in the text simultaneously. You can also insert as a table, an Excel Spreadsheet. There is option of Quick Tables too, which allows you to save a table format, which can be called later for quickly creating a table.

Illustrations

The various type of illustrations which can be inserted into the text of the document are: Picture, Clip Art, Shapes, SmartArt, and Charts. All of these have options, which are shown here.

Links

Among the various options which are here are: Hyperlink, Bookmark, and Cross-reference. These can be used in inserting these links into the text of the document.

Header & Footer

You can insert from here, Header, Footer and Page Numbers. Header appears on the top of each printed page. The content of the Footer appears at the bottom of the printed page. Header and Footer both of options of Editing and Removing them. Page number options are Top of Page, Bottom of Page, Page Margins, Current Position, Format Page Numbers and Remove Page Numbers.

Text

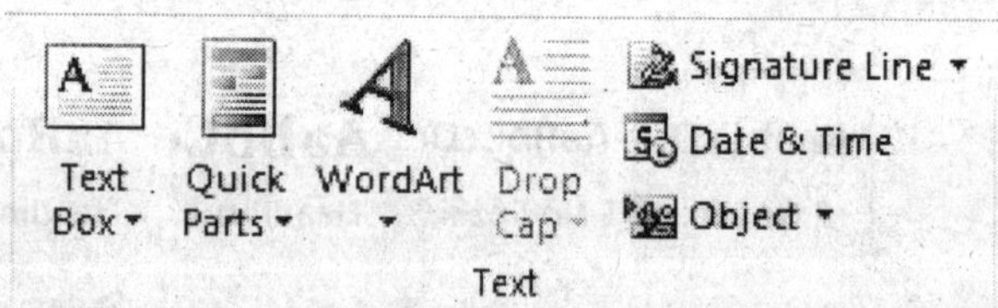

Various options here are: Text Box, Quick Parts, Word Art, Drop Cap, Signature Line, Date and Time, and Object. Text box creates a box which can be filled up with the text and is independent of the document text.

Quick Parts has the options of Document Property, Field, Building Blocks Organizer, Get More on Office Online, and Save Selection to Quick Part Gallery.

WordArt is an independent program which allows you to create and insert an independent text.

Drop Cap allows you to put a capital letter in the beginning of the text. It can cover 2-3 lines of the text to highlight the alphabet.

Signature Line allows you to insert a signature line.

Date and Time would insert date and time in the text, in the format selected by you.

Object allows you to insert objects in the text. It also allows you to insert text from another file.

Symbols

It has two options: Equation and Symbol. Equation allows you to enter equations in the text, after creating it using the various symbols available under it. It is quite a big topic and can be discussed in an advanced book. Symbol button allows you insert a symbol from the list shown here.

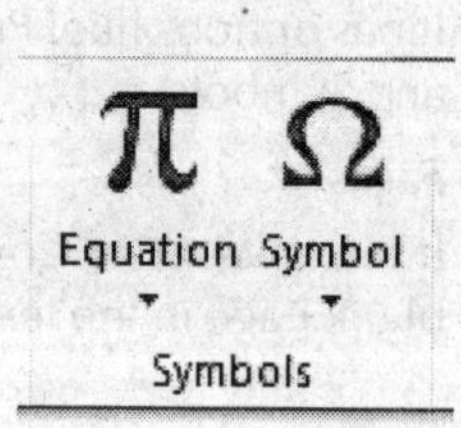

Now we come to Design.

Design Panel

It has the various options of changing the design of the text. Among the various important features are: Themes, Colors, Fonts, Paragraph Spacing, Effects, Set as Default, Watermark, Page Colours, Page Borders. Let us look at them one by one.

Themes

Pick a new theme to give your document instant style and just the right personality. Each theme uses a unique set of colors, fonts and effects to create a consistent look and feel.

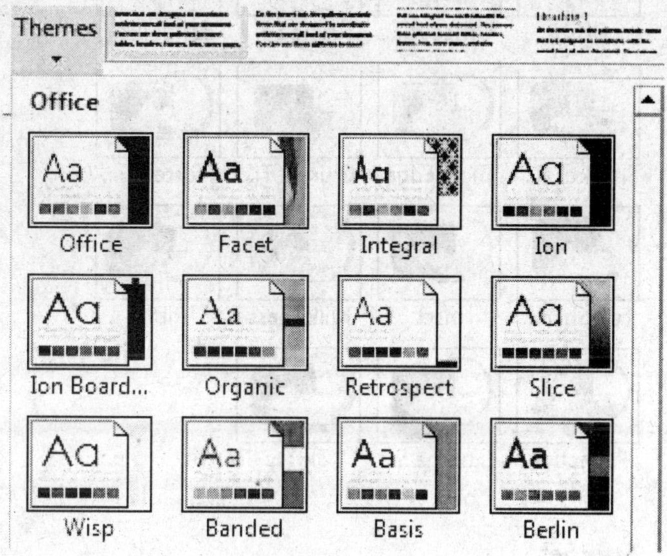

Document Formatting

You can choose any of the document formatting which are shown here. You can browse to have more options.

Colors

Quickly change all the colors used in your document by picking a different color palette. This will update the colors available to you in the color picker along with any theme color in your document. No matter what palette you choose, your document will look perfectly coordinated.

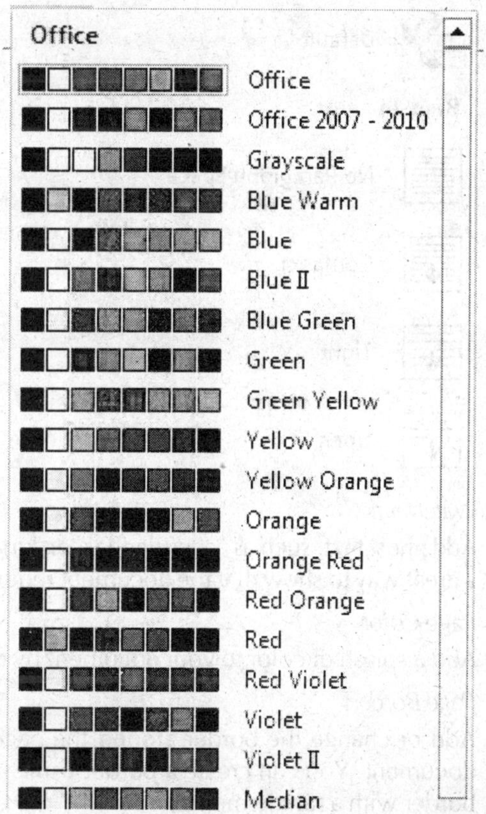

Fonts

Quickly change the text in your document by picking a new font set. This is an easy way to change all of your text at once. For this to work your text at once. For this to work, your text must be formatted using the 'body' and 'heading' fonts.

Paragraph Spacing

Quickly change the line and paragraph spacing of your document. This option will change the spacing of your entire document including new paragraphs. You can choose between predefined values or specify your own.

Effects

Quickly change the general look of objects in your document. Each option uses various borders and visual effects, such as shading and shadow, to give your objects a different look.

Set as Default

Use this look for all new documents. Save your current settings so that every time you create a blank document it will be formatted just the way you like. This is pefect if you have a favorite font or always want specific paragraph spacing.

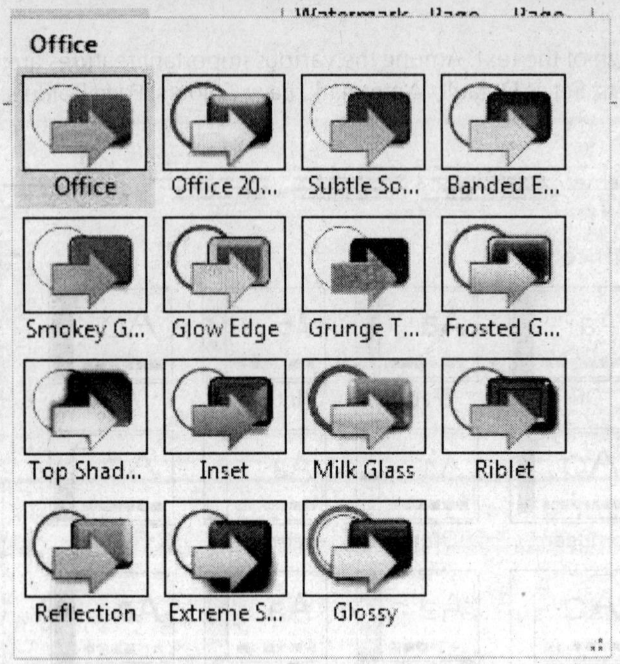

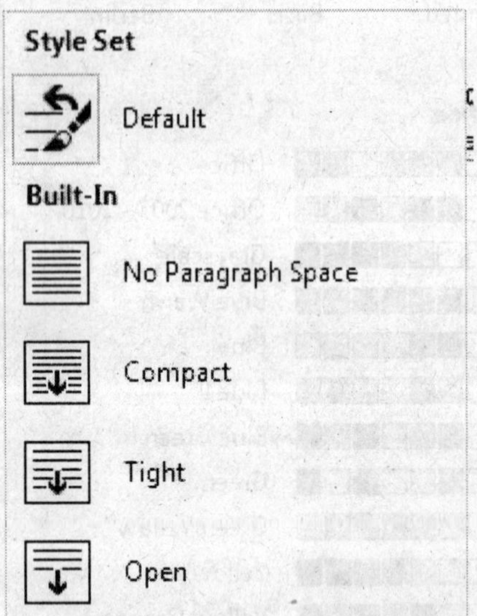

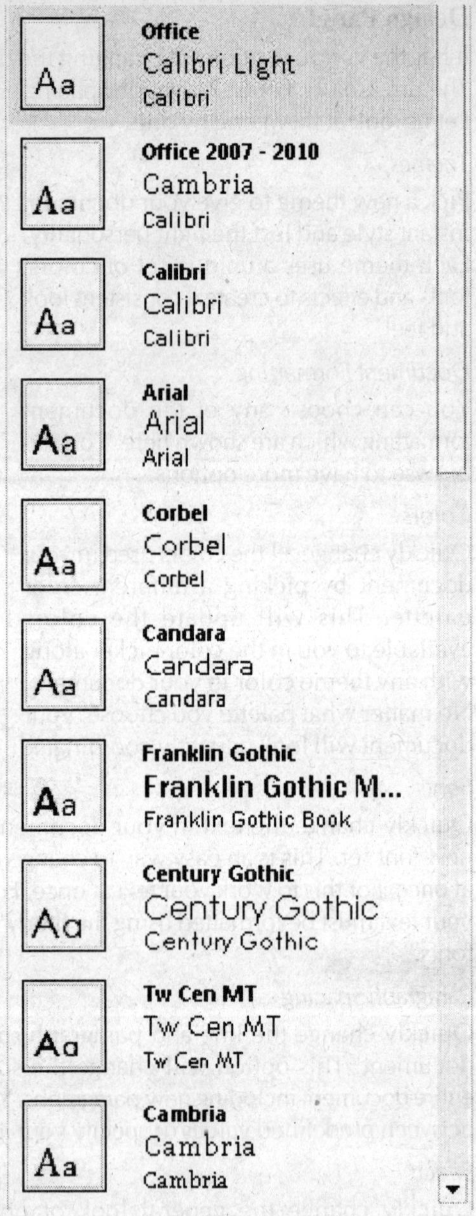

Watermark

Add ghost text, such as "confidential" or "urgent" behind the content on the page. The faint watermark is a great way to show that the document requires special treatment without distracting from the contents.

Page Color

Add a splash of color to your document by changing the color of the page.

Page Borders

Add or change the border around the page. A border draws focus and adds a stylish touch to your document. You can create a border using a variety of line styles, widths and colors, or choose an art border with a fun theme..

Page Layout Panel

It has the following options: Themes, Page Setup, Page Background, Paragraph, and Arrange.

Page Setup

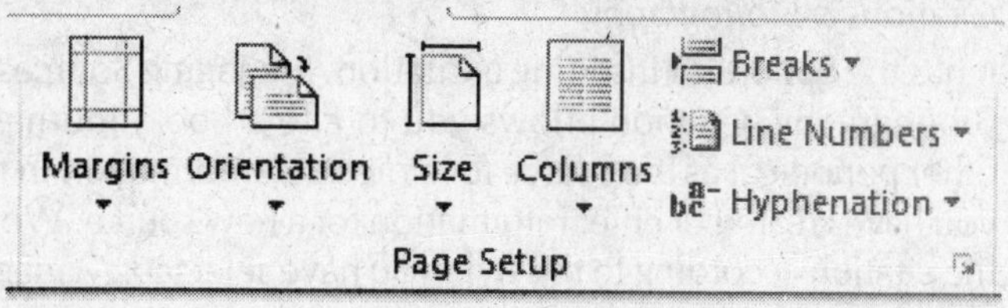

Among the various options available here are: Margins, Orientation, Size, Columns, Breaks, Line Numbers and Hyphenation.

Margins allows you to set margins of the page, i.e., margins from the left and right of the page.

Orientation has two options: Portrait and Landscape.

Size allows you to choose from the various size of the paper normally used globally.

Columns allow you to set the page into various columns with line in-between or not.

Breaks inserts break into the text in the form of line, page, etc.

Line Numbers are inserted using this option.

Hyphenation allows to have hyphens in the paragraph or not.

Paragraph

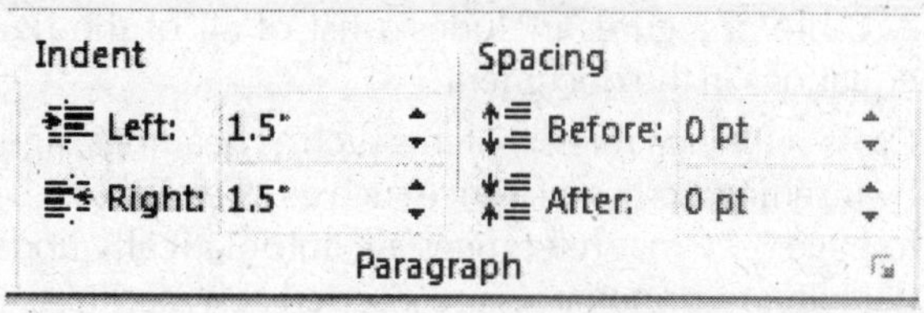

It has two main options: Indent and Spacing.

Indent allows you to set the left and right indent.

Spacing allows you to set the Before and After paragraph space.

Arrange

It has the following options: Position, Bring to Front, Send to Back, Text Wrapping, Align, Group and Rotate.

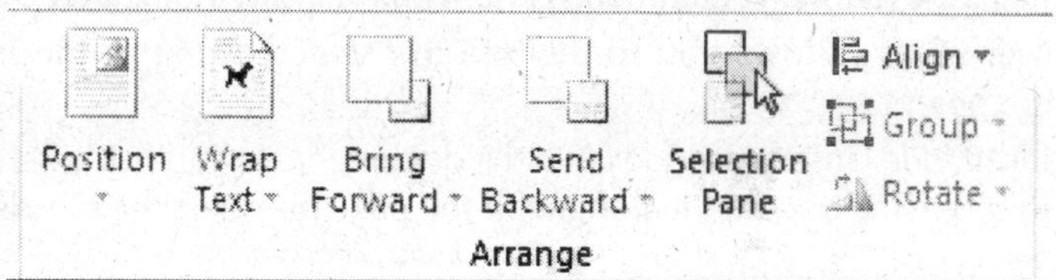

Position allows you to position the picture/object as per the options available.

Bring to Front and Send to Back are used when you have to rearrange the picture/object with respect to the text.

Align allows you to align the text, as per the options shown here.

Group allows you to group two or more objects together.

Rotate allows you to rotate the inserted object as per the options shown here.

References Panel

It has the following options: Table of Contents, Footnotes, Citations and Bibliography, Captions, Index, and Table of Authorities.

Table of Contents

It has the options: Table of Contents, Add Test and Update Table. Table of Contents allows you create table of contents of the text. Add Text allows you to set levels of the text. Update Table updates an existing table of contents.

Footnotes

It has the options: Insert Footnote, Insert Endnote, Next Footnote, and Show Notes. Insert Footnote allows you to insert a footnote in the text. Insert Endnote allows you to insert endnote. Next footnote allows to insert the next or prev footnote, endnote. Show notes shows all the notes in the text.

Citations & Bibliography

It has the options of Inserting a Citation, Managing Sources, Style, and Bibliography. Citation allows you to cite a book, journal article, or other periodical as the source for a piece of information in the document. Choose from the list of sources you have created or enter information for a new source. Word formats the citation according to the style you have selected. Manage Sources allow you to look into the source manager and manage it. Style allows you to choose from the various styles given. Bibliography allows you to maintain the various references.

Captions

This has the following options: Insert Caption, Insert Table of Figures, Update Table, and Cross-reference. Insert Caption allows you to add a caption to a picture or other image. A caption is a line of text that appears below an object to describe it.

Insert Table of Figures inserts a Table of Figures into the document. A Table of Figures includes a list of all of the figures, table, or equations in the document.

Cross-reference refers to items such as headings, figures, and tables by inserting a cross reference such as, "See Table 6 below" or "Turn to page 8." Cross references are automatically updated if the content is moved to another location. By default, cross references are inserted as hyperlinks.

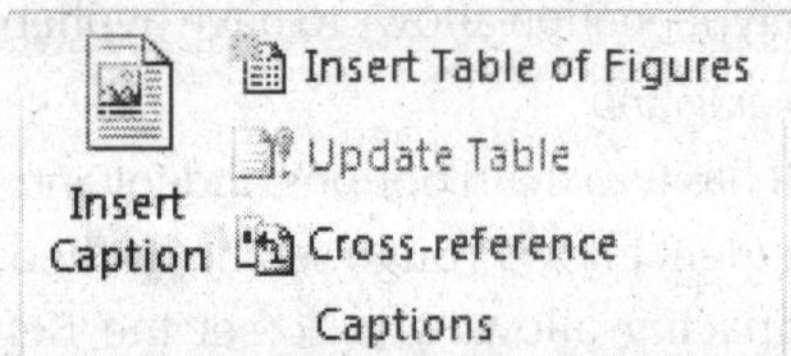

Index

It has the following commands: Mark Entry, Insert Index, and Update Index.

Mark Entry allows you to include the selected text in the index of the document.

Insert Index inserts an index into the document. An index is a list of keywords found in the document along with the page numbers the words appear on.

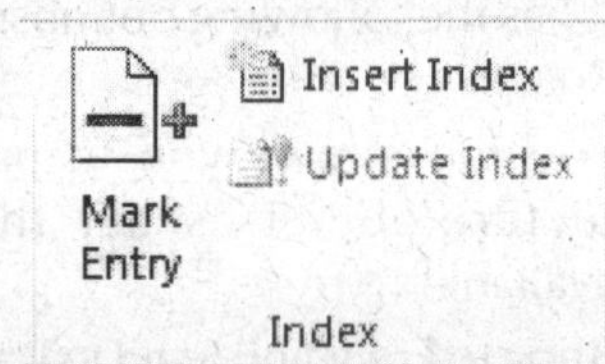

Table of Authorities

It has the option called Mark Citation, Insert Table of Authorities, and Update Table of Authorities. Mark Citation adds the selected text as an entry in the Table of Authorities.

Mailings Panel

It has the following options: Create, Start Mail Merge, Write & Insert Fields, Preview Results, and Finish.

Create

It has the following options: Envelopes, and Labels. Each one of them gives rise to a dialog box, which allows you to create envelopes and labels.

Start Mail Merge

It has options to Start Mail Merge, Select Recipients and Edit Recipients List.

Start Mail Merge allows you to select the options of Letters, E-Mail Messages, Evelopes, Labels, Directory or start the Step by Step Mail Merge Wizard.

Select Recipients allows you to choose the list of people you intend to send the letter to. You can type you own list, use your Outlook contacts, or connect to a database. It also has options to Type New List, Use Existing List or Select from Outlook Contacts.

Write & Insert Fields

It has the options to Highlight Merge Fields, Address Block, Greeting Line, Insert Merge Field, Rules, Match Fields, and Update Labels.

Highlight Merge Fields highlights the fields you have inserted into the document. This makes it easy to see what part of your form letter will be replaced by information from the recipient list you have chosen.

Addresss Block adds an address to your letter. You specify the formatting and location, and Word will replace it with actual addresses from your recipient list when you finish the mail merge.

Greeting Line adds a greeting line such as "Dear<<First Name>>", to your document.

Insert Merge Field adds any field from your recipient list to the document, such as "Last Name," "Home Phone," "Company Name," or any other field.

When you finish the mail merge, Word will replace these fields with the actual information from the recipient list.

Rules specifies rules to be added decision-making ability to the mail merge. For instance, you could use If...Then...Else to check the address of recipient and show a local phone number to recipients near you and an international phone number for recipients outside of your country.

Match Fields allows you to tell Word the meaning of different fields in your recipient list. For example, you can indicate that your custom field "Home" is equivalent to normal built-in field "Home Phone."

Update Labels allow you to create labels, update all the labels in the document to use information from the recipient list. For a mail merge to a printed letter or e-mail, this command is not necessary.

Preview Results

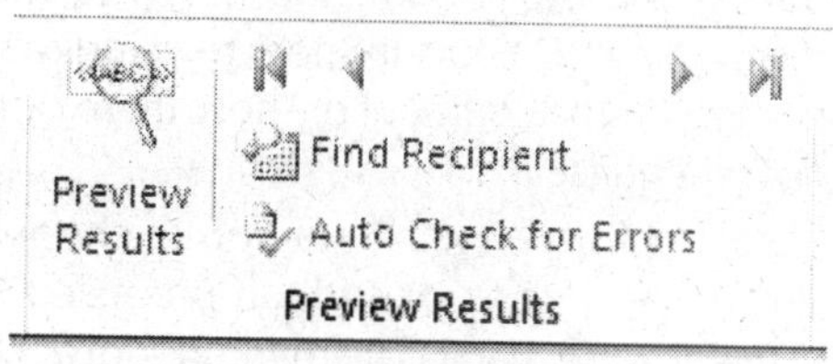

It has the options to Preview Results, Find Recipient, and Auto Check for Errors.

Preview Results replaces the merge fields in your document with acutal data from your recipient list so you can see what it looks like.

Find Recipient finds and previews a specific record in the recipient list by searching for text.

Auto Check for Errors specifies how to handle errors that occur when completing the mail merge. You also have the option of simulating the mail merge to see if any errors would occur.

Finish

It has the options to Finish & Merge. It completes the mail merge. You can create separate documents for each copy of the letter, send them all directly to the printer, or send them via e-mail.

Review Panel

It has the following options: Proofing, Comments, Tracking, Changes, Compare, and Protect.

Proofing

It has the following options: Spelling & Grammer, Research, Thesaurus, and Word Count.

Spelling & Grammar checks the spelling and grammar of text in the document.

Research opens the Research Task Pane to search through reference materials, such as dictionaries, encyclopedias, and translation services.

Thesaurus suggests other words with a similar meaning to the word you have selected.

Word Count finds out the number of words, characters, paragraphs, and lines in the document. You can also find the word count in the status bar at the bottom of the window.

Language

Translates the selected text into a different language. Translation ScreenTip enables a ScreenTip that translates words you pause your cursor over into another language.

Editing Language sets the language used to check the spelling and grammar of the selected text.

Comments

This has the following options: New Comment, Delete, Previous, and Next.

New Commnet adds a selection over the selection.

Delete command deletes an existing comment.

Previous locates the previous comment.

Tracking

This has the following options: Track Changes, Balloons, Final Showing Markup, Show Markup, and Reviewing Pane.

Track Changes trackes all changes made to the document, including insertions, deletions, and formatting changes. Change Tracking Options allows you to change the tracking options. Change User Name would allow you to change the user name.

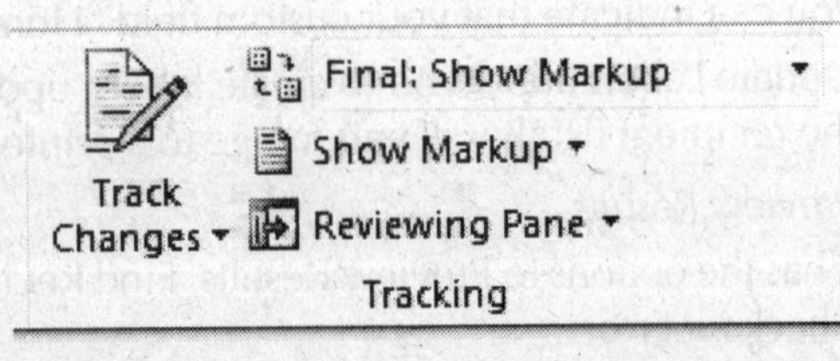

Balloons allow you to choose how to show revisions to the document. You can show revisions as balloons in the margins of the coument or show them directly within the document itself.

Display for Review allows you to choose how to view the proposed changes to the document. Final shows the document with all proposed changes included, Original shows the document before any changes were made. The markup shows what changes have been proposed.

Show Markup allows you to choose what kind of markup to show in the document. You can hide or show comments, insertions and deletions, formatting changes, and other kinds of markup.

Reviewing Pane shows revisions in a separate window.

Changes

This has the following options: Accept, Reject, Previous, and Next.

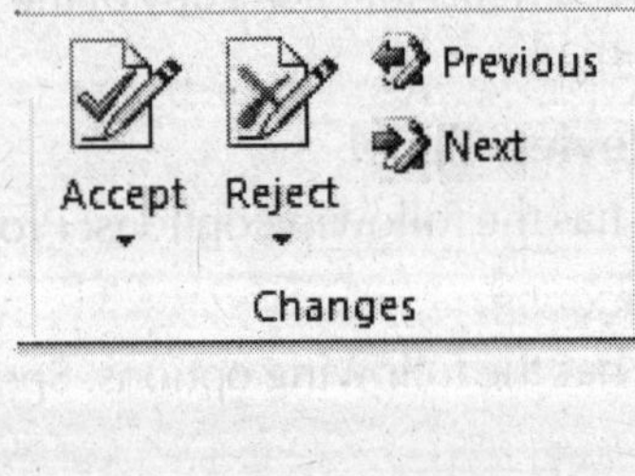

Accept and Move to Next allows you to access other options such as accepting all changes in the document.

Reject and Move to Next allows you to access other options such as rejecting all changes in the document.

Previous Change allows you to navigate to the previous revision in the document so that you can accept or reject it.

Next Change allows you to navigate to the next revision in the document so that you can accept or reject it.

Compare

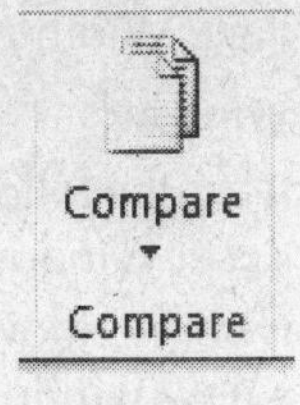

This has the following options: Compare, and Show Source Documents.

Compare compares or combines multiple versions of a document.

Show Source Documents allows you to choose which source documents to show. You can show the original document, the revised document, or booth.

Protect

This has only one option: Protect Document.

It restricts how people can access the document.

View Panel

It has the following options: Document Views, Show/Hide, Zoom, Window, and Macros.

Views

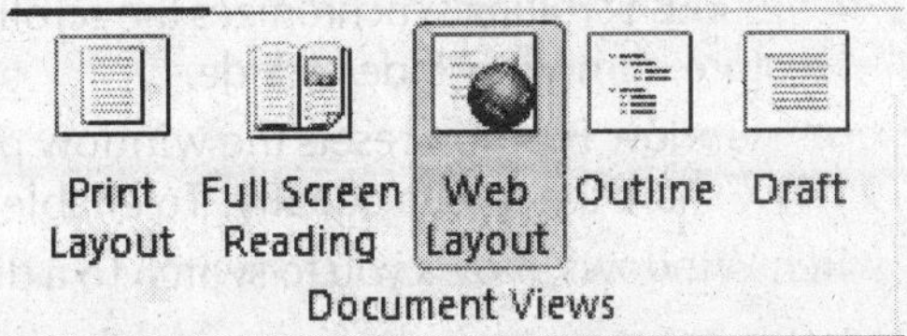

It has the following options: Print Layout, Full Screen Reading, Web Layout, Outline, and Draft.

Print Layout views the document as it will appear on the printed page.

Full Screen Reading allows you to view the document in full screen Reading View in order to maximize the space available for reading or commenting on the document.

Web Layout allows you to view the document as it would look as a Web page.

Outline View allows you to view the document as an outline and show the outlining tools.

Draft View allows you to view the document as a draft to quickly edit the text.

Show

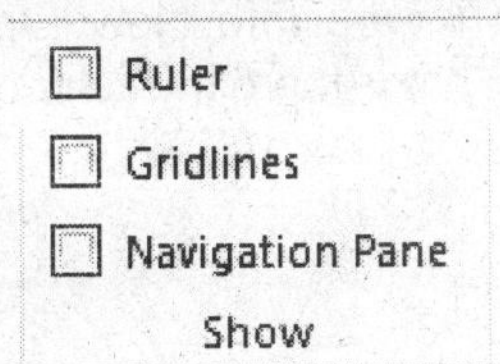

It has the following options: Ruler, Gridlines, Message Bar, Document Map, and Thumbnails.

Ruler allows you to view the rulers, used to measure and line up objects in the document.

Gridlines turns on gridlines to which you can align objects in the document.

Message Bar opens the Message Bar to complete any required actions on the document.

Document Map opens the Document Map, which allows you to navigate through a structural view of the document.

Thumbnails opens the Thumbnails pane, which you can use to navigate a long document through small pictures of each page.

Zoom

It has the following options: Zoom, 100%, One Page, Two Pages, and Page Width.

Zoom opens the Zoom dialog box to specify the zoom level of the document. In most cases, you can alos use the zoom controls in the status bar at the bottom of the window to quickly zoom the document.

100% zooms the document to 100% of the normal size.

One Page zooms the document so that an entire page fits in the window.

Two Pages zooms the document so that two pages fit in the window.

Page Width zooms the document so that the width of the page matches the width of the window.

Window

It has the following options: New Window, Arrange All, Split, View Side by Side, Synchronous Scrolling, Reset Window Position, and Switch Windows.

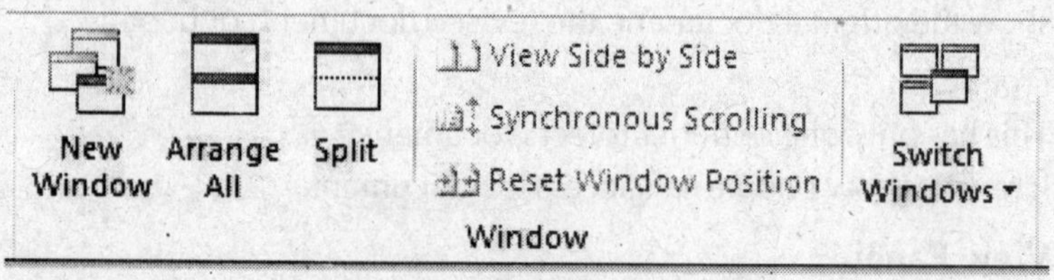

New Window allows you to open a new window containing a view of the current document.

Arrange All tiles all open program windows side-by-side on the screen.

Split Window splits the current window into two parts so that you can view different sections of the document at the same time.

View Side by Side allows you to view two documents side-by-side so that you can compare their contents.

Synchronous Scrolling synchronizes the scrolling of two documents so that they scroll together. To enable this feature, turn View Side by Side.

Reset Window Position resets the window position of the documents being compared side-by-side so that they share the screen equally. To enable this feature, turn on View Side by Side.

Switch Windows allows you to switch to a different currently open window.

Macros

It has only one option, i.e., Macros.

Macros command allows you to view macros. Click here to record a macro or to access other macro options.

File Button

Besides, the commands mentioned till now, we have a set of commands, under the so called File Button. These are the commands which can be used just by a clik. Given below are the various options available.

They are: Info, New, Open, Save, Save As, Print, Share, Export, Close, Account and Options. Want to see what is there in each one of them. Go through the pages next to see them.

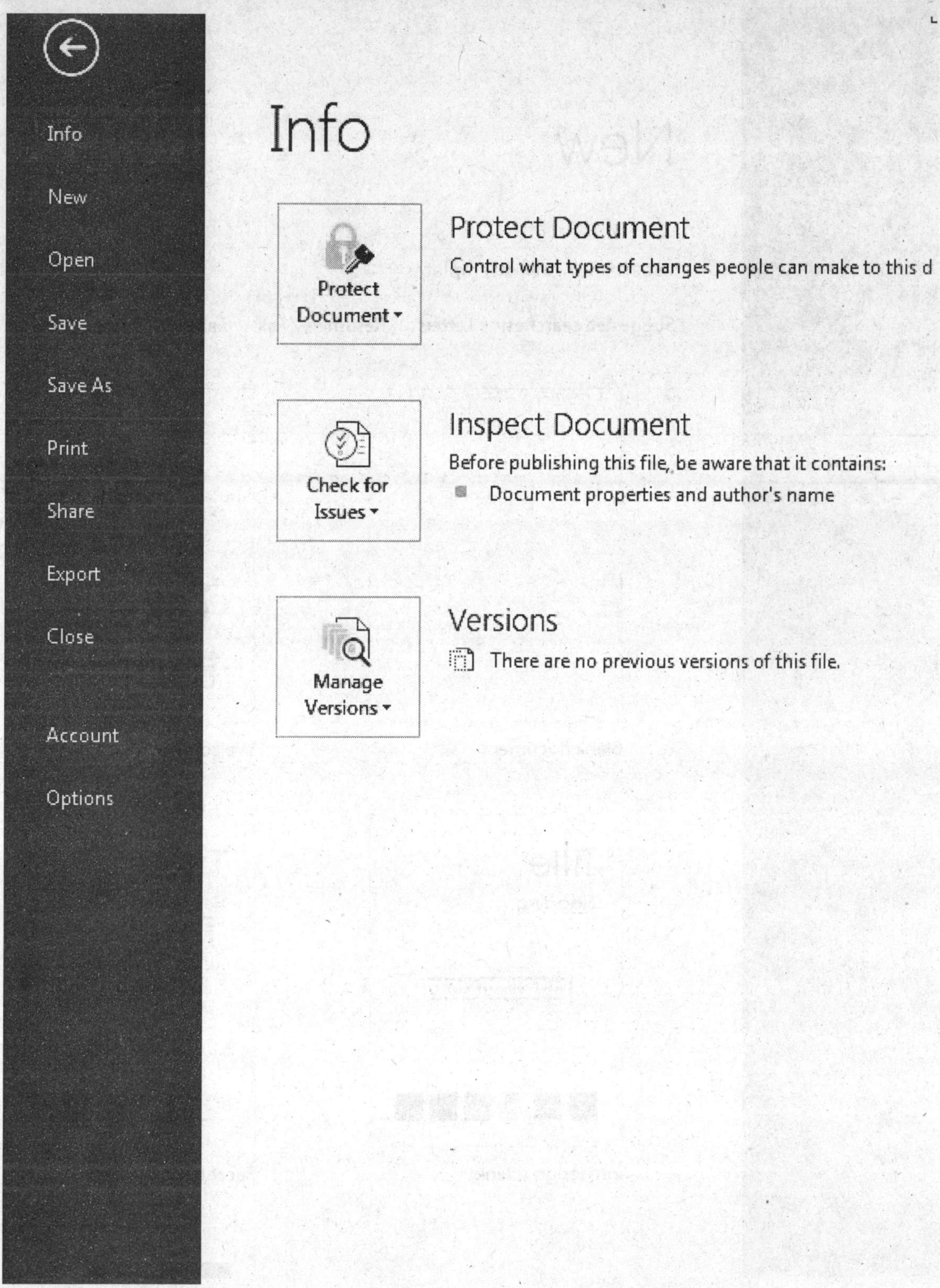
Info
New
Open
Save
Save As
Print
Share
Export
Close
Account
Options
Info
Protect Document ▾
Protect Document
Control what types of changes people can make to this d
Check for Issues ▾
Inspect Document
Before publishing this file, be aware that it contains:
Document properties and author's name
Manage Versions ▾
Versions
There are no previous versions of this file.

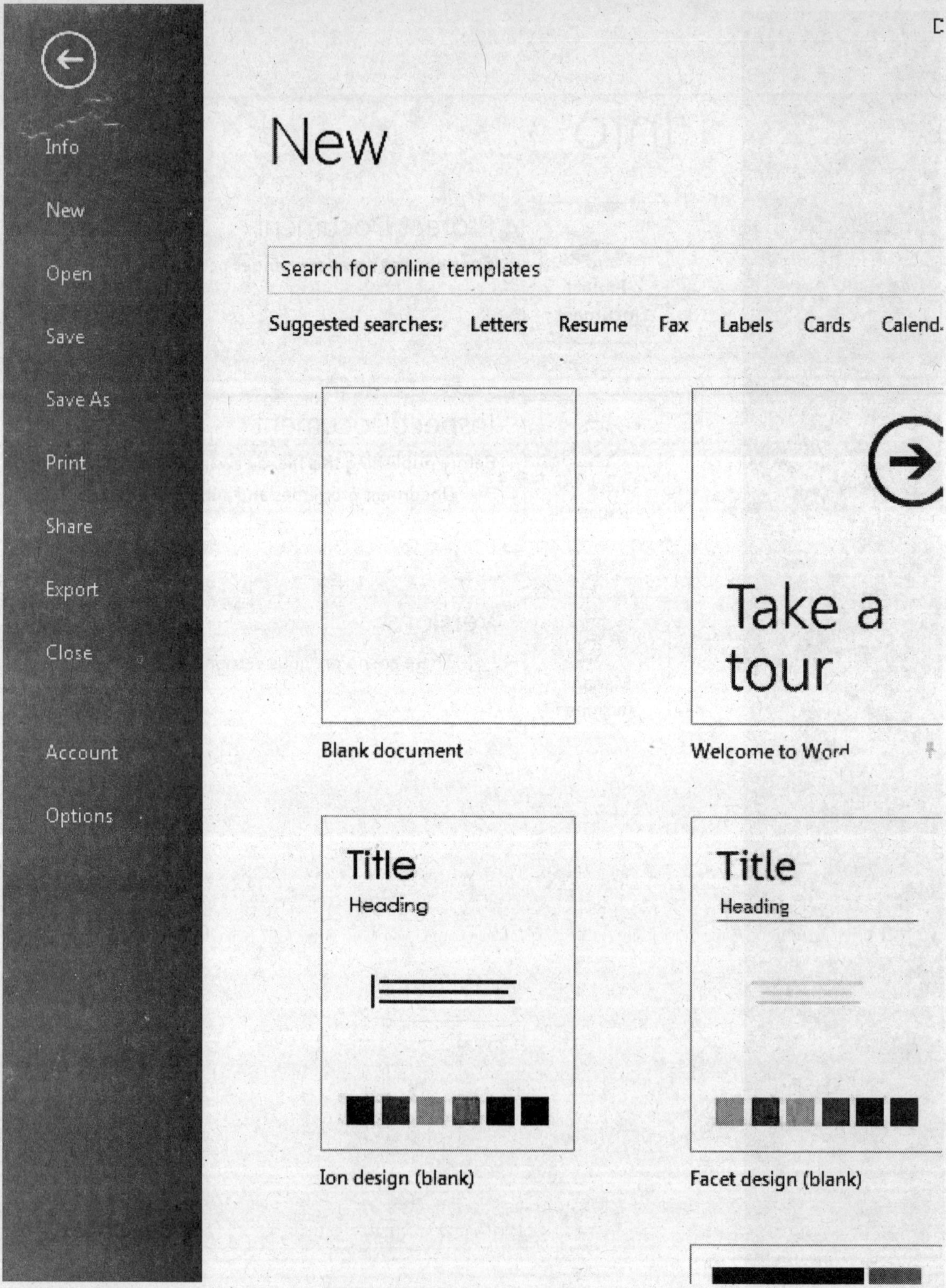
Info
New
Open
Save
Save As
Print
Share
Export
Close
Account
Options
New
Search for online templates
Suggested searches: Letters Resume Fax Labels Cards
Take a tour
Blank document
Title
Heading
Ion design (blank)
Title
Heading
Facet design (blank)

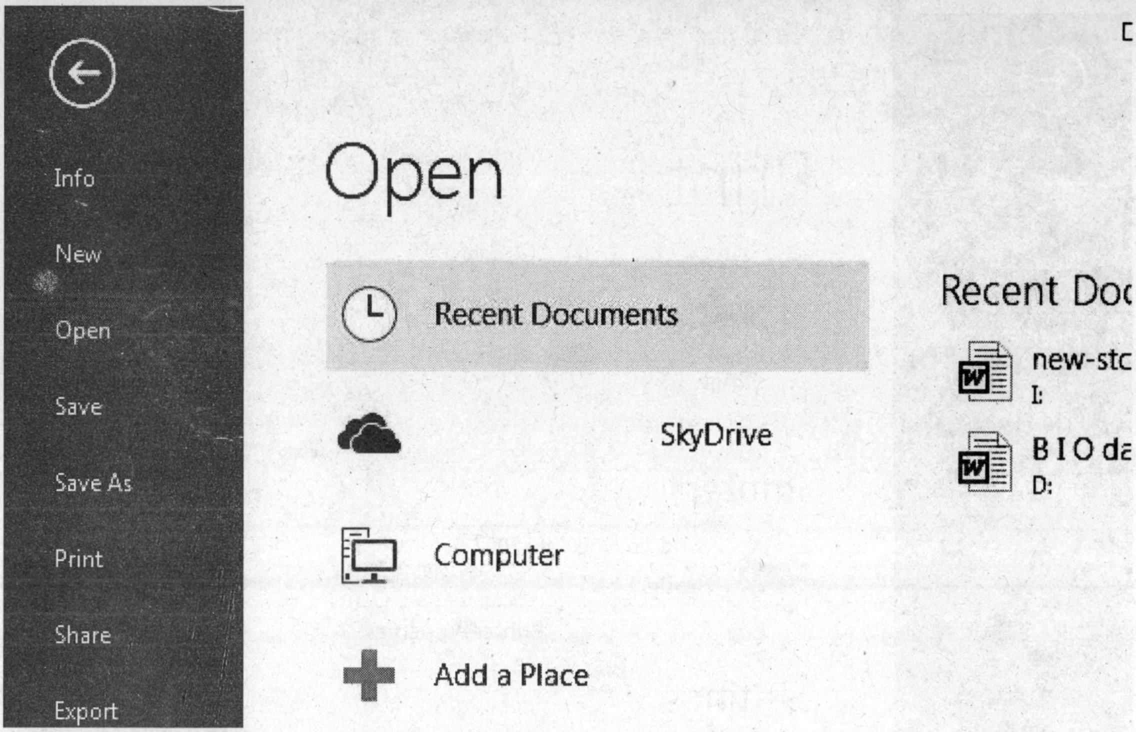
Info
New
Open
Save
Save As
Print
Share
Export
Open
Recent Documents
SkyDrive
Computer
Add a Place
Recent Doc
new-stc
I:
B I O da
D:

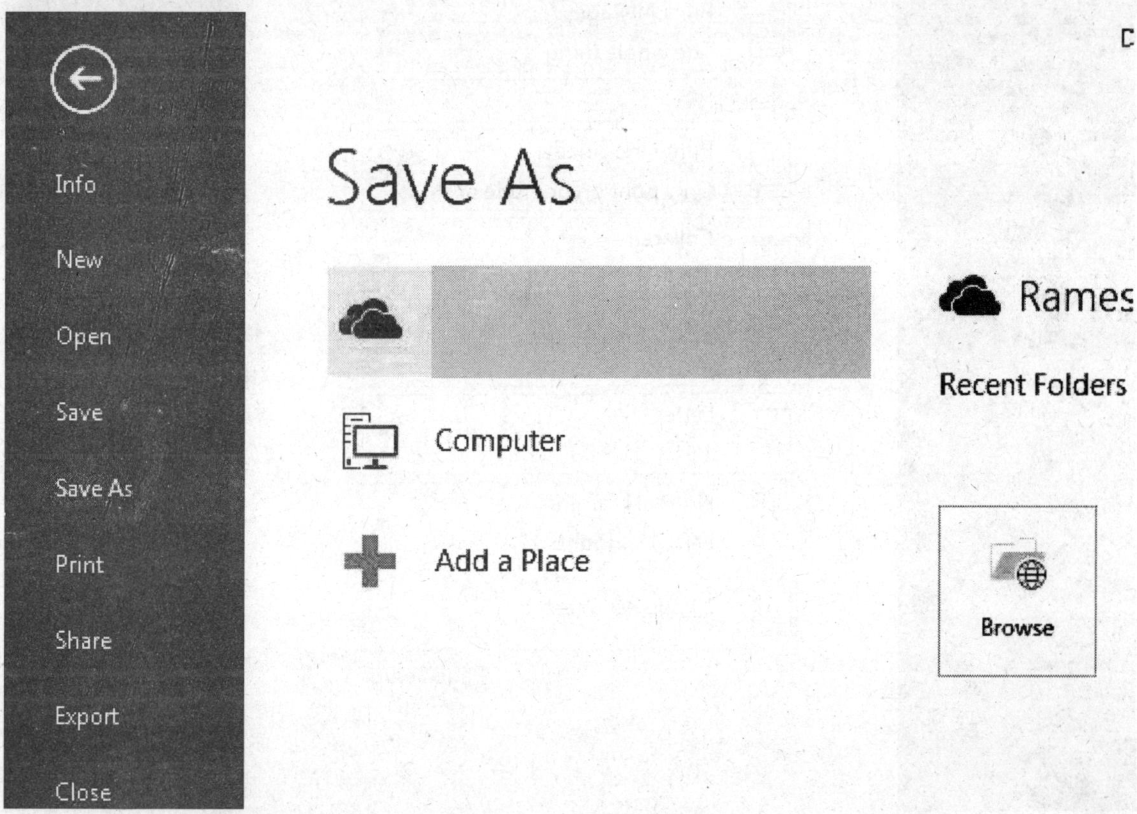
Info
New
Open
Save
Save As
Print
Share
Export
Close
Save As
Computer
Add a Place
Rames
Recent Folders
Browse

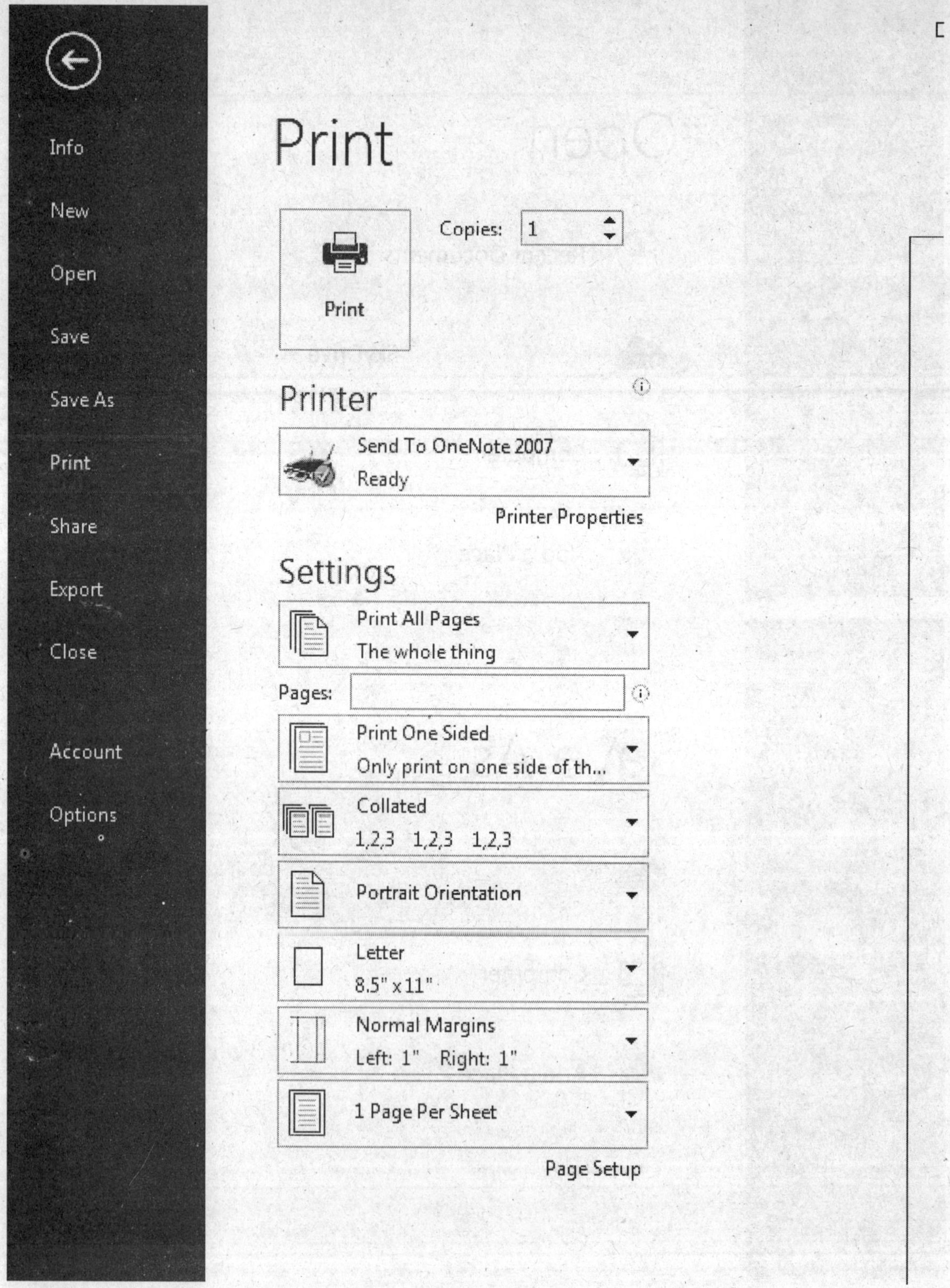
Info
New
Open
Save
Save As
Print
Share
Export
Close
Account
Options
Print
Print
Copies: 1
Printer
Send To OneNote 2007
Ready
Printer Properties
Settings
Print All Pages
The whole thing
Pages:
Print One Sided
Only print on one side of th...
Collated
1,2,3 1,2,3 1,2,3
Portrait Orientation
Letter
8.5" x 11"
Normal Margins
Left: 1" Right: 1"
1 Page Per Sheet
Page Setup

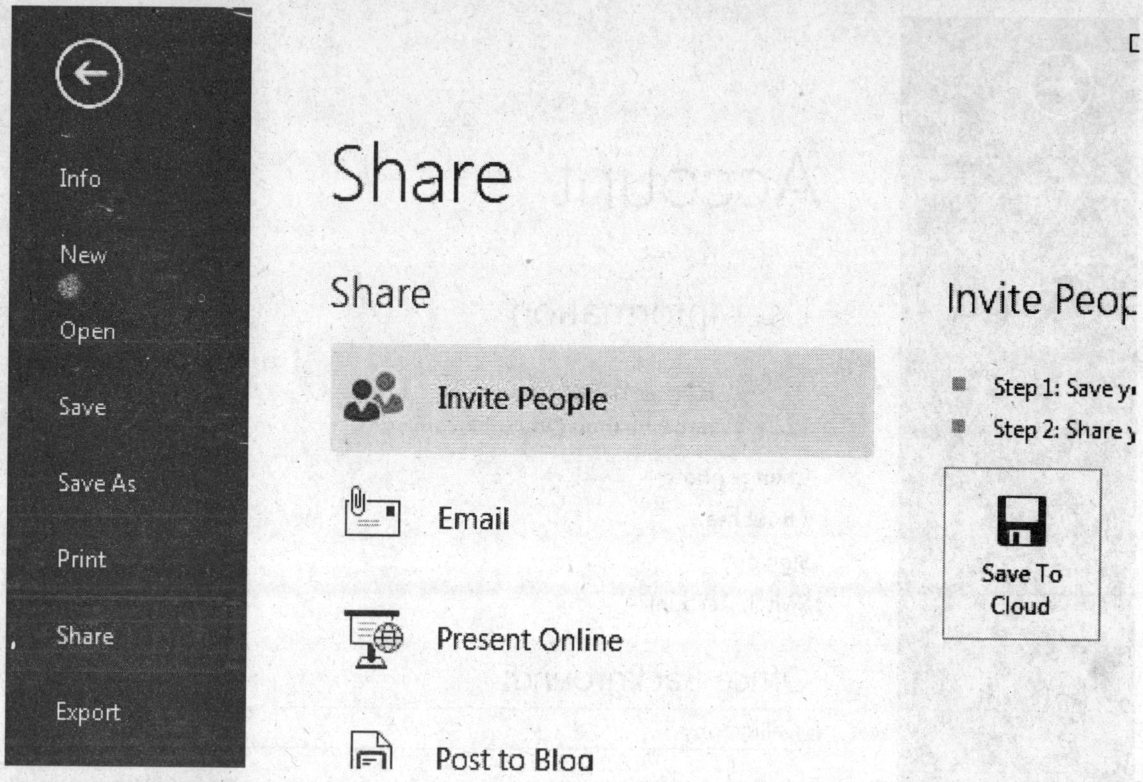
Info
New
Open
Save
Save As
Print
Share
Export
Share
Share
Invite People
Email
Present Online
Post to Blog
Invite Peop
Step 1: Save y
Step 2: Share y
Save To
Cloud

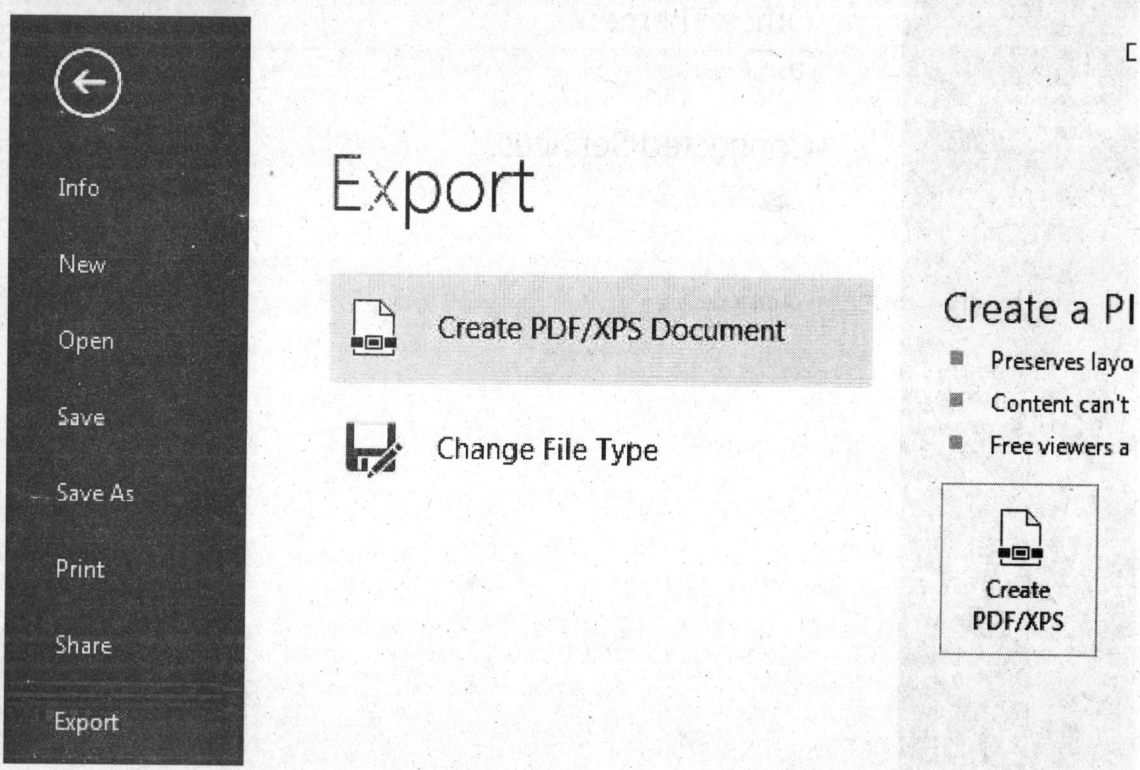
Info
New
Open
Save
Save As
Print
Share
Export
Export
Create PDF/XPS Document
Change File Type
Create a Pl
Preserves layo
Content can't
Free viewers a
Create
PDF/XPS

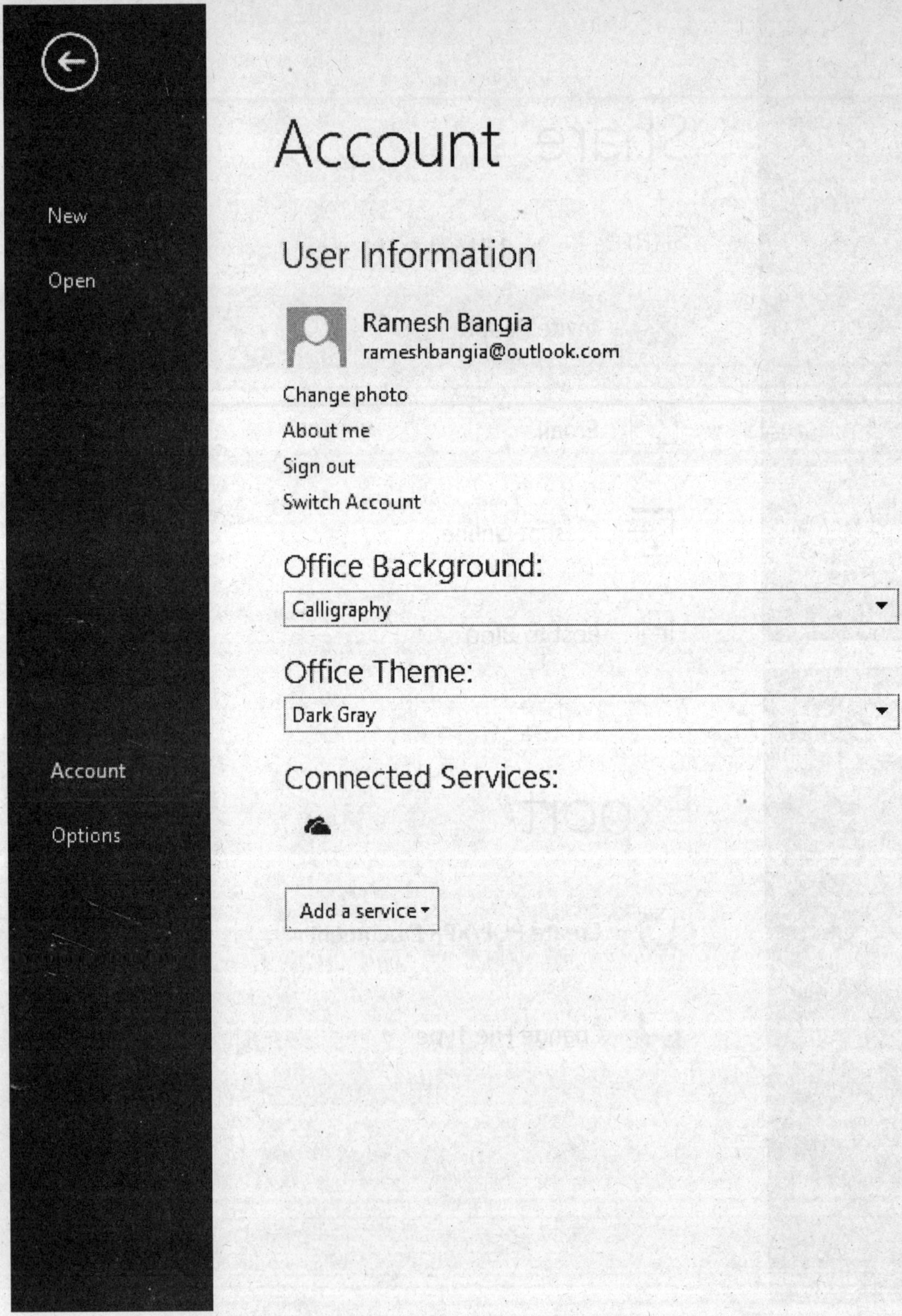
New
Open
Account
Options
Account
User Information
Ramesh Bangia
rameshbangia@outlook.com
Change photo
About me
Sign out
Switch Account
Office Background:
Calligraphy
Office Theme:
Dark Gray
Connected Services:
Add a service

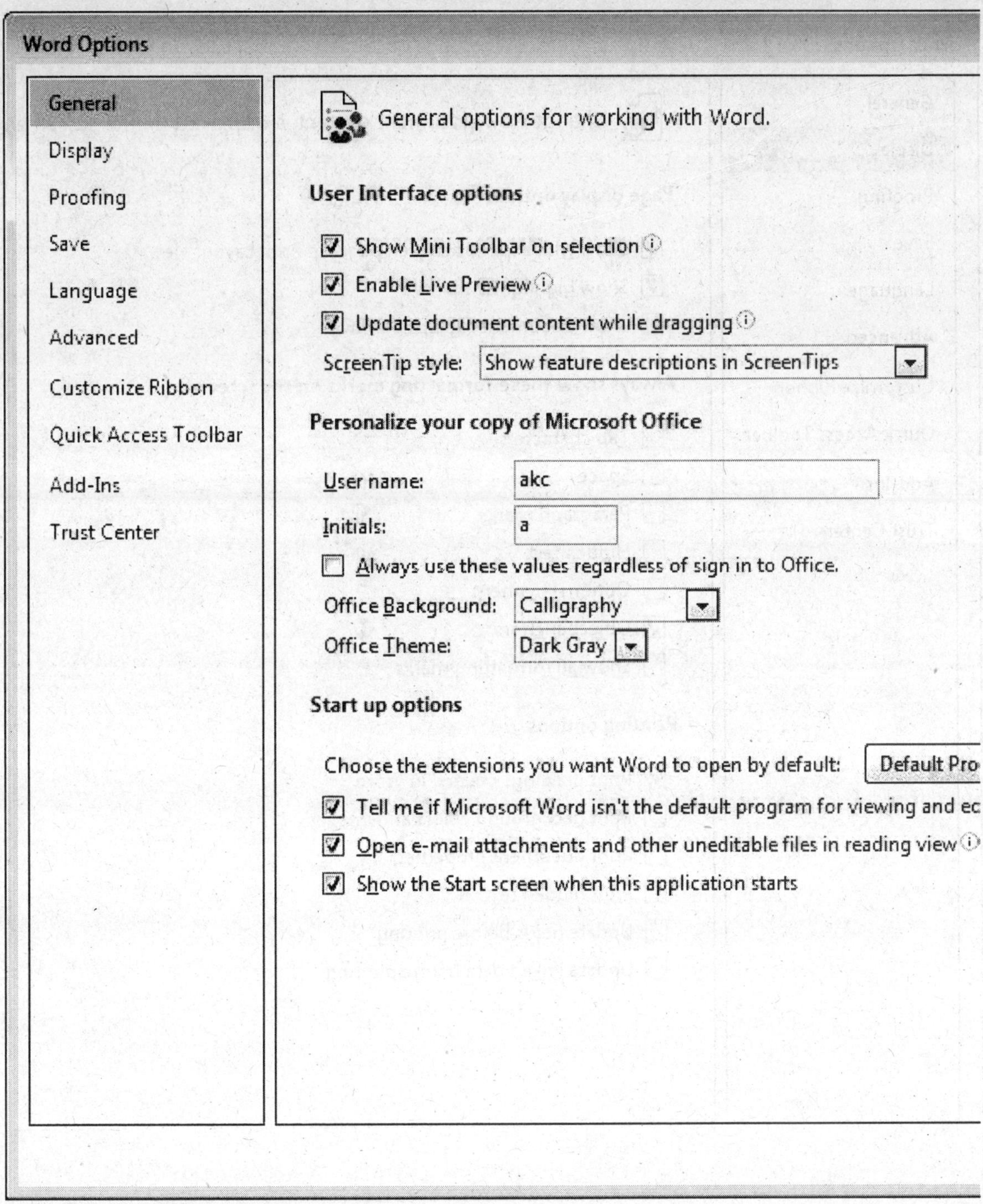
Word Options
General
Display
Proofing
Save
Language
Advanced
Customize Ribbon
Quick Access Toolbar
Add-Ins
Trust Center
General options for working with Word.
User Interface options
Show Mini Toolbar on selection
Enable Live Preview
Update document content while dragging
ScreenTip style:
Show feature descriptions in ScreenTips
Personalize your copy of Microsoft Office
User name:
akc
Initials:
a
Always use these values regardless of sign in to Office.
Office Background:
Calligraphy
Office Theme:
Dark Gray
Start up options
Choose the extensions you want Word to open by default:
Default Pro
Tell me if Microsoft Word isn't the default program for viewing and ec
Open e-mail attachments and other uneditable files in reading view
Show the Start screen when this application starts

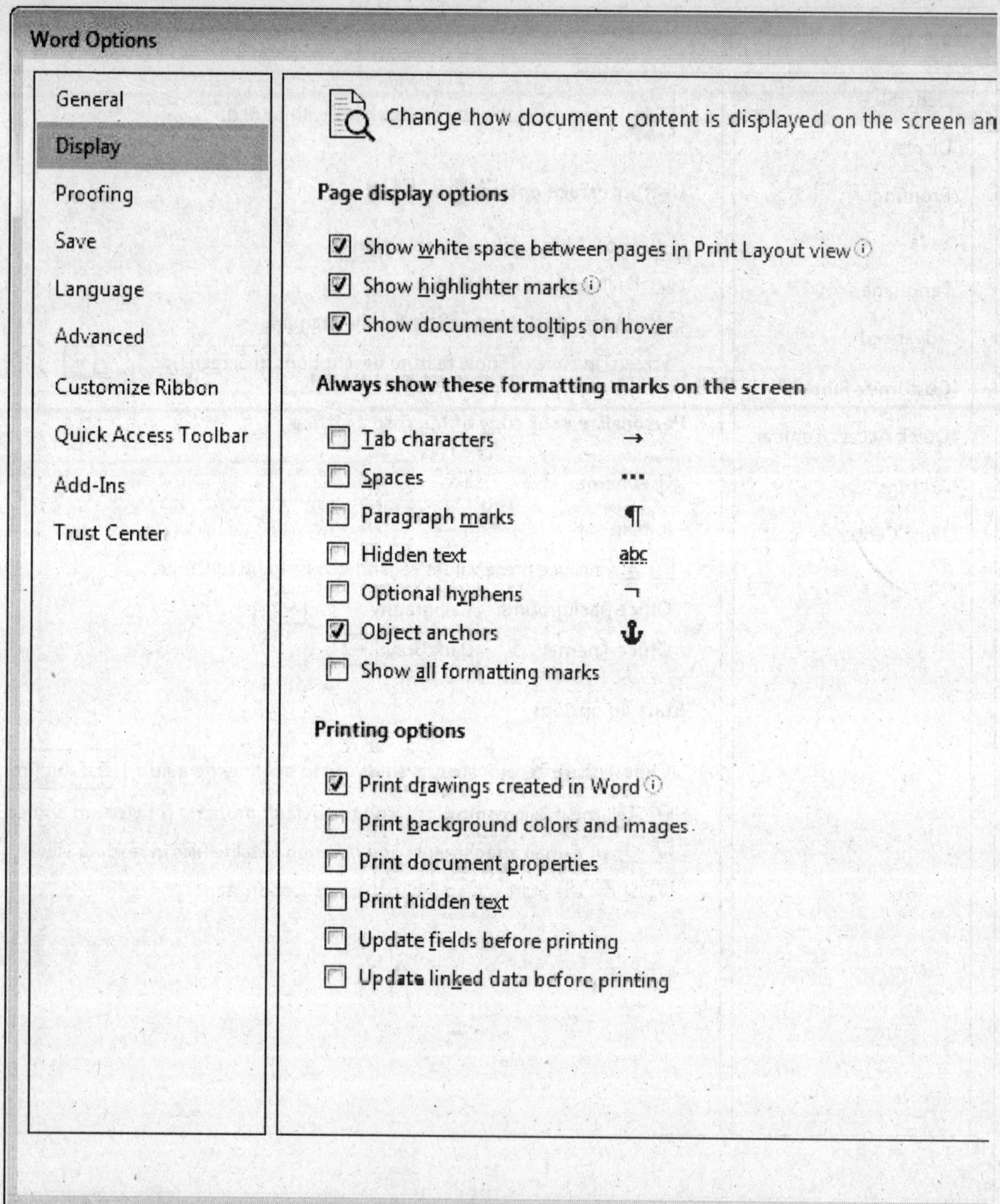
Word Options
General
Display
Proofing
Save
Language
Advanced
Customize Ribbon
Quick Access Toolbar
Add-Ins
Trust Center
Change how document content is displayed on the screen an
Page display options
Show white space between pages in Print Layout view
Show highlighter marks
Show document tooltips on hover
Always show these formatting marks on the screen
Tab characters →
Spaces ···
Paragraph marks ¶
Hidden text abc
Optional hyphens ¬
Object anchors
Show all formatting marks
Printing options
Print drawings created in Word
Print background colors and images
Print document properties
Print hidden text
Update fields before printing
Update linked data before printing

CHAPTER 3

Working with a Document in Microsoft Word 2013

Introduction

The best way to learn about a new software is to use it. It is like jumping into the swimming pool to learn swimming. What we will do here is that we will type our document and learn the various commands side by side.

Working with Documents in Microsoft Word 2013

The best way to learn about a new software is to use it. It is like jumping into the swimming pool to learn swimming. What we will do here is that we will type our document and learn the various commands side by side. Starting Word 2013 is easy so I am not discussing that here. Let us start a new document here. This can again be done from the Start button. After you have opened Word 2013 you can either click at New from the Office button.

Supposing we have to create a document in the form of a letter written to the General Manager of Telephones complaining him of the inflated bills. The text of the letter is shown next. Now that you have opened a new document, do not worry about any typing mistakes or any formatting, just type the text as it is.

Text of the document follows:

13th April, 2013
To,
The General Manager
Mahanagar Telephones Nigam Limited
Khurshid Lal Bhawan
New Delhi - 110 001

Ref: Telephone No. 4611098

Sir,
I am in receipt of bill for the above telephone number dated 1.10.2010 for an amount of Rs. 4,678.90. This bill is to be paid by 21.10.2010. While going through the bill, I notice that I have been charged at two accounts for the calls which have not been made by me. These enteries are:

Called Id	***Duration***	***Amount***
0017249873769	120	1,008.00
0013245934234	60	675.90

As you can notice that both these entries pertain to **International calls** and since my phone does not have this facility, these calls could not have been made from my phone.

I hope that you would look into and send me the revised bill, so that I can make the payment in time.

Hoping for an early action,

Thanking you,

Yours faithfully,
Amitabh Bachan

3695 Ballimaran, Delhi - 110 006

As you may notice that there are few red and green wavy lines. The red lines, show that the word is incorrectly typed as per the dictionary available with the system and the word/words under whom the green line is, show that the words are grammatically wrong. This is the opinion of the software, you may beg to differ from it. Since most of the proper names like Shah Rukh Khan, are shown as wrong.

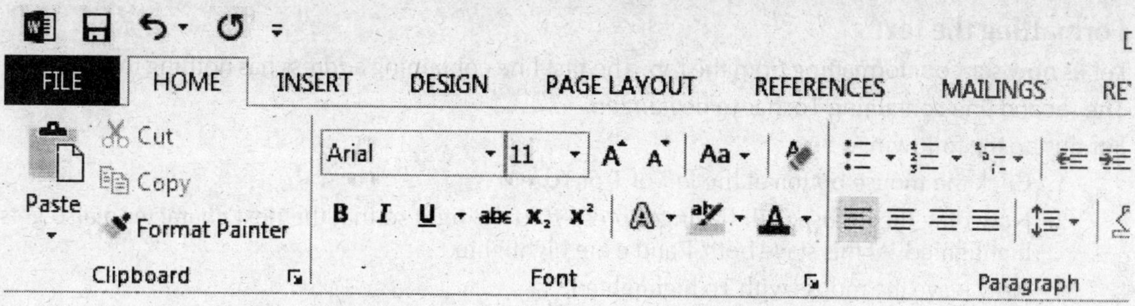

Yours faithfully, 13th April, 2013

To,

The General Manager
Mahanagar Telephones Nigam Limited
Khurshid Lal Bhawan
New Delhi - 110 001
Ref: Telephone No. 4611098

Sir,

I am in receipt of bill for the above telephone number dated 1.10.2010 for an amour
have been charged at two accounts for the calls which have not been made by me.

Called Id	*Duration*	*Amount*
0017249873769	120	1,008.00
0013245934234	60	675.90

As you can notice that both these entries pertain to International calls and since my

I hope that you would look into and send me the revised bill, so that I can make the

Hoping for an early action,

Thanking you,

Amitabh Bachan
3695 Ballimaran, Delhi - 110 006

This is just the raw text which has been typed. Now we have to do the formatting. But, before that, lest the file gets tangled in power failure or something, we must save the file.

Saving the file

It is the process by which you give the name to the file and save under that name. Since our letter pertains to the inflated bill, we will call our file as Bill. For saving, just select the Save option under Office button. You will get the following dialog box. Just type the name Bill in the space provided for typing the filename and click Save. Your file will be saved under this name and automatically the title bar will show the name of the file on the top of the Word 2013 screen.

Now we come to other fomatting tools.

Formatting the text

Let us now start our formatting from the top. The first line containing address has nothing to be done. The second line containing To, has to be *italized*.

For this do the following:

1. Click the mouse button at the left of T of To.
2. Now drag the mouse, still having it pressed to the right so that the next character o also gets highlighted. At this stage both T and o are highlighted.
3. Now leave the mouse with To highlighted.
4. With the mouse, click at I in the formatting toolbar to make To as *To*.
5. See how To looks in the next figure.

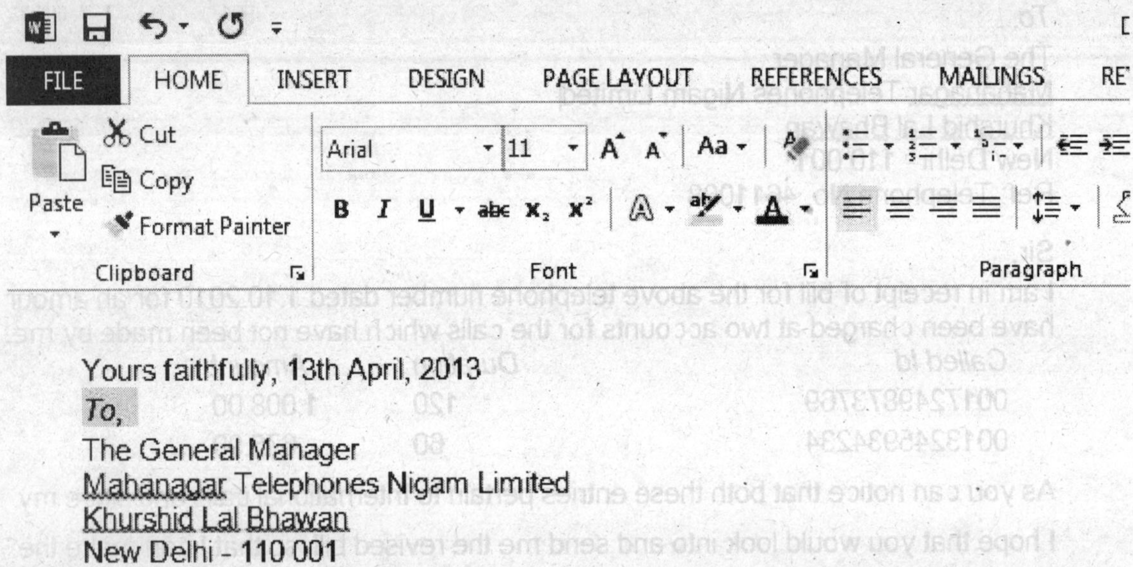

Now we come to the line having The General Manager. This line has to be made bold. This is how we do it.

1. Click the mouse button at the left of T of The General Manager.
2. Since we had highlighted the matter using mouse in the case of To, we will use a different approach here. Press Shift key and start pressing right arrow key ⇨. You will see that as the right arrow key is pressed the matter on the right gets highlighted. So highlight the matter till the point you want it to highlight. In this case highlight till r of Manager.
3. Now leave the shift key.
4. With the mouse, click at B in the formatting toolbar to make the highlighted text as **Bold**.
5. In the figure next, see how the text looks now.

Next in the line is the address, whose last line New Delhi - 110 001 has to be underlined. Word 2013 allows you the option of underlining the word with one or more lines. This option is available under Font. But for the time being, we will stick to single underline.

For this do the following:

1. Click the mouse button at the left of N of New Delhi - 110 001.

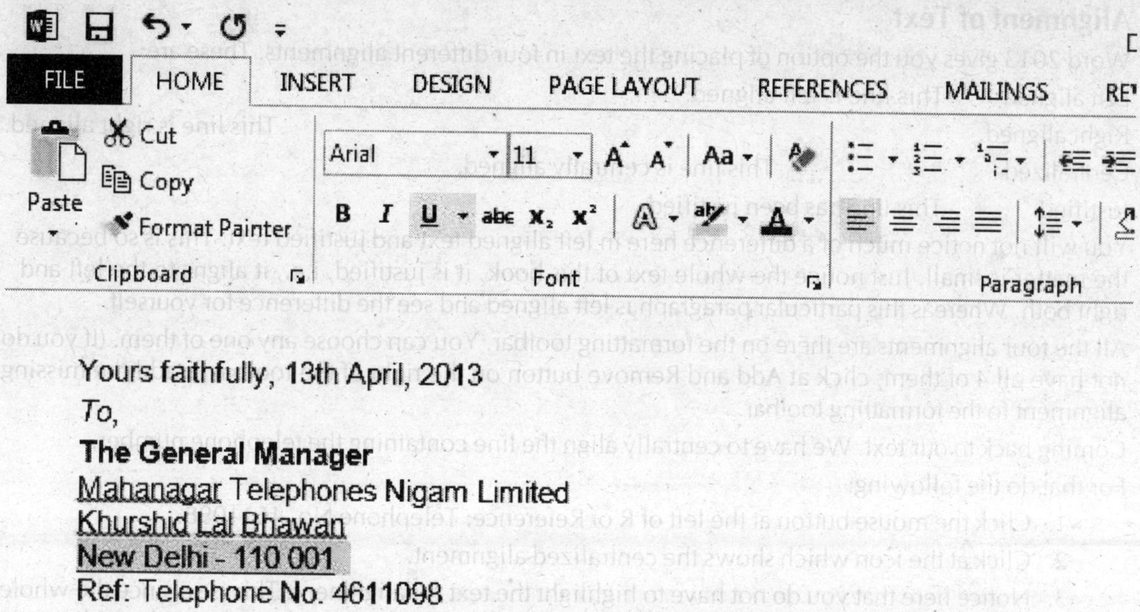

2. Using any of the two methods described above, highlight the text to be underlined.
3. With the mouse, click at U in the formatting toolbar to make the highlighted text **Underlined**.
4. You can see the text underlined next.

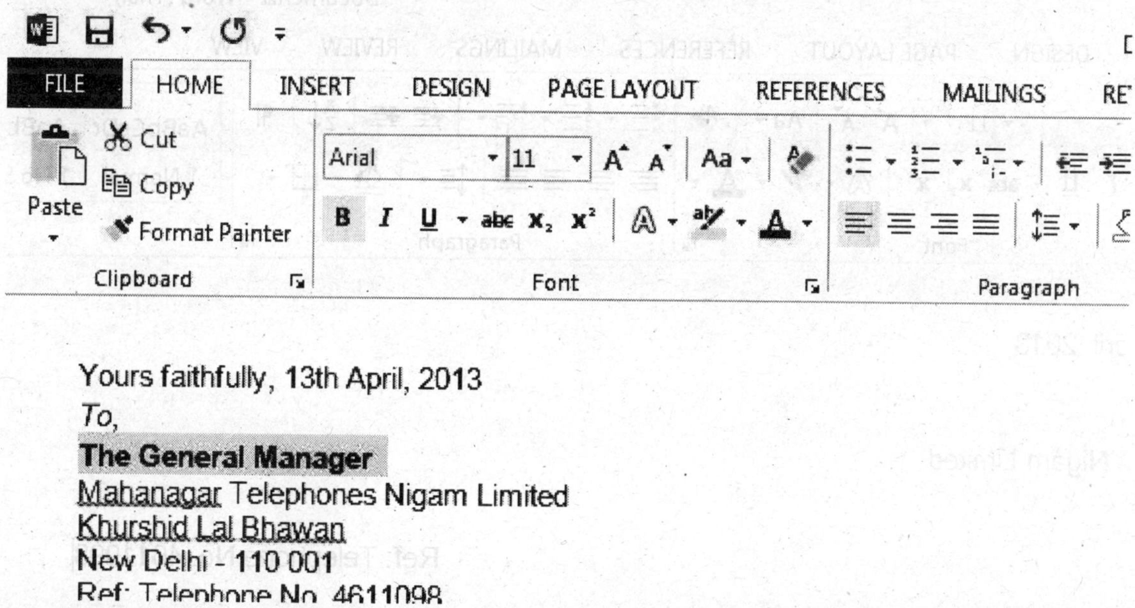

Coming down now you see the line containing the telephone number. This line has to be underlined and centralized. I am not describing here the method to underline this line since it is similar to the one followed by you in the above case. I am sure you can do it yourself. Let us now concentrate on alignment. Let us see how it is done in Word 2013.

Alignment of Text

Word 2013 gives you the option of placing the text in four different alignments. These are:

Left aligned This line is left aligned.

Right aligned This line is right aligned.

Centralized This line is centrally aligned.

Justified This line has been justified.

You will not notice much of a difference here in left aligned text and justified text. This is so because the matter is small. Just notice the whole text of this book, it is justified, i.e., it aligns to the left and right both. Whereas this particular paragraph is left aligned and see the difference for yourself.

All the four alignments are there on the formatting toolbar. You can choose any one of them. (If you do not have all 4 of them, click at Add and Remove button on the right of the toolbar to add the missing alignment to the formatting toolbar.

Coming back to our text. We have to centrally align the line containing the telephone number.

For that do the following:

1. Click the mouse button at the left of R of Reference: Telephone No. 4611098.
2. Click at the icon which shows the centralized alignment.
3. Notice here that you do not have to highlight the text for alignment. This is so since the whole matter of the paragraph has to be aligned to the same alignment. It is not possible to align one word to one alignment and another word to another alignment.
4. You can see the text underlined and centralized aligned in the figure next.

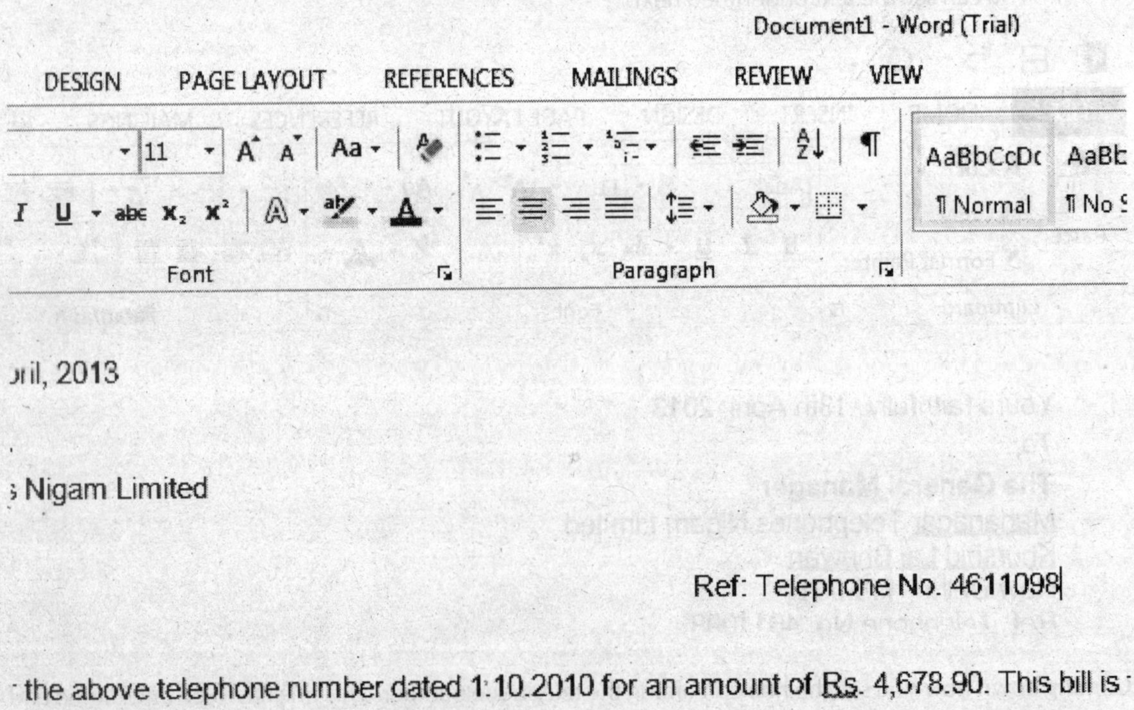

Now that the next lines have nothing much to be done, expect that International calls and Amitabh Bachan have to be made bold. This I presume you will be able to do without any difficulty.

It is time to save the document again so as to make sure that the changes made by you are stored in the hard disk.

Next, let us try to put some fancy things on the text. First among them is Font.

Applying fonts

It is upto you to select the same font for the whole text or have different fonts for different paragraphs. Let us see how it is done..

1. Click at any place in the text with the mouse.
2. Click at Select All in the Edit menu or simply press Ctrl and then A. This will highlight the whole text in the document.
3. Now you can select the font of your liking in the whole text. You can also change the size of the font too.
4. Select Arial for font and size 12 for the whole text in the Formatting toolbar.
5. This will make the whole text 12 points and will have Arial as the font.
6. The previous changes made by you in terms of **Bold**, *Italics* will remain intact and will not be disturbed by doing this.
7. Now if you want you can change the font of particular items like address, etc., to make it more decorative.

Now that our letter is ready, we can just print it, but before that we must check the spelling in the document so as no typological errors remain in the document.

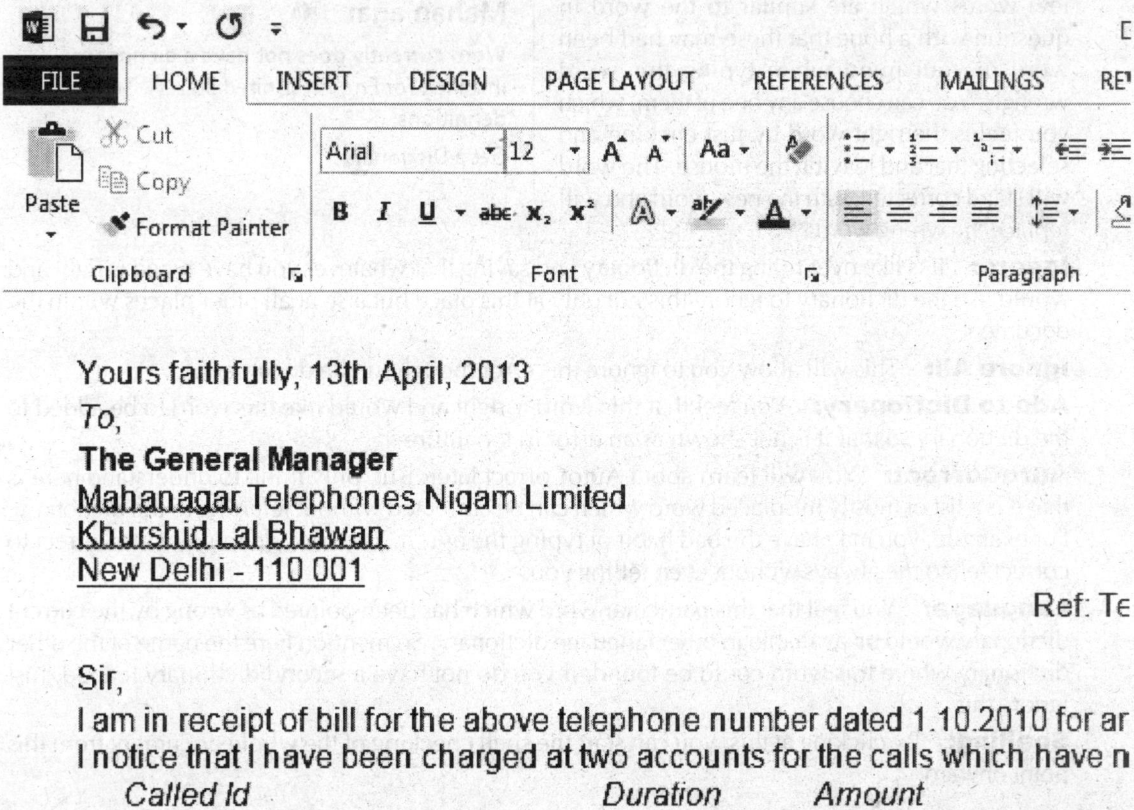

Spell Checking

As was mentioned in the options, Word 2013 points out the spelling errors by underling the word/words with red wavy line. Since our document is just one page long. It is not difficult to pin point the errors.

There are two methods of correcting these errors. One method is to correct these errors one by one, picking them up. Secondly, you spell check the whole document. Let us do both on our document.

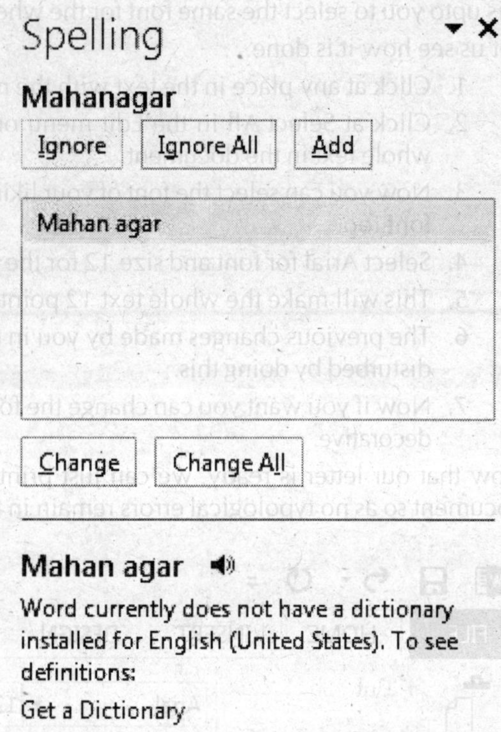

Looking from top to bottom of the text in the document file Bill, you will see few of the words underlined by wavy red line. Few of them are the proper words and thus cannot be corrected.

Words like Mahanagar is basically a *Hindi* word, so it cannot be in the dictionary of Word 2013 and that is why it has been shown as an error. Similar is the case with enteries which is wrong and needs to be corrected. For this follow the following procedure:

1. Click with the mouse at any place within the word to be corrected, in this case enteries.
2. Now right click the mouse button.
3. A pop-menu will pop-up as shown next.
4. Among the various options are:

Alternative words: Word 2013 displays few words which are similar to the word in question with a hope that these may had been word in your mind while typing this word wrongly. You can choose any one of them, which you feel is the right word by just clicking and selecting that and leaving the mouse. The word will stand corrected with the new word and will replace the wrong word.

Ignore: It is like over ruling the dictionary and saying that whatever you have typed is right and would like the dictionary to ignore this not only at this place but also at all other places within the document.

Ignore All: This will allow you to ignore this error thoughout the document.

Add to Dictionary: You feel that this word is right and would like this word to be added to the dictionary so that it is not shown as an error in the future.

AutoCorrect: You will learn about AutoCorrect later. But, only thing to understand here is that it is a list of mostly misplaced word which can be corrected without referring to the dictionary. For example, you may have the bad habit of typing *the* as *teh*. You can add this to AutoCorrect to correct *teh* to *the* always without even telling you.

Language: You feel that this particular word which has been pointed as wrong by the current dictionary would be available in other language dictionary. So mention here the name of the other dictionary where this word could be found. If you do not have a second dictionary loaded, just ignore this.

Spelling: By clicking at this, you can start the spell checking of the whole document from this point onward.

Look Up: It looks for an alternative word in the Thesaurus.

Cut, Copy and Paste: These can be used for transferring the word to some other place in the document by cutting or copying it at this place and pasting it there.

5. In our case we will accept entries as the correct substitute for the wrong word enteries.

Since there is no other word which is to be corrected here. The corrected text would now look like the one shown next. Now we come to the second way of spell checking which is checking the whole document. In this case place the cursor at the beginning of the text in the document. In our case we will place the cursor at the left of 1 of 11th January.

From here do either of the following to start the spell checking.

1. Select Spelling and Grammar from the Tools menu.

   Or

2. Press F7

   Or

3. Click at Spell Grammar in Proofing panel of Review.

This will initiate the spell checking process and will start the spell checking of the document with each word of the document being searched with the similar word with the words available in the dictionary. If not found it will point out.

In our case it will select *Mahanagar* of **Mahanagar Telephones Nigam Limited.** As was mentioned before it is a proper *Hindi* word, so it cannot be corrected. Ignore it to proceed further. Other words in the document are also correct. So keep clicking Ignore for all of them till you reach the end of the document and it stops checking the spelling of the document. After this there is no other word to correct and the spell checking ends with a dialog box, saying that the spelling checking is complete.

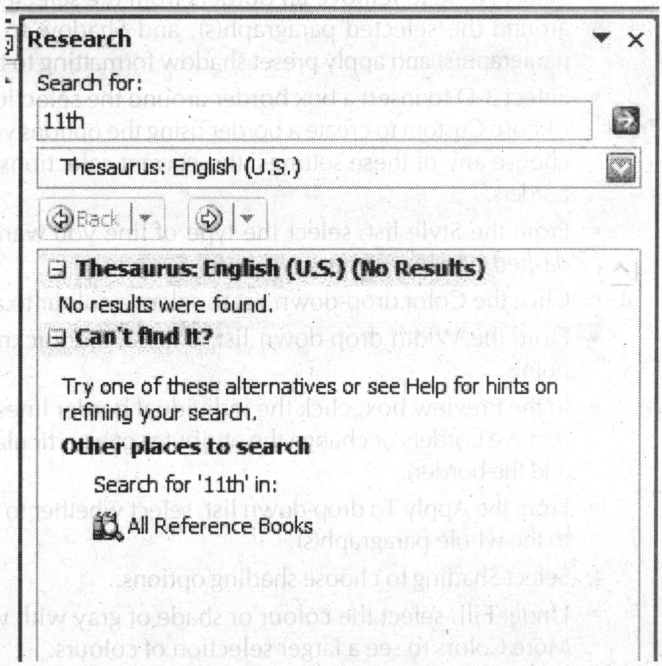

Remember, you can spell check a portion of the text or a word by just highlighting it and then clicking at Spell Checking Icon.

Then there is another option called Thesaurus.

Consulting Thesaurus

Thesaurus is there to help you find Synonym, words with similar meanings and Antonym, words with opposite meanings. Using the thesaurus not only helps your vocabulary, but gives you alternatives to using the same word over and over again throughout your text.

Let us try to use this option in our text. We would like to see the alternatives to the word Bill. For this we do the following:

1. Select the word bill in the second line of the paragraph.
2. Now select Thesaurus from the Proofing panel.
3. You will get the dialog box as shown here.
4. The options given here are Invoice as the main. But there are others too like statement, check, etc.
5. You have the option to select a new word Invoice or other or let the bill remain as it is.

Borders and Shading

Word 2013 allows you to highlight headlines, captions, and other text of importance by applying a border or shading to that text. You can apply it to a piece of text or to the full text.

Apply Borders and Shading

1. Select the text on which you want to apply Borders or Shading. Basically the rules to follow this are:
   - If no text is selected, the paragraph where the cursor is, will be taken as the starting point.
   - If you select text within a single paragraph, but the paragraph mark itself is not included in the selection, the results affect only the selected text.
   - If you select text included in more than one paragraph (so that at lease one paragraph mark is included in the selection), the results affect all the paragraphs in which any of the selected text resides.
2. Open the Design Panel, and select Page Border.
3. Click Borders to work with options available under it.
   - Under Setting, click one of the preset border options.
   - Select None to remove all borders from the selected paragraph(s), Box to insert a box border around the selected paragraph(s), and Shadow to insert a box border around the selected paragraph(s) and apply preset shadow formatting to the border.
   - Select 3-D to insert a box border around the selection and apply preset 3D border formatting. Choose Custom to create a border using the options you click in the Preview window. When you choose any of these settings, the current selections in Style, Colour, and Width apply to the borders.
   - From the Style list, select the type of line you want to use for the border, including *dotted, dashed*, and *wavy lines*.
   - Click the Color drop-down list to select a colour to apply to the border.
   - From the Width drop-down list, choose the thickness of the border line from ¼ point to 6 points.
   - In the Preview box, click the individual border lines or use the border line buttons to apply or remove borders or change the attributes of a particular border (select the attributes first and then add the border).
   - From the Apply To drop-down list, select whether to apply the border to just the selected text or to the whole paragraph(s).
4. Select Shading to choose shading options.
   - Under Fill, select the colour or shade of gray with which you want to fill the selection. Click More Colors to see a larger selection of colours.

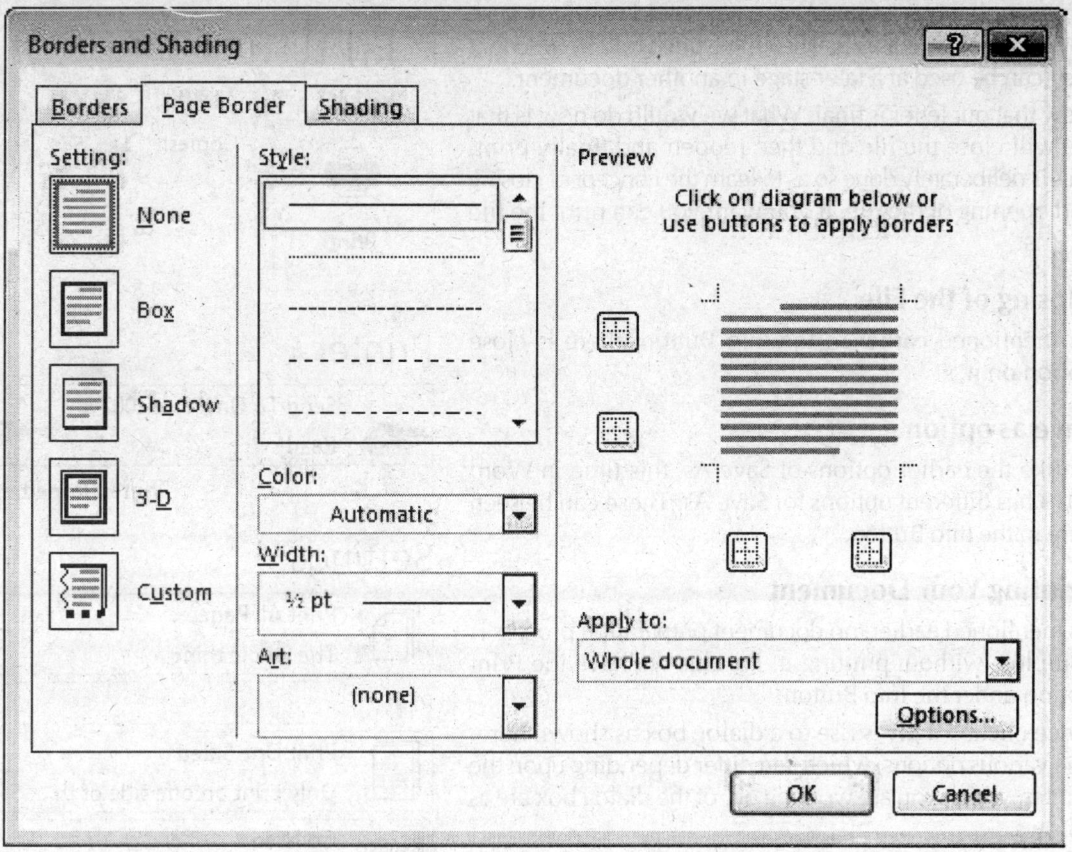

- From the Patterns Style drop-down list, choose a shading percentage for the colour you selected under Fill or a pattern of lines such as Lt Horizontal or Dk Trellis.
- If you selected a pattern of lines, select the Color of the lines from the drop-down list. The Fill colour then becomes the background colour for the pattern.
- From the Apply To drop-down list select whether to apply the shading options to just the selected text or to the whole paragraph(s).

5. Click Ok.

You can use all these options of Borders and Shading from the Tables and Border toolbar, which can be called from toolbar options. This will allow you to select shading colours, border line styles, border line colours, and border line widths, etc.

Following are the button on the toolbar that apply to borders and shading.

Button	***Description***
Line Style	Sets the style of the border lines (dotted, dashed, wavy, double, and so on)
Line Weight	Sets the thickness of the border lines
Border Color	Sets the colour of the border lines
Borders	Specifies where the border appears (top, bottom, left, right, or box)
Shading Color	Sets the colour of the background shading for the paragraph (you cannot specify the percentage)

Since our letter is a formal one, we would not like to use any of these decorations. They have been told here so that they can be used at a later stage in another document.

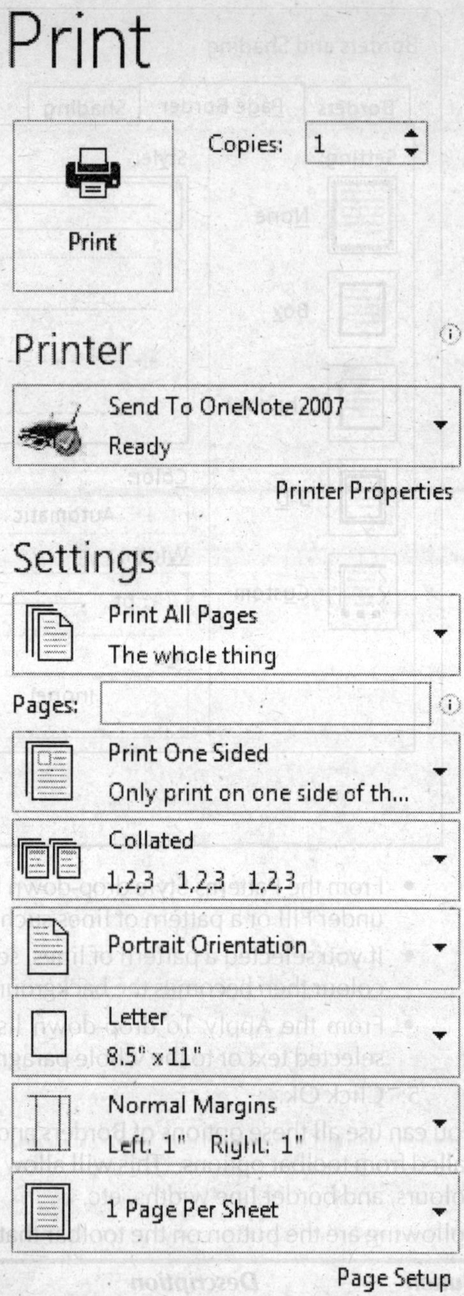

Now that our letter is final. What we would do now is that we will close the file and then reopen and finally print. This is deliberately done so as to learn the concept of closing and opening of the file. If you want you can print the file as it is.

Closing of the File

As mentioned earlier in the Info Button, there is close option on it.

Save as option

Unlike the earlier options of Save As, this time in Word 2013 has different options for Save As. These can be seen here in the Info Button.

Printing Your Document

As mentioned earlier, no document preparation process is complete without printing it. For this we have the Print option under the Info Button.

Once clicked it gives rise to a dialog box as shown here. The various options, which can differ depending upon the printer, which you are working on, of the dialog box are as follows:

Print All Pages: Select to print all pages in the file.

Print One Sided: Select to print one side of the paper or on both sides of the paper.

Collated: Yoy can select to have the pages collated in case of multiple copies being printed.

Orientation: You may select from Portrait or Landscape.

Page Size: Select the page size from the various page sizes options available.

Normal Margins: You can choose to have normal margins or set up your own margins as required.

Page Per Sheet: You can choose to print multiple pages printed on the sheet.

Zoom: Pages per sheet allows you to print 1 to 16 pages of the document on one sheet. Scaling allows you to scale your document to the various sizes of the paper.

Once you are sure that you have selected all the options required by you, just click Ok to for document to start printing. However, do not forget to have the Printer ON before giving the final print command.

Editing the Document

Now that you have printed the document, you may want to either correct few words which you have realized that they do not look good in the letter. Even otherwise you may want to enhance the overall look of the letter. Besides this you would also learn how to do the tailor's job, i.e., Cut, Copy and Paste. There are other options too which may not be used in this letter but are quite useful overall for editing. Let us start with the proofing tools.

Editing Tools

Many editing functions are performed on selected text, such as cut, copy, move, and delete. There are various tools provided by Word to help you edit text:

Cut, Copy: Cutting and copying items places them on the Clipboard and you can paste these items anywhere in the document, wherever required. These items can be text, graphics, tables and any other object which is there in the word document. Cut and Copy can be performed using mouse and key strokes.

Paste: It is the command used to paste whatever is available on the Clipboard to paste it in the document. This is also done by the use of mouse and key strokes.

Move: It is an action associated with the mouse. However, if you cut and paste from one place to another, it can also be called move.

Insert Mode: It is the feature that adjusts spacing when you add new text to the document.

Overtype Mode: This option replaces the existing text with your new text.

Delete: It is an action you should reserve for text you want to permanently remove. Deleted text is not placed in the Clipboard. You can delete text with either mouse or key strokes.

Undo and Redo: Using these commands you can reverse the tasks performed earlier.

All these commands are available on the toolbar in the Home menu.

For either cutting or copying, you have to highlight the part of the text on which you want to perform this operation. All these commands have their keyboard strokes associated with them too.

Let us now learn few options of Word 2013 which help us in correcting our document with minimum efforts.

AutoCorrect

It is a handy feature of Word 2013 which automatically corrects common typing, capitalization, and spelling errors for you, as you type. It also enables you to type shortcuts that AutoCorrect replaces with the full text, such as typing BOMBAY and having AutoCorrect replace it with MUMBAI. This has been neccesiated due to the fact that the name of the city has been changed as thus. Although Word 2013 has a number of default AutoCorrect entries, you can add your own common misspellings and shortcuts.

It only checks whole words, so if you type TEH, Word won't replace it with THE until your press the spacebar, period, or some other key that indicates that the word is complete. It is also useful tool for applying formatting options. In a business letter, for example, you might want your company name to always appear in a certain font and size, regardless of the font you are using for the letter. By creating an AutoCorrect entry of your company name with formatting options, you eliminate the need to format while you type, or to run search and replace when you are finished with the letter.

Add AutoCorrect Entries Without Formatting

1. From the Info button, select Options, and then Proofing, AutoCorrect options.
2. Click Replace Text as You Type to place a check mark there, if it isn't already checked.

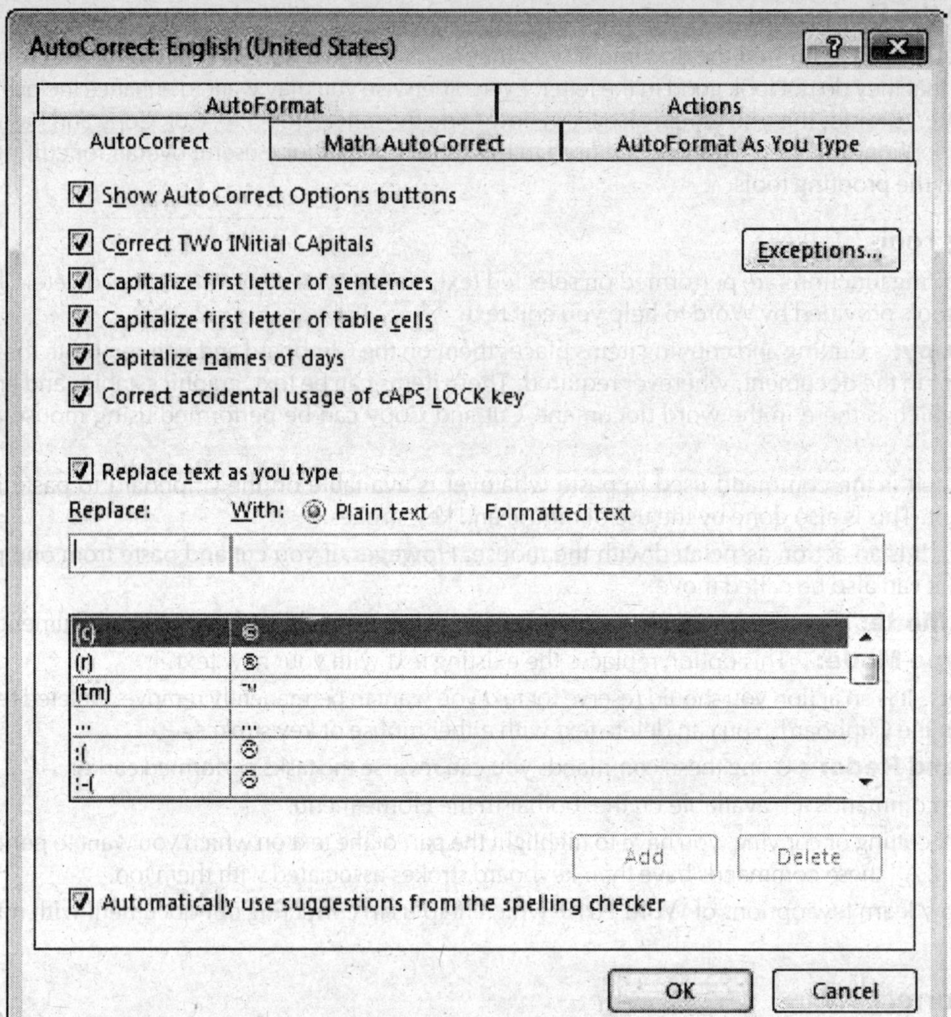

3. In the replace box, enter the text you want AutoCorrect to automatically replace for you, such as your initials or a word you commonly misspell.
4. Click Plain Text if it is not selected to inserted text without formatting options.
5. Choose Add. If the text in the Replace box is already listed, choose Replace to replace the existing replacement text with the text you entered in the With box.
6. Click Ok.

Text your new AutoCorrect entry by typing the word in a document and pressing the Spacebar.

Add New AutoCorrect Entries with Formatting

1. Type the text in your document and format it.
2. Select the text. To store paragraph formatting with your entry, include the paragraph mark at the end of the text, in your selection.
3. From the Info button, select Options and Proofing and AutoCorrect Options. The AutoCorrect dialog box appears.

4. In the Replace text box, type a name for the AutoCorrect entry (an abbreviation, or the entire word or phrase).
5. Click Formatted Text.
6. To save the entry and close the dialog box, click Add.

Here you have an option for Math AutoCorrect tool, which allows you to create mathematical characters, by just writing the english word for it.

AutoFormat

Word 2013 has automated a lot of small, tedious chores that we had to do manually in older word processing programs. Many of these are formatting chores, and Word collects them under the term AutoFormat. You can control what formatting chores Word 2013 performs automatically in the AutoFormat panels of the AutoCorrect dialog box. The benefit of using AutoFormat is that you can concentrate more on the content of your document and less on the details of formatting.

AutoFormat works on two different ways—as you type or on command.

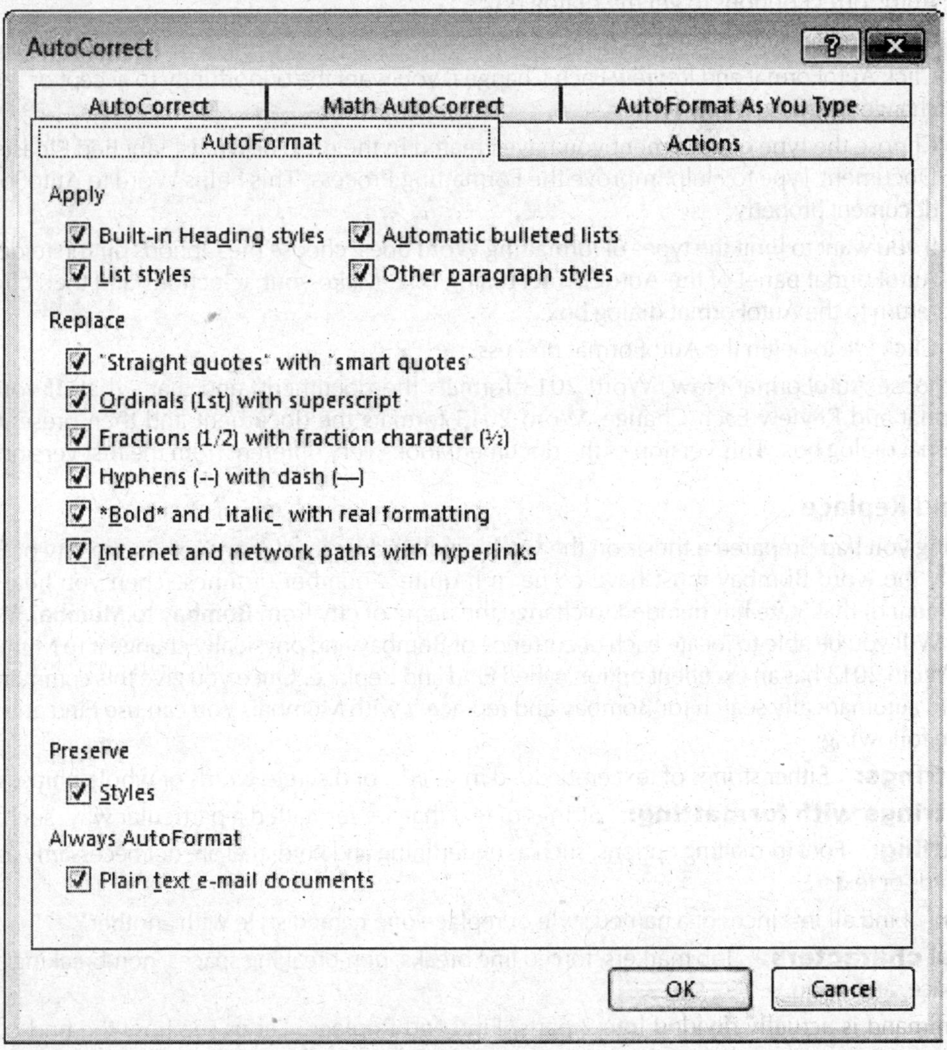

AutoFormat as You Type

Automatically formats headings, bulleted and numbered lists, borders, numbers, symbols, and so on, as you type.

AutoFormat on Command

Automatically formats selected text or the entire document in one pass. You don't have to do anything to activate AutoFormat. By default, AutoFormat as You Type is enabled—you just enter text and Word formats it as you go. You can change the default to AutoFormat on Command, which allows you to manually run AutoFormat. This is similar to the way in which you can spell check a document—as you type, or manually, using the menu commands or toolbar icons.

AutoFormatting Text

1. To AutoFormat a block of text, select it. To AutoFormat the entire document, make sure that no text is selected.
2. From the Office button, select Word Options followed by Proofing options. From here click at AutoCorrect options to get the dialog box.
3. Click AutoFormat.
4. Click AutoFormat and Review Each Change if you want the opportunity to accept or reject each change proposed by Word.
5. Choose the type of document you have created in the drop-down list labelled Please Select a Document Type to Help Improve the Formatting Process. This helps Word to AutoFormat the document properly.
6. If you want to limit the types of formatting Word does, choose the Options button to display the AutoFormat panel of the AutoCorrect dialog box. Make your selections and then click Ok to return to the AutoFormat dialog box.
7. Click Ok to begin the AutoFormat process.

If you choose AutoFormat Now, Word 2013 formats the document, and that's that. If you choose AutoFormat and Review Each Change, Word 2013 formats the document and then presents a new AutoFormat dialog box. This version of the document looks very different from the first version.

Find and Replace

Supposing you had prepared a thesis on the working of middle level managers in the city of Bombay. Naturally the word Bombay must have come in it quite a number of times. Then you hear that the Government of that State has decided to change the name of city from **Bombay** to **Mumbai**. What will you do? Will you be able to locate each occurrence of Bombay and physically change it to Mumbai? No! For this Word 2013 has an excellent option called Find and Replace. Once you give this command, Word 2013 will automatically search for Bombay and replace it with Mumbai. You can use Find and Replace to do the following:

Text strings: Either strings of text embedded in words, or discrete words or whole phrases.

Text strings with formatting: Strings of text that are formatted a particular way, such as Bold.

Formatting: Font formatting options, such as underlining and bold, that are not necessarily associated with words or text.

Styles: Find all instances of a named style or replace one named style with another.

Special characters: Tab markers, forced line breaks, non-breaking spaces, non-breaking hyphens, whitespace, and so on.

This command is actually divided into 2 parts, Find and Replace. Let us see how the find command works first.

Find

This command will find for you the exact text which is mentioned in its box and will stop for further action. Normally the finding of the text starts from the position where the cursor is. If you have selected some text, the finding will be restricted to that block of text only. So if you have to select the entire text, then it is advised to put the cursor at the beginning of the text in the document.

To start the Find command, click at Find in the Home menu.

Find and Replace dialog box, as shown here will appear.

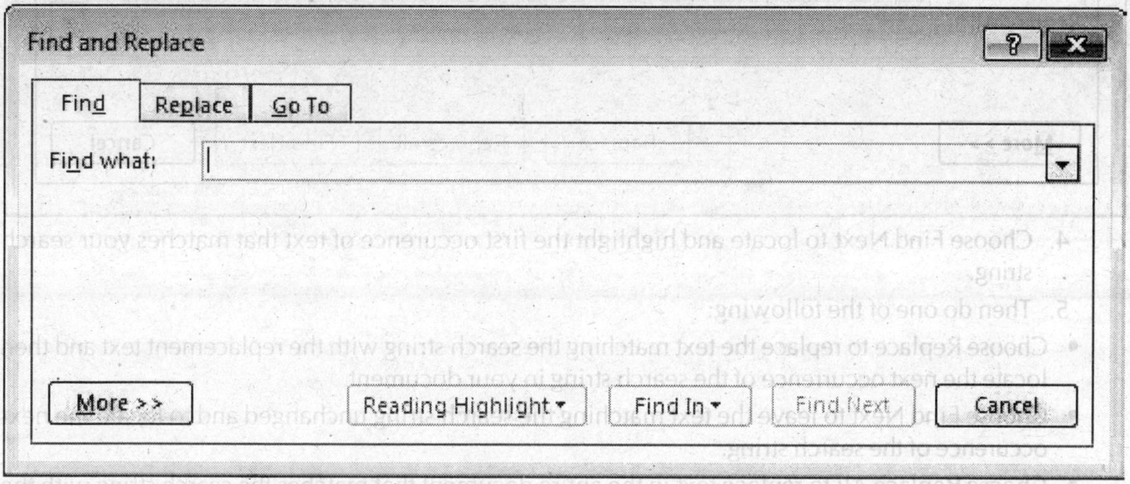

This is how you will use the Find command.

1. Type the text that you are seeking in the Find What? text box. This word or phrase is also referred to as the search string.
2. Choose the More button (if necessary) to specify search options.
3. Choose Find Next. Find looks through the document for text that matches your search strings. When it finds matching text, Word highlights the text in the document and stops. The Find and Replace dialog box remains on screen.
4. Choose Find Next if you want to continue the search for another instance of the search string. Click Cancel or press Esc to close the dialog box and return to the document. The text in the document is still highlighted.

When Word finishes the entire document, or if it could not find the search string in the document, a dialog box displays a message to that effect. Choose Ok to continue working in the document.

Replace Text

Next step after finding the required text is to replace it with some other text. For this we would call the command called Replace. To get the replace command click at Replace in the Home menu. Now on the Find and Replace dialog box click at the Replace panel and do the following:

1. Type the text you want to replace in the Find What text box (in this case, *Bombay*). You can leave this field blank if you have to search for a formatting only. However, you have to search for something.
2. Type the text you want to replace it with in the Replace With text box (in this case, *Mumbai*). If you search for text and leave this field blank, you are in effect telling Word to delete all instances of the search strings, because they would be replaced by a blank.
3. Choose the More button (if necessary) to specify search options.

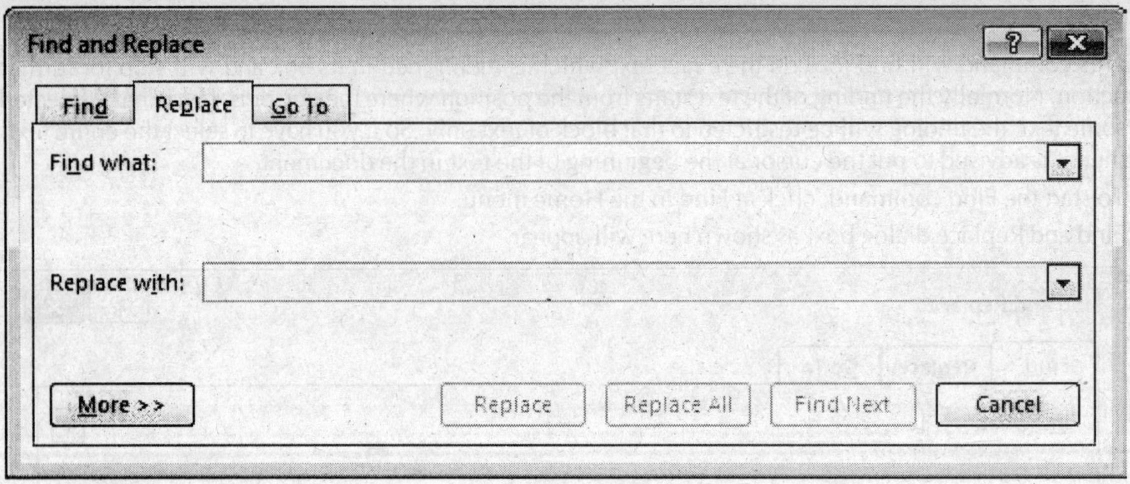

4. Choose Find Next to locate and highlight the first occurence of text that matches your search string.
5. Then do one of the following:

- Choose Replace to replace the text matching the search string with the replacement text and then locate the next occurrence of the search string in your document.
- Choose Find Next to leave the text matching the search string unchanged and to locate the next occurence of the search string.
- Choose Replace All to replace text in the entire document that matches the search string with the replacement text.

6. Choose Cancel. Alternatively, press Esc to close the Find and Replace dialog box and return to the your document.

When Word has finished searching through the document and has replaced all occurrences of the search text or can't find any further occurrences, a message box appears. Click Ok to return to your document.

Word Count

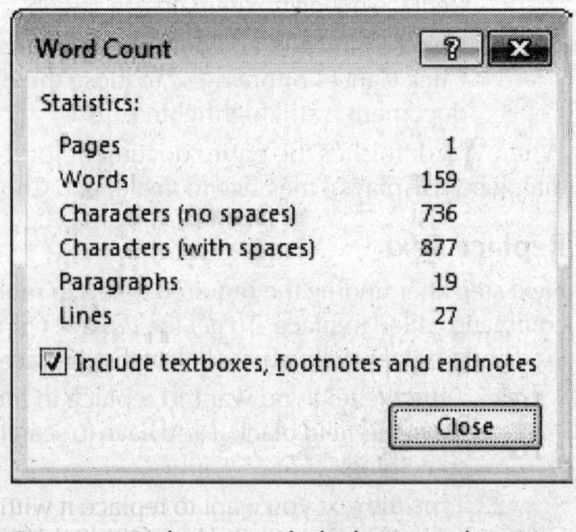

Printed documents longer than one page should have page numbers. You can set up page numbering in two ways. Either insert a page number code while editing headers and footers, or insert page numbers from the Insert menu. Both methods insert a page number code in you documents' header or footer, but there are two differences.

1. Click the Insert panel and select Page Numbers to open the Page Numbers dialog box.
2. From the Position drop-down list, select the position on the page where you want your page numbers to appear. The options are:

   Top of the Page (Header)

   Bottom of the Page (Footer)
3. From the alignment drop-down list, select Left, Center, or Right to specify the horizontal position of the page number in relation to the right or left margins.
4. If you want the page number to appear on the first page, Show number on first page to place

check mark there. Deselecting this option creates a separate header or footer for the first page.

5. Click Ok.

When you insert a page number, Word automatically switches you to Print Layout view so you can scroll to the portion of the page where the page number appears to check its appearance.

Header and Footer

As you must be knowing that Header appears on the top of the page and Footer appears on the bottom of the page. Word 2013 allows you to put both of them on the document pages. Once clicked they give you the options to choose from.

Headers and footers can vary within a document. Choices include:

1. The same header and footer on every page.
2. A different header and footer for the first page only
3. Different headers and footers for odd numbered pages than those on even numbered pages.
4. Different headers and footers for each section of the document.

Footnotes and Endnotes

These are used in the documents to provide references to the source documents for the document text, to provide more detailed explanations and definitions that might otherwise distract the reader if left in the main body of the document.

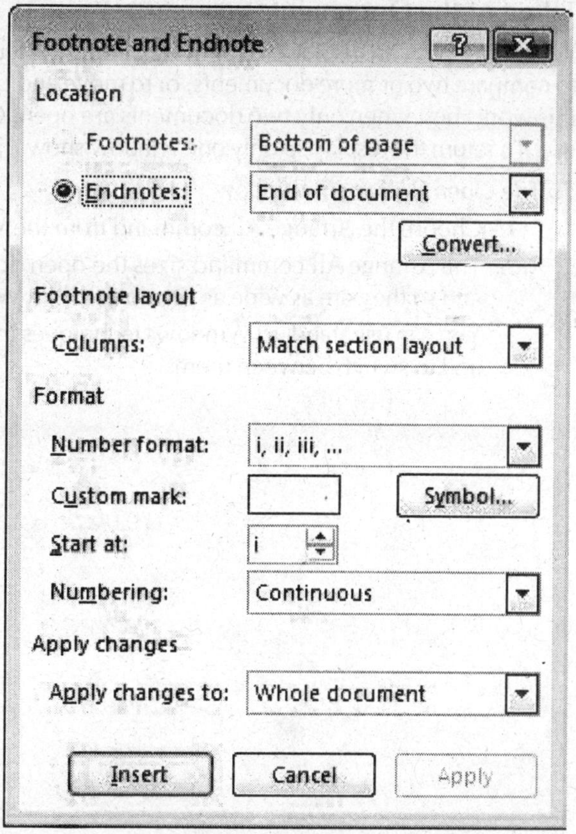

The two parts to each footnote or endnote are the reference mark—a number, character, or combination of characters appearing in the body of the document—and the note text. You may automatically number the marks or create your own custom marks. If you use the automatic numbering, Word renumbers the note reference marks if you add, delete, or move notes. The note can be of any length and format, and you can format the line that separates the notes from the body of the document. To view the note text, rest the mouse pointer on the note reference mark. The note text appears in a pop-up box above the mark. Double-click the note reference mark to display the note text in a note pane at the bottom of the screen. If you are using Print Layout view, footnotes display at the bottom of the page, endnotes at the end of the document.

Add a Footnote or Endnote

1. Place curosr where you want the note reference mark to appear.
2. Choose the Reference menu and select Insert Footnote. The Footnote dialog box appears.
3. Select Footnote or Endnote.
4. Under Numbering, select AutoNumber or Custom Mark. If you choose Custom Mark, insert the symbol or symbols for the reference mark

or choose Symbol to open the Symbol dialog box. Choose a font, click the symbol you want to use, and then click Ok.

5. Choose Ok to close the Footnote and Endnote dialog box.
6. Type the note text in the footnote pane. Apply formatting as desired or, better yet, reformat the Footnote text style (which automatically appears in the Style list when you insert your first footnote).
7. Choose Close to close the footnote pane or click in the document to continue typing.

Splitting Panes

You can split a document window into two panes. Then, you can display different portions of the same document at the same time. This lets you compare two portions of a single document. It also makes it easier for you to move or copy text from one portion of a document to another. When you make a change to the document from either pane, the change is applied to the same document. As a result, the change can be found in both panes.

Splitting Document into Two Panes

1. Choose the New window command from the View panel, drag the separator bar to where you want to split the window, and click the left mouse button.
2. Use Remove Split to remove the split.

Tiling of the Documents

With tiling you can display two or more different documents at the same time. This makes it easy for you to compare two or more documents, or to move and copy text from one document to another. However, this works best when only two documents are open. Otherwise, the windows get too small for effective use. To return the display so only one window shows, just maximize the window that you want dispalyed.

To Tile Open Document Window

1. Choose the Arrange All command from the View menu.
2. The Arrange All command sizes the open documents windows so they are all the same height and so they are as wide as possible within Word's application window.
3. You can use standard Windows techniques to move, size and maximize the document windows and to switch between them.

CHAPTER 4

Customizing Microsoft Word 2013

Introduction

You can fine tune Word 2013 according to your likings. For this you have to choose the various tools which you feel are useful for you and ignore others. First we will set the vaious options in the Options and then go on to set the options in the toolbars.

Setting Options

Default settings specify what options are in effect when you start a document or set up how a particular operation works unless you change the settings. If you do not like the default settings used by Word 2013 for fonts, margins, file locations, styles, and so on, Word 2013 allows you to change the defaults. After you make the modifications, your new settings become the default for documents created from that moment onwards.

Options menu is available under Office Button under the name Word Options. This allows you to set the various settings according to your usage of Word 2013. First among them is Popular.

General Options

As you would notice that various options have been ticked and others have been left blank. Each one of them signifies something. Let us look at them, one by one:

Show Mini Toolbar on selection

Select this option to show the Mini Toolbar when you select text. The Mini Toolbar provides quick access to formatting tools.

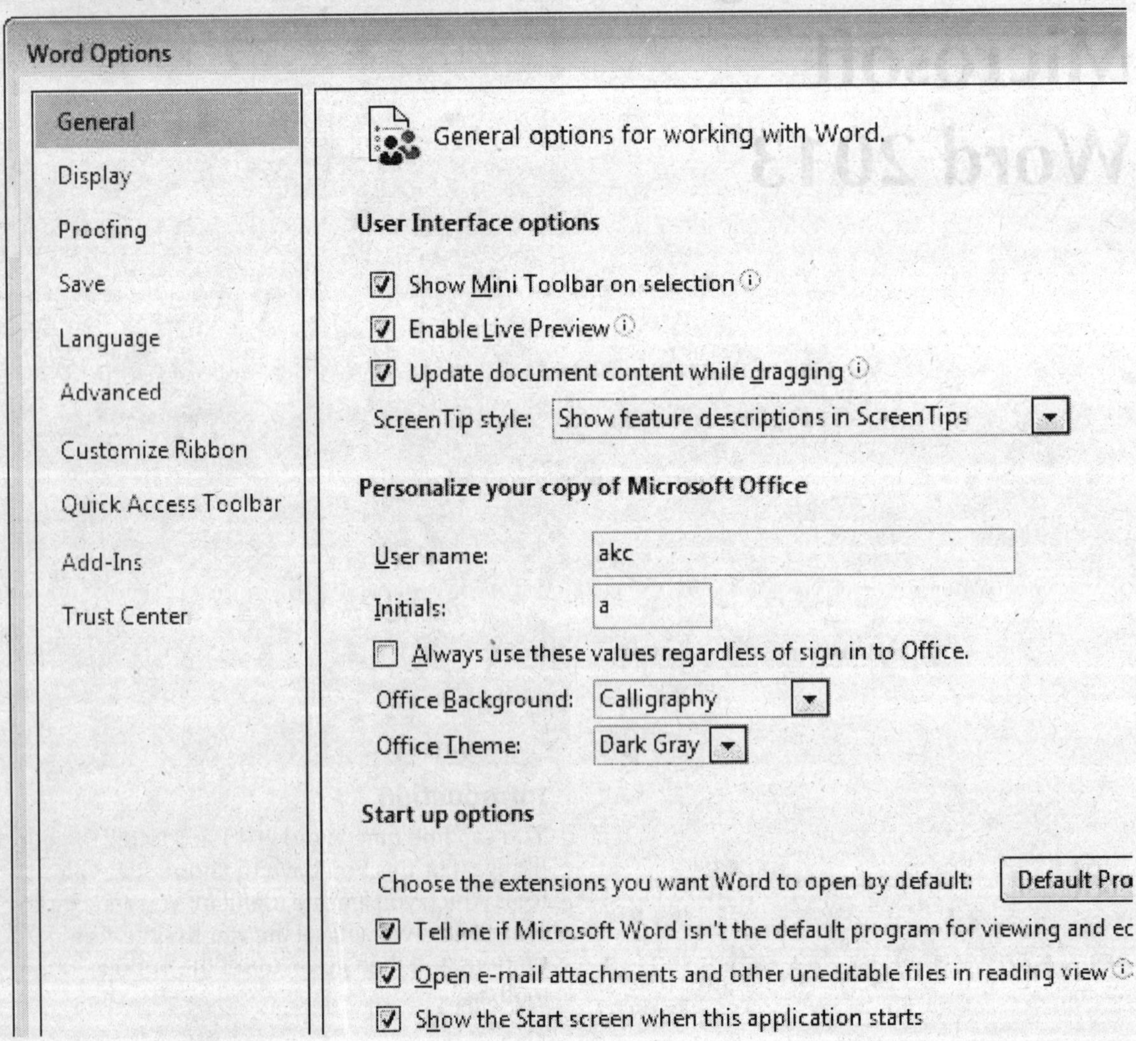

Enable Live Preview

Select this option to preview the effects of formatting changes in the document.

Show Developer tab in the Ribbon

Select this option to show the Developer tab on the Ribbon in 2013 Microsoft Office system programs. The Developer tab includes macro and form authoring tools, as well as XML-related features. Clear this check box to hide the Developer tab.

Always use ClearType

Selected by default, this option turns on ClearType to make the text easier to read. If you change this setting, you must restart Microsoft Office Word for the setting to take effect.

Notes

- This setting applies to all Office programs.
- On computers running Microsoft Windows XP, turning this option on overrides the ClearType setting in Windows. This option is not available on computers running Microsoft Windows Vista.

Open e-mail attachments in Full Screen Reading view

Selected by default, this option displays documents in Full Screen Reading view when they are opened from e-mail attachments. Clear this check box to open e-mail attachments in Print Layout view.

Color scheme

Select an option from the list to change the color scheme of the programs.

ScreenTip style

Select a style from the list to control the display of the names of buttons and additional helpful information. Select Show feature descriptions in ScreenTips for names and helpful information, select Don't show feature descriptions in ScreenTips for button names only, or select Don't show ScreenTips for neither.

Personalize your copy of Microsoft Office

User name

Type a name in the User name box to change your user name.

The name that appears here will be associated with revisions that you make when you review documents by using the Track Changes feature. It is also the author name that is associated with the documents that you create. For example, in predesigned cover pages that include the author name, the name that appears in the User name box is used automatically.

Initials

Type your initials in the Initials box to change the initials that are associated with your user name.

The initials that appear here are associated with comments that you add when you review documents.

Choose the languages you want to use with Office

Click Language Settings to turn on the features necessary for the languages you want to use in 2013 Microsoft Office system.

Display Options

This has the following options:

Show white space between pages in Print Layout view

Select this option to display the top and bottom margins of the page, including the content of headers and footers.

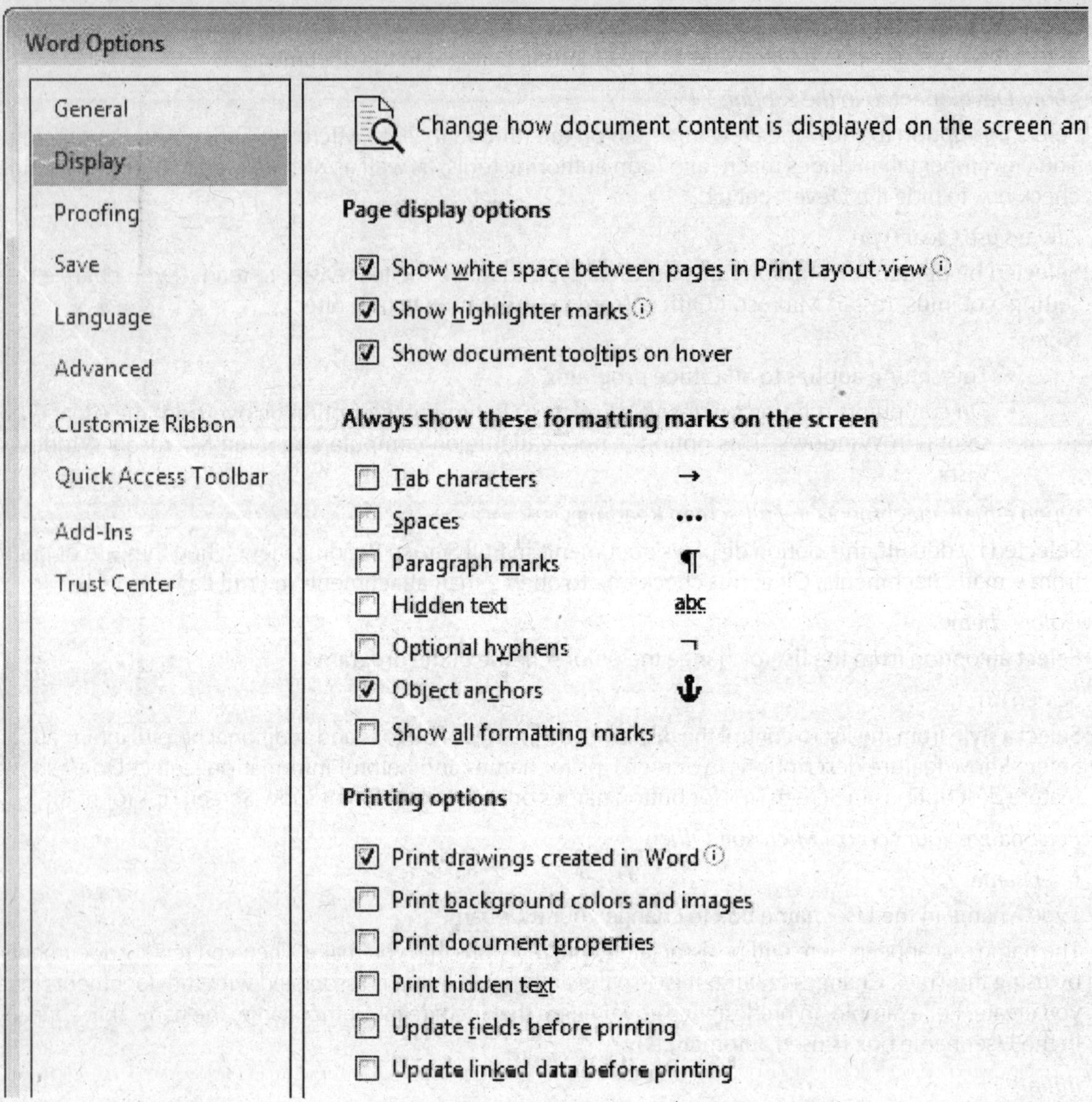

Show highlighter marks

Select this option to display highlighted text on the screen and in printed documents.

Show document tooltips on hover

Select this option to display information such as URLs and reviewers' comments in yellow pop-up boxes. The tooltips appear when you rest your mouse pointer on a hyperlink, comment reference mark, or similar content.

Always show these formatting marks on the screen

Tab characters

Select this option to display tab characters as arrows.

Spaces

Select this option to display spaces between words as dots.

Paragraph marks

Select this option to display ends of paragraphs with the paragraph symbol.

Hidden text

Select this option to display a dotted line under text that is formatted as hidden.

Optional hyphens

Select this option to display hyphens that indicate where to divide a word at the end of a line. Optional hyphens are not printed unless a word actually breaks at the end of a line. When a word breaks at the end of the line, the optional hyphen is printed as a regular hyphen.

Object anchors

Select this option to display objects anchors, which indicate that an object is attached to a specific paragraph.

Show all formatting marks

Select this option to display all the formatting characters that are listed in the Always show these formatting marks on the screen section, whether or not the check box associated with each one is selected. When you turn this option off, only the formatting characters indicated by the selected check boxes in the Always show these formatting marks on the screen section are displayed. You can quickly turn this option on or off by clicking Show/Hide ¶ in the Paragraph group of the Home tab.

Printing options

Print drawings created in Word

Select this option to print all drawing objects, such as shapes and text boxes. Clearing this check box may speed your printing process because Word prints a blank box in place of each drawing object.

Print background colors and images

Select this option to print all background colors and images. Clearing this check box may speed your printing process.

Print document properties

Select this option to print the document's summary information on a separate page after the document is printed. Word stores summary information on the Document Information Panel.

Print hidden text

Select this option to print all text that has been formatted as hidden. Word does not print the dotted underline that appears under the hidden text on the screen.

Update fields before printing

Select this option to update all the fields in a document before you print it.

Update linked data before printing

Select this option to update all linked information in a document before you print it.

Proofing Options

This has the following sections; AutoCorrect options, When correcting spelling in Microsoft Office programs, When correcting spelling and grammar in Word, Exception for. Let us see them in details.

AutoCorrect options

Change how Word corrects and formats text as you type.

It has a button called AutoCorrect Options. This will give rise to various optional dialog boxes which are self suggestive and can be clicked at the required options.

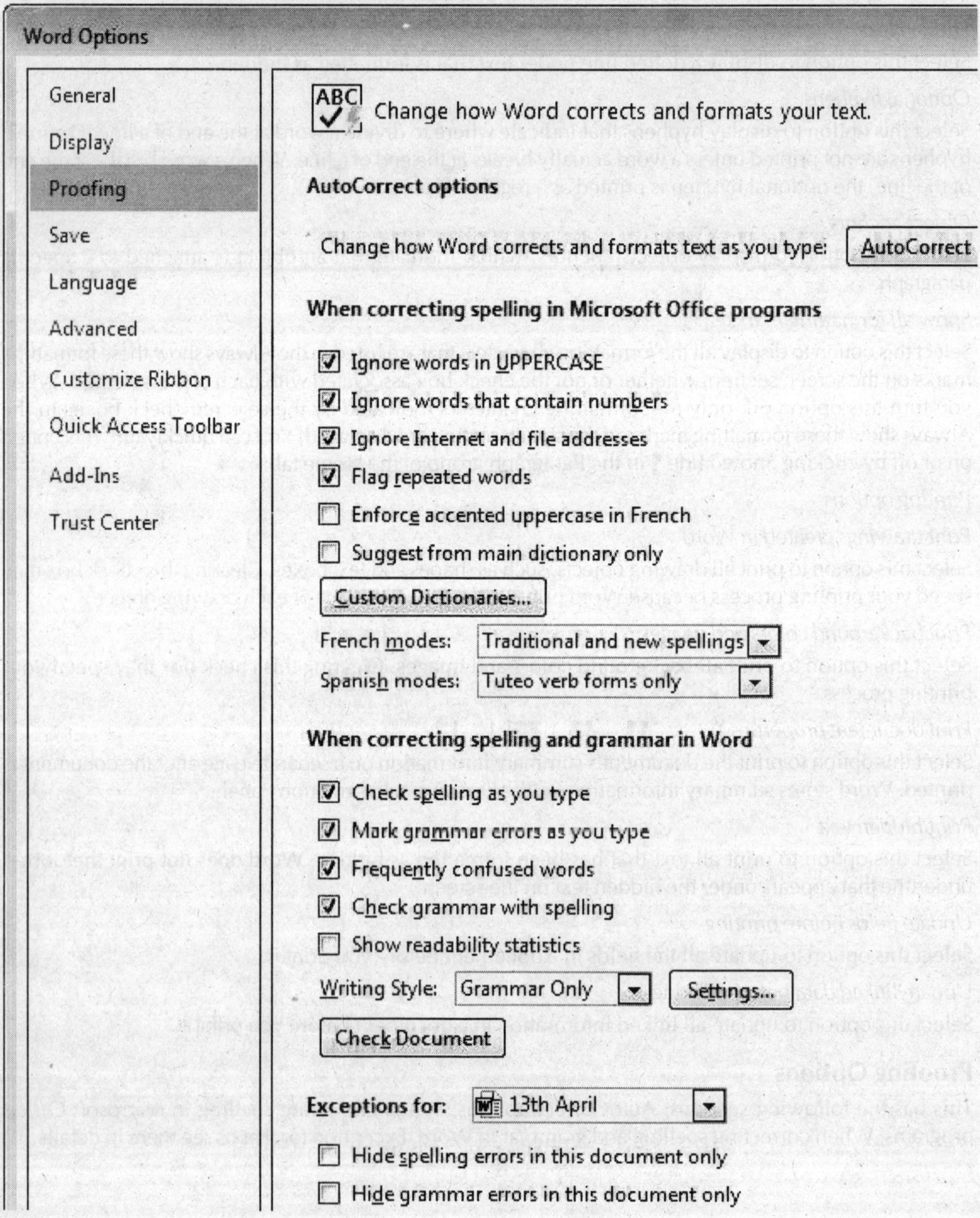

Now we come to the other options.

When correcting spelling in Microsoft Office programs

It has the following options.

Ignore words in UPPERCASE

Ignore words that contain numbers

Ignore Internet and file addresses

Flag repeated words

Enforce accented uppercase in French

Suggest from main dictionay only

French modes

These are self defined and no more description is needed for them.

When correcting spelling and grammar in Word

It has the following options.

Check spelling as you type

Use contexcual spelling

Mark gammar errors as you type

Check grammar with spelling

Show readability statistics

Writing Style

These are self defined and no more description is needed for them.

Exceptions for:

It has the following options.

Hide spelling errors in this document only

Hide grammar errors in this document only

These are self defined and no more description is needed for them.

Save Options

This dialog box has the following options.

Save files in this format

This option sets the default file format that is used when you save documents. If your documents are used in different versions of Microsoft Office Word, as Web pages, or in other programs, you can select the file format that you most frequently use. In this list, select the file format that you want to use.

Save AutoRecover information every

Word automatically creates an AutoRecover file at the interval that you specify in the minutes box. The interval must be a positive number from 1 to 120. If your computer stops responding, or you lose power unexpectedly, the AutoRecover file is opened the next time that you start Word. The AutoRecover file may contain unsaved information that would otherwise be lost from your original document.

AutoRecover does not replace the Save command. You must still save your document when you finish working on it.

AutoRecover file location Displays the default

In the text box, type the path that you want to use as the AutoRecover file location.

Default file location

Type the path that you want Word to use as the location the first time that you use the Open, Save, or Save As command when you start Word, or click Browse to locate the folder. If you want to type a path to a network server location for the default file location, enter the path by using the UNC syntax: \\servername\foldername. You must restart Word to apply the new default file location to a network server.

This option controls the default behavior the first time that you use the Open, Save, or Save As commands when you start Word. Whenever you save a document, you can override these settings by selecting a different location or format in the Open, Save or Save As dialog box.

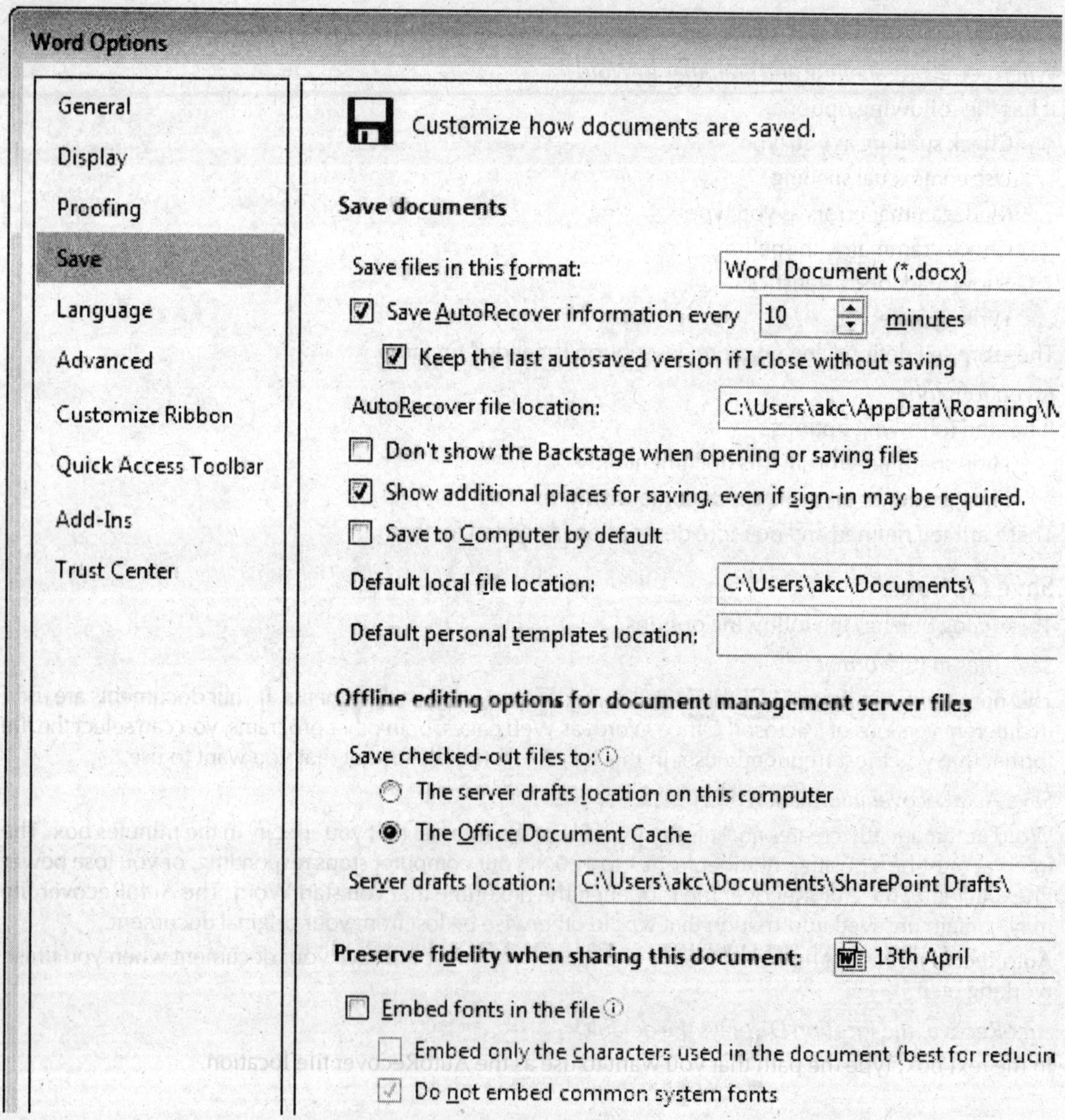

Offline editing options for the document management server files

Save checked-out files to

This option specifies the location where you want to save checked-out documents.

- The server drafts location on this computer Click this to save checked-out files to the folder that is specified in the Server drafts location box to save checked-out files.
- The web server Click this to save checked-out files to the Web server.

Server drafts location Displays the default server drafts location. In the text box, type the path that you want to use as the server drafts location, or click Browse to locate the server drafts location.

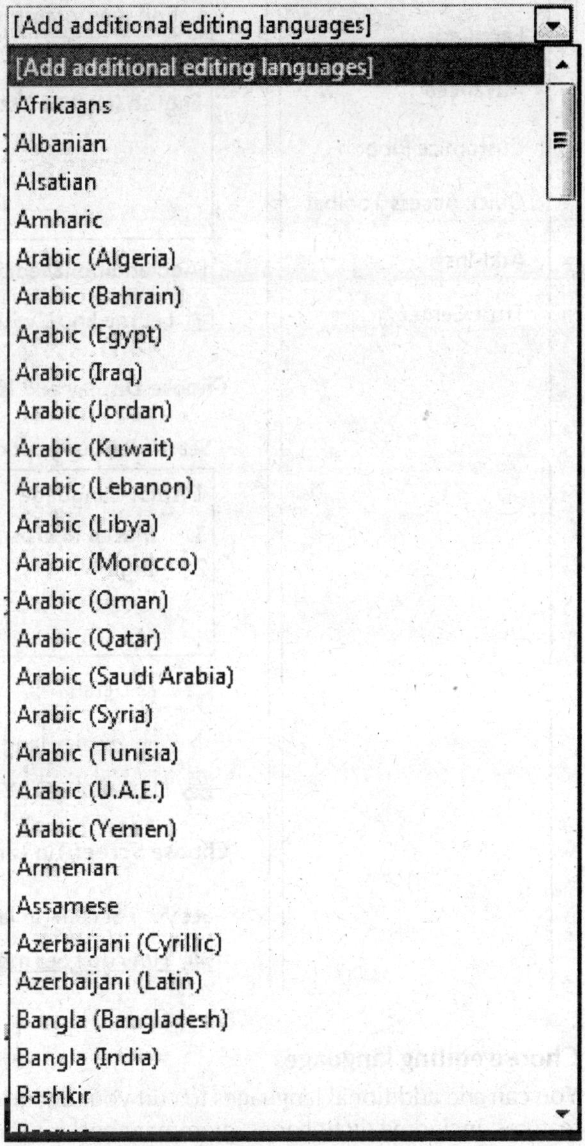

Preserve fidelity when sharing this document

Preserve fidelity when sharing this document Select the name of a document that is already open, or click All New Documents to make the fidelity settings apply to all documents that you will create.

Embed fonts in the file

Select this option to save the fonts that are used in the document with the file, if the fonts are allowed to be embedded. When this option is on, other readers can see and can use the fonts in your document, even if they do not have the fonts installed on their computer. Turning on this option increases file size. For more information about embedding fonts, see Embedding TrueType on the Microsoft.com Web site.

- Embed only the characters used in the document (best for reducing file size) Select this option to embed only the fonts that you actually use in a document. If you use 32 or fewer characters of a font, Word embeds only those characters. This option is most useful for documents that other users plan to view or print only, because the unembedded font characters and styles aren't available for editing. This option is available only when you select the Embed fonts in the file option.
- Do not embed common system fonts Select to embed fonts only if they are not commonly installed on computers running Microsoft Windows and 2013 Microsoft Office system software. This option is available only when you select the Embed fonts in the file option.

Language Options

This has the following options.

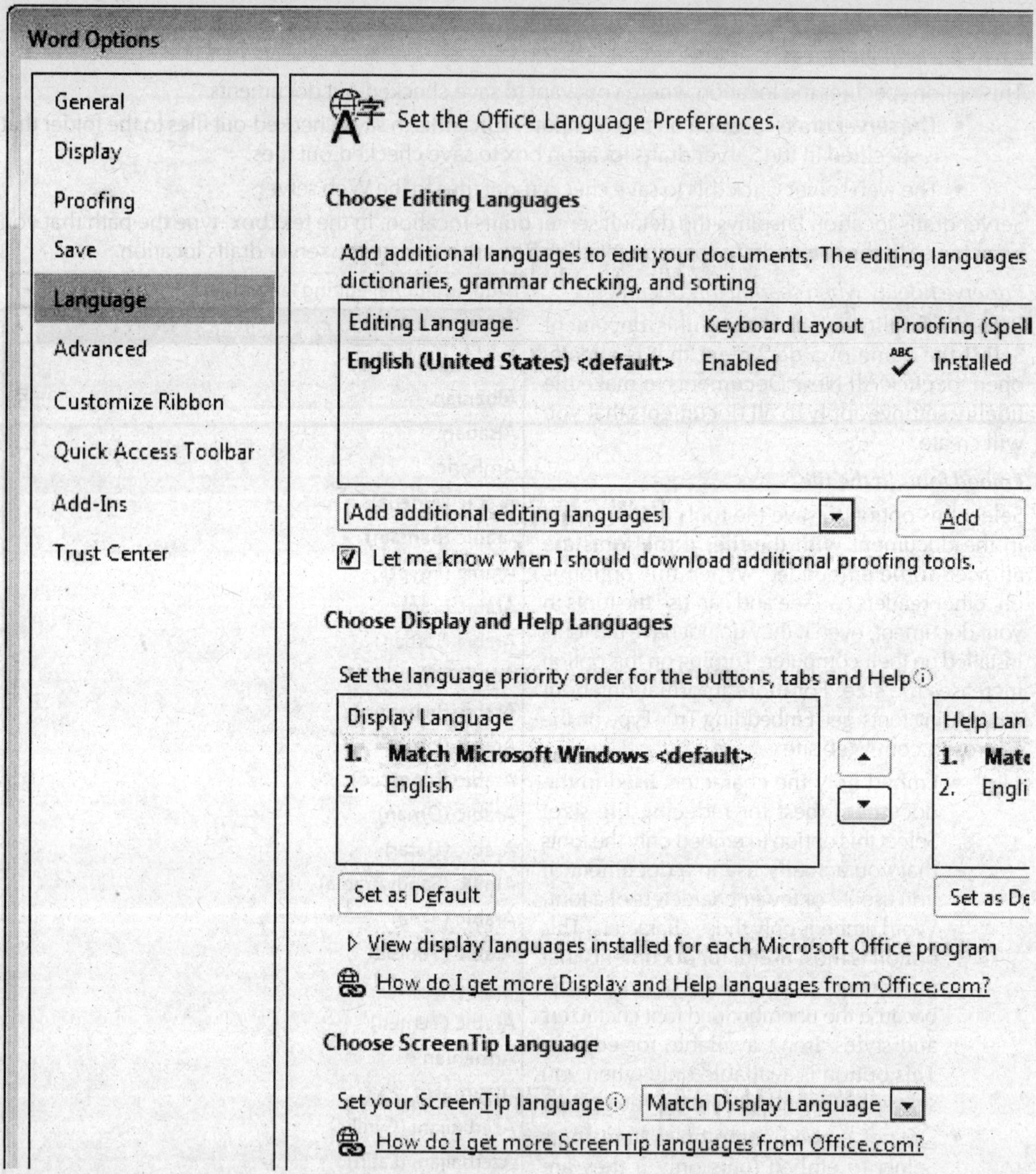

Choose editing languages

You can add additional languages to edit your documents. The editing Languages set language-specific features, including dictionaries, grammar checking, and sorting.

Add additional Editing Lanaguages

This is a pop-up menu which gives you the list of various languages, one or more of them can be chosen for editing purposes.

Choose display and Help languages

Using this option you can set the lanauge priority order for the Ribbon, tabs and Help.

Choose ScreenTip Language

Using this option you can set the language for your ScreenTips.

Advanced Options

This has the following options.

Editing options

Typing replaces selected text

Select this option to delete the selected text when you begin to type. If you clear this check box, Microsoft Office Word inserts new text in front of the selected text and does not delete the selected text.

When selecting, automatically select entire word

Select this option to select entire words when you select part of one word and then part of the next word. Turning this option on also causes Word to select a word and the space that follows it when you double-click a word.

Allow text to be dragged and dropped

Select this option to be able to move or copy selected text by dragging it. To move text, select the text, and then drag it to a new location. To copy text, select the text, and then hold down the CTRL key while you drag the selection to its new location.

Use CTRL + Click to follow hyperlink

Select this option to make it easier to edit the text of hyperlinks. When this option is turned on, you must press CTRL while you click the link to follow the link. When this option is turned off, clicking the link causes Word to jump to the destination of the link, which makes it more difficult to edit the text of the link.

Automatically create drawing canvas when inserting AutoShapes

Select this option to place a drawing canvas around drawing objects or ink drawings and writing when you insert them into your document. A drawing canvas helps you to arrange drawing objects and pictures and to move them as a unit.

Use smart paragraph selection

Select this option to select the paragraph mark when you select a whole paragraph. If you include the paragraph mark when you cut and paste a paragraph, you don't leave a blank paragraph, and your formatting automatically stays with the paragraph.

Use smart cursoring

Select this option to specify that the cursor moves as you scroll up or down. When you press the LEFT ARROW, RIGHT ARROW, UP ARROW, or DOWN ARROW keys after you scroll, the cursor responds at the page currently in view, not at its previous position.

Use the Insert key to control overtype mode

Select this option to turn overtype mode on and off by pressing the INSERT key.

- Use overtype mode Select this option to replace existing text as you type, one character at a time. If the Use the Insert key to control overtype mode is selected, you can turn this option on and off by pressing the INSERT key on your keyboard.

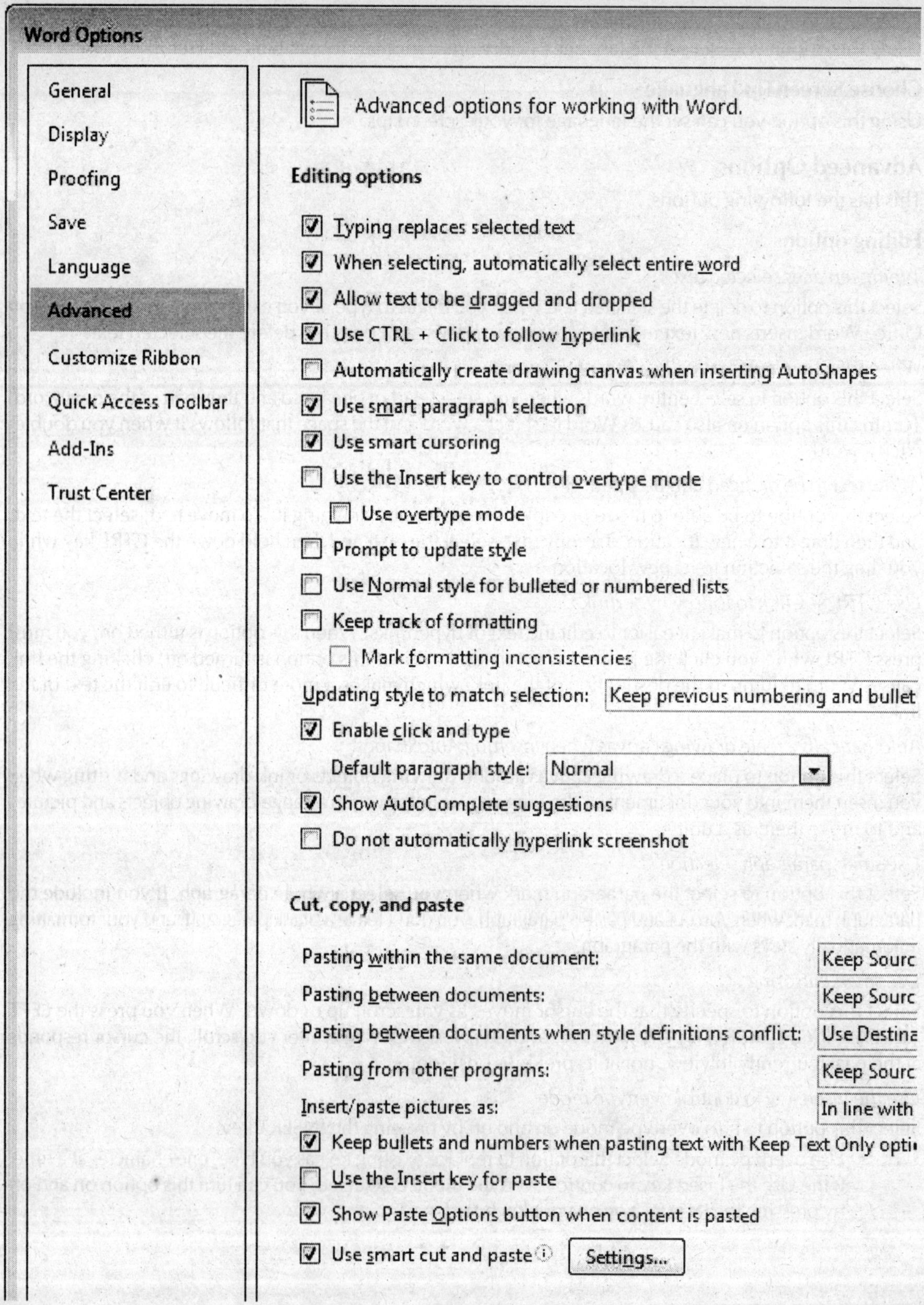
Word Options
General
Display
Proofing
Save
Language
Advanced
Customize Ribbon
Quick Access Toolbar
Add-Ins
Trust Center
Advanced options for working with Word.
Editing options
Typing replaces selected text
When selecting, automatically select entire word
Allow text to be dragged and dropped
Use CTRL + Click to follow hyperlink
Automatically create drawing canvas when inserting AutoShapes
Use smart paragraph selection
Use smart cursoring
Use the Insert key to control overtype mode
Use overtype mode
Prompt to update style
Use Normal style for bulleted or numbered lists
Keep track of formatting
Mark formatting inconsistencies
Updating style to match selection:
Keep previous numbering and bullet
Enable click and type
Default paragraph style:
Normal
Show AutoComplete suggestions
Do not automatically hyperlink screenshot
Cut, copy, and paste
Pasting within the same document:
Keep Sourc
Pasting between documents:
Keep Sourc
Pasting between documents when style definitions conflict:
Use Destina
Pasting from other programs:
Keep Sourc
Insert/paste pictures as:
In line with
Keep bullets and numbers when pasting text with Keep Text Only opti
Use the Insert key for paste
Show Paste Options button when content is pasted
Use smart cut and paste
Settings...

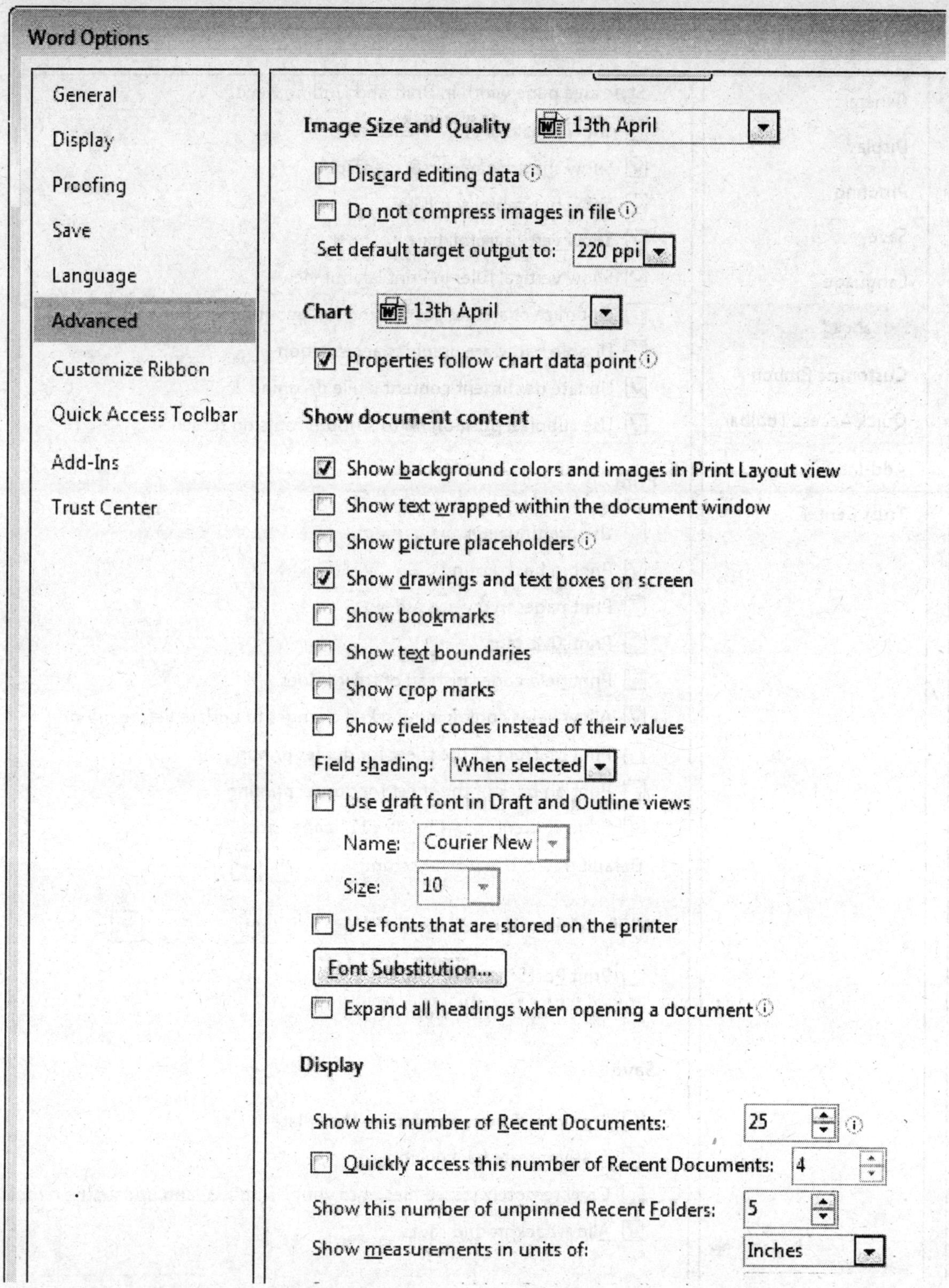
Word Options
General
Display
Proofing
Save
Language
Advanced
Customize Ribbon
Quick Access Toolbar
Add-Ins
Trust Center
Image Size and Quality
13th April
Discard editing data
Do not compress images in file
Set default target output to:
220 ppi
Chart
13th April
Properties follow chart data point
Show document content
Show background colors and images in Print Layout view
Show text wrapped within the document window
Show picture placeholders
Show drawings and text boxes on screen
Show bookmarks
Show text boundaries
Show crop marks
Show field codes instead of their values
Field shading:
When selected
Use draft font in Draft and Outline views
Name:
Courier New
Size:
10
Use fonts that are stored on the printer
Font Substitution...
Expand all headings when opening a document
Display
Show this number of Recent Documents:
25
Quickly access this number of Recent Documents:
4
Show this number of unpinned Recent Folders:
5
Show measurements in units of:
Inches

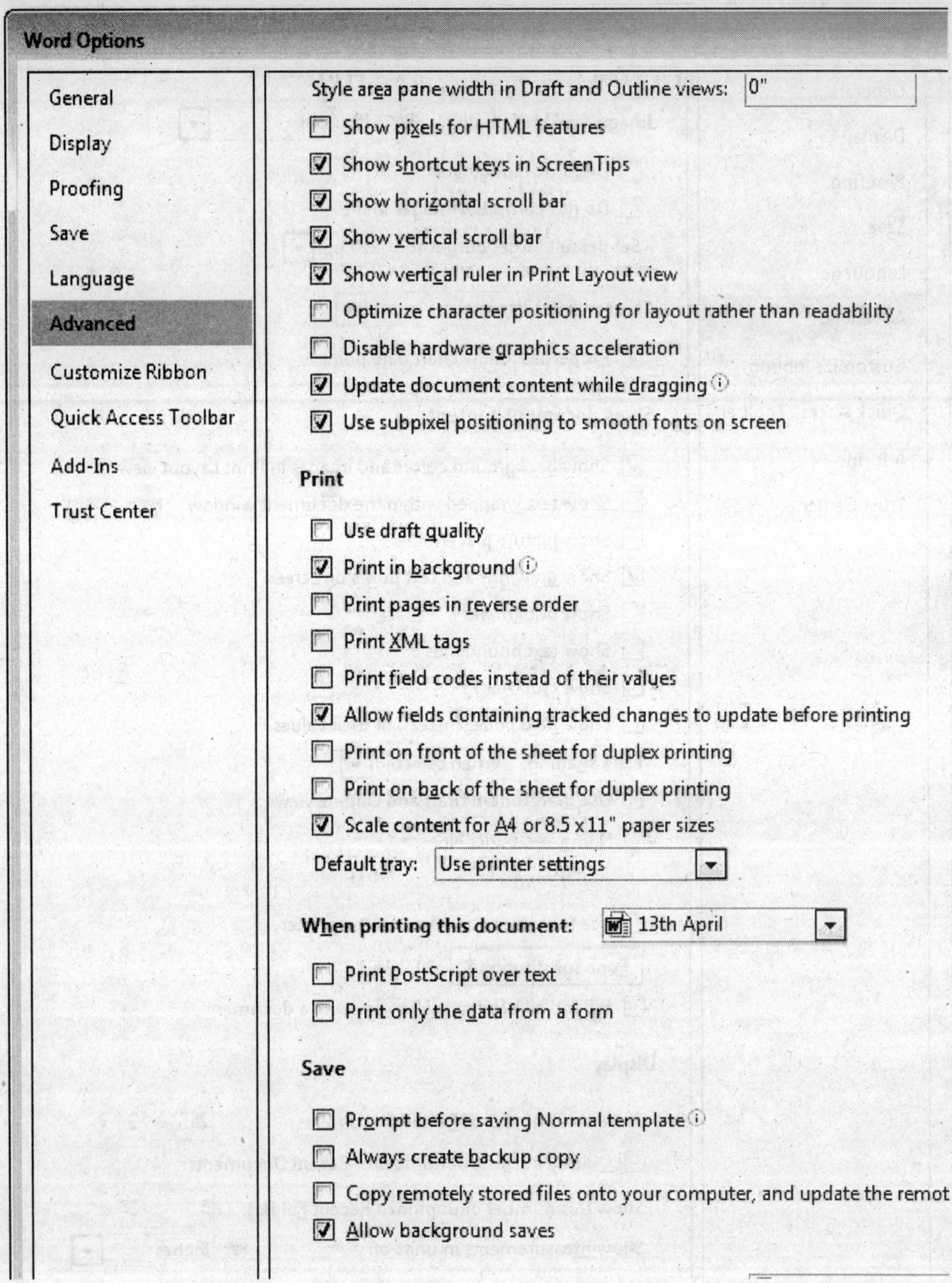
Word Options
General
Display
Proofing
Save
Language
Advanced
Customize Ribbon
Quick Access Toolbar
Add-Ins
Trust Center
Style area pane width in Draft and Outline views: 0"
Show pixels for HTML features
Show shortcut keys in ScreenTips
Show horizontal scroll bar
Show vertical scroll bar
Show vertical ruler in Print Layout view
Optimize character positioning for layout rather than readability
Disable hardware graphics acceleration
Update document content while dragging
Use subpixel positioning to smooth fonts on screen
Print
Use draft quality
Print in background
Print pages in reverse order
Print XML tags
Print field codes instead of their values
Allow fields containing tracked changes to update before printing
Print on front of the sheet for duplex printing
Print on back of the sheet for duplex printing
Scale content for A4 or 8.5 x 11" paper sizes
Default tray: Use printer settings
When printing this document: 13th April
Print PostScript over text
Print only the data from a form
Save
Prompt before saving Normal template
Always create backup copy
Copy remotely stored files onto your computer, and update the remot
Allow background saves

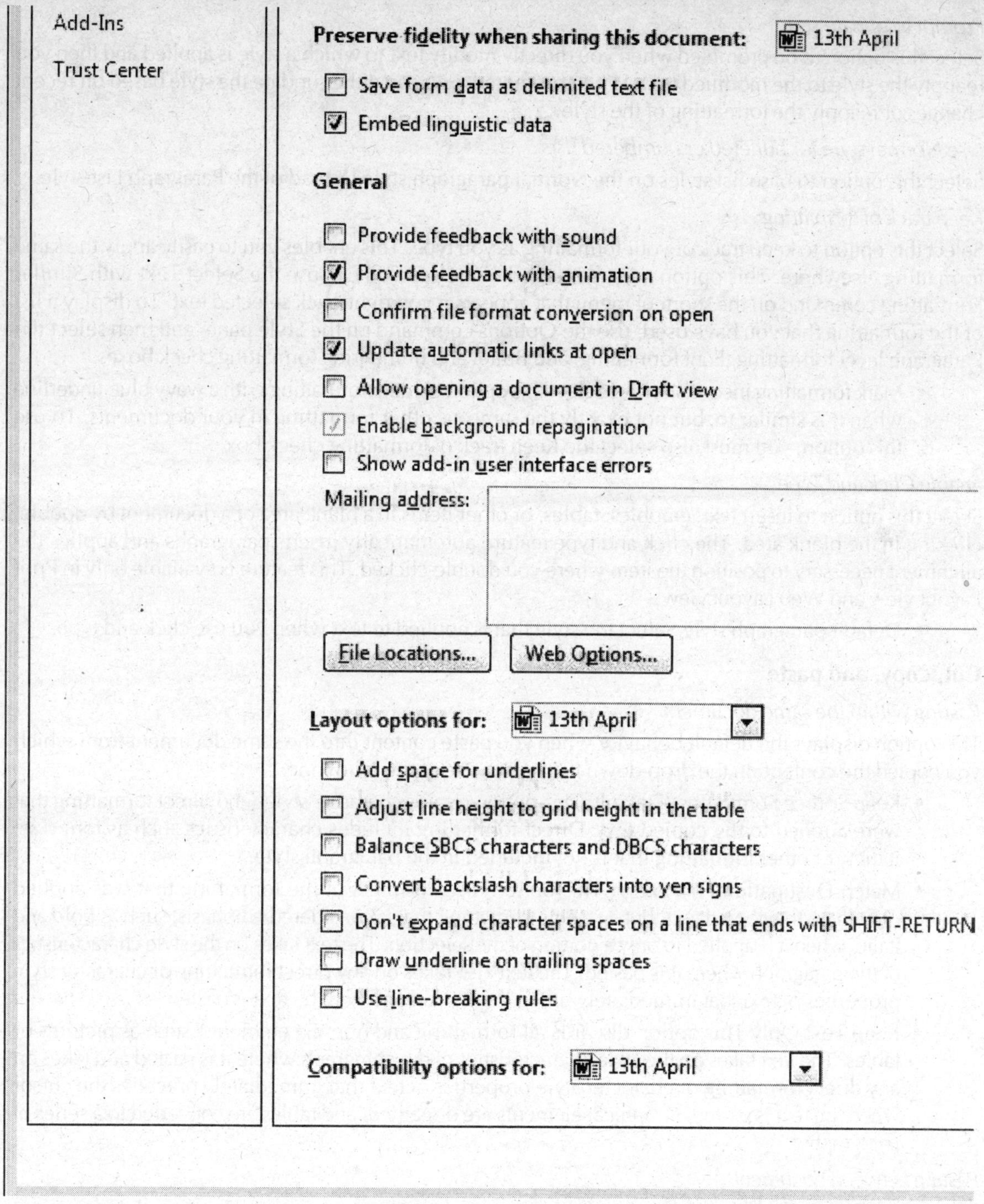
Add-Ins
Trust Center
Preserve fidelity when sharing this document:
13th April
Save form data as delimited text file
Embed linguistic data
General
Provide feedback with sound
Provide feedback with animation
Confirm file format conversion on open
Update automatic links at open
Allow opening a document in Draft view
Enable background repagination
Show add-in user interface errors
Mailing address:
File Locations...
Web Options...
Layout options for:
13th April
Add space for underlines
Adjust line height to grid height in the table
Balance SBCS characters and DBCS characters
Convert backslash characters into yen signs
Don't expand character spaces on a line that ends with SHIFT-RETURN
Draw underline on trailing spaces
Use line-breaking rules
Compatibility options for:
13th April

Prompt to update style

Select this option to be prompted when you directly modify text to which a style is applied and then you reapply the style to the modified text. When prompted, you can either update the style based on recent changes or reapply the formatting of the style.

Use Normal style for bulleted or numbered lists

Select this option to base list styles on the Normal paragraph style instead of the Paragraph List style.

Keep track of formatting

Select this option to keep track of your formatting as you type. This enables you to easily apply the same formatting elsewhere. This option must be turned on before you can use the Select Text with Similar Formatting command on the shortcut menu that appears if you right-click selected text. To display a list of the formatting that you have used, use the Options command on the Style pane, and then select the Paragraph level formatting, Font formatting, and Bullet and numbering formatting check boxes.

- Mark formatting inconsistencies Select this option to mark formatting with a wavy blue underline when it is similar to, but not exactly the same as, other formatting in your documents. To use this option, you must also select the Keep track of formatting check box.

Enable Click and Type

Select this option to insert text, graphics, tables, or other items in a blank area of a document by double-clicking in the blank area. The click and type feature automatically inserts paragraphs and applies the alignment necessary to position the item where you double-clicked. This feature is available only in Print Layout view and Web Layout view.

- Default paragraph style Select the style that is applied to text when you use click and type.

Cut, copy, and paste

Pasting within the same document

This option displays the default behavior when you paste content into the same document from which you copied the content. In the drop-down list, select one of the following:

- Keep Source Formatting (Default) This option retains character styles and direct formatting that were applied to the copied text. Direct formatting includes characteristics such as font size, italics, or other formatting that is not included in the paragraph style.
- Match Destination Formatting This option discards most of the formatting that was applied directly to the copied text, but it retains formatting that is considered emphasis, such as bold and italic, when it is applied to only a portion of the selection. The text takes on the style characteristics of the paragraph where it is pasted. The text also takes on any direct formatting or character style properties of text that immediately precedes the cursor when the text is pasted.
- Keep Text Only This option discards all formatting and nontext elements, such as pictures or tables. The text takes on the style characteristics of the paragraph where it is pasted and takes on any direct formatting or character style properties of text that immediately precedes the cursor when the text is pasted. Graphical elements are discarded, and tables are converted to a series of paragraphs.

Pasting between documents

This option displays the default behavior when you paste content that was copied from another document in Word. In the drop-down list, select one of the following:

- Keep Source Formatting (Default) This option retains formatting that was applied to the copied text. Any style definition that is associated with the copied text is copied to the destination document.

- Match Destination Formatting This option discards most formatting that was applied directly to the copied text, but it retains formatting that is considered emphasis, such as bold and italic, when it is applied to only a portion of the selection. The text takes on the style characteristics of the paragraph where it is pasted. The text also takes on any direct formatting or character style properties of text that immediately precedes the cursor when the text is pasted.
- Keep Text Only This option discards all formatting and nontext elements, such as pictures or tables. The text takes on the style characteristics of the paragraph where it is pasted and takes on any direct formatting or character style properties of text that immediately precedes the cursor when the text is pasted. Graphical elements are discarded, and tables are converted to a series of paragraphs.

Pasting between documents when style definitions conflict

This option displays the default behavior when you paste content that was copied from another document in Word, and the style that is assigned to the copied text is defined differently in the document where the text is being pasted. In the drop-down list, select one of the following:

- Keep Source Formatting This option retains the look of the copied text by assigning the Normal style to the pasted text and applying direct formatting. Direct formatting includes characteristics such as font size, italics, or other formatting to mimic the style definition of the copied text.
- Use Destination Styles (Default) This option retains the style name that is associated with the copied text, but it uses the style definition of the document where the text is being pasted. For example, you copy Heading 1 text from one document to another. In one document, Heading 1 is defined as Arial bold, 14-point, and in the document where you're pasting the text, Heading 1 is defined as Cambria bold, 16-point. When you use the Use Destination Styles option, the pasted text uses Heading 1 style, Cambria bold, 16-point.
- Match Destination Formatting This option discards the style definition and most formatting that was applied directly to the copied text, but it retains formatting that is considered emphasis, such as bold and italic, when it is applied to only a portion of the selection. The text takes on the style definition in the document where the text is being pasted.
- Keep Text Only This option discards all formatting and nontext elements, such as pictures or tables. The text takes on the style characteristics of the paragraph where it is pasted and takes on any direct formatting or character style properties of text that immediately precedes the cursor when the text is pasted. Graphical elements are discarded, and tables are converted to a series of paragraphs.

Pasting from other programs

This option displays the default behavior when you paste content that was copied from another program. In the drop-down list, select one of the following:

- Keep Source Formatting (Default) This option retains the formatting of the copied text.
- Match Destination Formatting This option discards most formatting that was applied directly to the copied text, but it retains formatting that is considered emphasis, such as bold and italic, when it is applied to only a portion of the selection. The text takes on the style characteristics of the paragraph where it is pasted. The text also takes on any direct formatting characteristics of text that immediately precedes the cursor when the text is pasted.
- Keep Text Only This option discards all formatting and nontext elements, such as pictures or tables. The text takes on the style characteristics of the paragraph where it is pasted and takes on any direct formatting or character style properties of text that immediately precedes the cursor when the text is pasted. Graphical elements are discarded, and tables are converted to a series of paragraphs.

Insert/paste pictures as

This option displays how Word inserts pictures relative to the text in your document. You can insert images inline with text, allow images to move with text, or you can wrap text around, in front of, or behind an image. In the drop-down list, select one of the following:

- In line with text This option inserts the graphic in a paragraph as if it were text. The graphic moves as you add or delete text. You can drag the graphic to reposition it the same way that you drag text.
- Square This option wraps the text around all sides of a square around the graphic. The graphic does not move as you add or delete text, but you can drag the graphic to reposition it.
- Tight This option wraps the text around the graphic in an irregular shape around the actual image. The graphic does not move as you add or delete text, but you can drag the graphic to reposition it.
- Behind text This option inserts the graphic so that the graphic floats on its own layer behind the text. There is no border around the graphic. The graphic does not move as you add or delete text, but you can drag the graphic to reposition it.
- In front of text This option inserts the graphic so that the graphic floats on its own layer in front of the text. There is no border around the graphic. The graphic does not move as you add or delete text, but you can drag the graphic to reposition it.
- Through This option wraps the text around the graphic, including filling the space created by a concave shape, such as a crescent moon. The graphic does not move as you add or delete text, but you can drag the graphic to reposition it.
- Top and bottom This option prevents text from wrapping on the sides of the graphic. The graphic does not move as you add or delete text, but you can drag the graphic to reposition it.

Keep bullets and numbers when pasting text with Keep Text Only option

Select this option to convert numbering and bullets into text symbols.

Use the Insert key for paste

Select this option to use the INSERT key to insert the contents of the Office Clipboard into a document.

Show Paste Options buttons

Select this option to display the Paste Options button when you paste content. You can use the Paste Options button to override or modify the settings you make in this section of the Word Options dialog box.

Use smart cut and paste

Select this option to automatically adjust formatting as you paste text. After you select this check box, you can click Settings to set additional options for pasting.

- Settings Click this to open the Settings dialog box. Use this dialog box to control spacing and formatting when merging, cutting, and pasting text.

Show Document Content

Show background colors and images in Print Layout view

Select this option to display background colors and images.

Show text wrapped within the document window

Select this option to wrap text to the document window, so that it is easier to read on the screen.

Show picture placeholders

Select this option to display an empty box in place of each picture in your documents. This option speeds the process of scrolling through a document that contains a large number of pictures.

Show drawings and text boxes on screen

Select this option to display objects that are created with the Word drawing tools in Print Layout view or Web Layout view. Clear this check box to hide drawings and possibly speed the display of documents that contain many drawings. Drawings will be printed even if you clear this check box.

Show text animation

Select this option to display text animations on your screen. Clear the check box to see how the text will look when printed. Use this option when viewing animated text in documents that were created in a version of Word earlier than Word 2013. The current version of Word no longer provides the ability to create animated text.

Show bookmarks

Select this option to display bookmarks on the screen. If you assign a bookmark to an item, the bookmarked item appears in brackets ([...]). If you assign a bookmark to a location, the bookmark appears as an I-beam. The brackets and the I-beam do not appear in printed documents.

Show smart tags

Select this option to display a purple dotted underline beneath text that is recognized as a smart tag.

Show text boundaries

Select this option to display dotted lines around text margins, columns, and paragraphs. The boundaries are for layout purposes; they do not appear in printed documents.

Show crop marks

Select this option to display the corners of the margins.

Show field codes instead of their values

Select this option to display field codes instead of field results in your documents. For example, you may see { TIME @\"MMMM, d, YYYY" } instead of February 4, 2008. Clear this check box to view field results.

Regardless of this setting, you can always switch between displaying field codes and field code results by pressing ALT + F9.

Field shading

This option displays whether and when fields are shaded. In the list, select Always or When Selected to shade your fields. Shading fields makes them easy to identify. The shading appears on the screen but not in the printed document.

Use draft font in Draft and Outline views

On computers with extremely limited resources, select this option to speed the screen display of documents.

- Name Select the font to use for drafts of your documents. This option is available only when you select the Use draft font in Draft and Outline views check box.
- Size Select the point size of the draft font. This option is available only when you select the Use draft font in Draft and Outline views check box.

Font Substitution

Click this to open the Font Substitution dialog box. Use this option to determine whether the active document uses any fonts that are not available on your computer. If the document uses fonts that are not on your computer, you can use the dialog box to specify a substitute font.

Display

Show this number of Recent Documents

Enter the number of items, between 1 and 50, to display in the Recent Documents list. Only the first nine files in the list are assigned an accelerator key. You can open these documents by pressing 1 through 9 after you have pressed ALT+F.

Show measurements in units of

Select the measurement unit that you want to use for the horizontal ruler and for measurements that you type in dialog boxes.

Style area pane width in Draft and Outline views

Type a positive decimal, such as 0.5, in the box to open the style area, which displays the names of the styles applied to text. To close the style area, enter 0.

Show pixels for HTML features

Select this option to use pixels as the default unit of measurement in dialog boxes that are related to HTML features.

Show all windows in the Taskbar

Select this option to display an icon on the Microsoft Windows taskbar for each open window in a Microsoft Office program. Clearing this check box places a single icon for each open program on the taskbar.

Show shortcut keys in ScreenTips

Select this option to display shortcut keys in ScreenTips.

Show horizontal scroll bar

Select this option to display the horizontal scrollbar at the bottom of the document window.

Show vertical scroll bar

Select this option to display the vertical scroll bar at the side of the document window.

Show vertical ruler in Print Layout view

Select this option to display the vertical ruler at the side of the document window. Make sure that you also select the Ruler check box in the Show/Hide group on the View tab of the Ribbon.

Optimize character positioning for layout rather than readability

Select this option to display character positioning accurately as it will appear in the printed document with respect to blocks of text. Spacing between characters may be distorted when this option is turned on. For best readability on the screen, turn this option off.

Print

Use draft quality

Select this option to print the document with minimal formatting, which may speed the printing process. Many printers do not support this function.

Print in background

Select this option to print documents in the background, which allows you to continue to work while you print. This option requires more available memory to allow you to work and print at the same time. If working with your document while printing becomes unacceptably slow, turn this option off.

Print pages in reverse order

Select this option to print pages in reverse order, beginning with the last page in your document. Do not use this option when you print envelopes.

Print XML tags

Select this option to print the XML tags for the XML elements that are applied to an XML document. You must have a Schema attached to the document, and you must apply elements that are provided by the attached Schema. The tags appear in the printed document.

Print field codes instead of their values

Select this option to print field codes instead of field results — for example, { TIME @\"MMMM, d, YYYY" } instead of February 4, 2008.

Print on front of the sheet for duplex printing

Select this option to print the front of each sheet when printing on a printer that does not have duplex capability. Pages will print in reverse order so that when you flip the stack to print on the back, the pages will print in the proper order.

Print on back of the sheet for duplex printing

Select this option to print the back of each sheet when printing on a printer that does not have duplex capability. Pages will print in ascending order so that they correspond to a stack of pages that were printed on the front in reverse order.

Scale content for A4 or 8.5 x 11" paper sizes

Select this option to automatically adjust documents that are designed for 8.5-by-11-inch paper to fit A4 paper and to adjust documents that are designed for A4 paper to fit 8.5-by-11-inch paper. This option takes affect only if the A4 or 8.5-by-11-inch paper in the printer does not match the paper size that is set on the Page Layout tab of Word. This option affects printouts only; it does not affect formatting.

Default tray

This option displays the printer tray that is used by default. To follow the settings in your printer, select Use printer settings. To choose a particular tray, select it in the list. The choices in the list depend on your printer's configuration.

When printing this document

When printing this document

Select the document that these printing settings apply to. In the list, select the name of a document that is already open, or select All New Documents to make the setting apply to all documents that you will create.

Print PostScript over text

Select this option to print PostScript code when a document contains PRINT fields.

Print only the data from a form

Select this option to print the data that is entered into an online form without printing the form.

Save

Prompt before saving Normal template

Select this option to display, when you close Word, a message that asks if you want to save any changes that were made to the default template. Because changes to the default template will affect any new documents that you create, you may want to be alerted when the template has changed. Clearing this check box automatically saves changes without prompting you.

Always create backup copy

Select this option to create a backup copy of a document each time you save the document. Each backup copy replaces the previous backup copy. Word adds the phrase "Backup of" to the file name and applies the file extension .wbk to all backup copies. The backup copies are saved in the same folder as your original document.

Copy remotely stored files onto your computer, and update the remote file when saving

Select this option to temporarily store a local copy of a file that you store on a network or removable drive. When you save the local copy, Word saves your changes to the original copy. If the original file is not available, Word prompts you to save the file in another location to avoid data loss.

Allow background saves

Select this option to save your document while you work. A progress meter appears in the status bar when Word performs a background save.

Preserve fidelity when sharing this document

Preserve fidelity when sharing this document

Select the document that these settings apply to. In the list, select the name of a document that is already open, or select All New Documents to make the setting apply to all documents that you will create.

Save smart tags as XML properties in Web pages

Select this option to save all of the smart tags in a document as Extensible Markup Language (XML) within a Hypertext Markup Language (HTML) file.

Save form data as delimited text file

Select this option to save the data that is entered into an online form as a single, tab-delimited text file in plain text format. You can then import the contents of that file into a database.

Embed linguistic data

Select this option to save linguistic data, such as speech and handwritten text.

Embed smart tags

Select this option to save smart tags as part of your document.

General

Provide feedback with sound

Select this option to add sounds to certain actions or events in Word and other programs in 2013 Microsoft Office system. For example, Word can play a sound when it completes a process. To change the sound that is associated with an event, open the folder for sounds and audio devices in Control Panel. Your computer must have a sound card to play most sounds.

Provide feedback with animation

Select this option to animate the movement of your pointer in Word and the other Office programs. This option also provides animated cursors for actions such as printing, saving, automatic formatting, and find-and-replace operations.

Confirm file format conversion on open

Select this option to choose the file converter that Word uses to open files that were created in another program. Clear this check box if you want Word to select a converter automatically.

Update automatic links at open

Select this option to automatically update any content that is linked to other files each time you open a document.

Allow opening a document in Draft view

Select this option to be able to open a document in Draft view.

To make a document open in Draft view by default, you need to turn on this option and then on the View tab in the Document Views group, click Draft. Make some kind of change to the document, and then save the document.

Allow background open of Web pages

Select this option to open Web page documents in the background while you work. A progress meter appears in the status bar when Word opens the page in the background.

Enable background repagination

Select this option to repaginate documents automatically as you work. This option is available in Draft and Outline views only. Clearing this check box prevents page numbers from updating (when displayed in the status bar) until you switch to Print Layout view.

Show add-in user interface errors

Select this option to display error messages from programs that customize the user interface. This option is especially useful for authors of software solutions, because it provides information for debugging customizations to the user interface.

Mailing address

Type the address that you want Word to use as the default return address for envelopes and letters.

File Locations

Click this to see the default storage location for documents, templates, and other items that you create and use in Word. In the File Locations dialog box, click the item you want to change, and then click Modify to set a new default location.

Caution

The default locations for templates and the Startup folder are treated as trusted locations. If you change the location, be sure that the new folder is a secure location.

Web Options

Click this to open the Web Options dialog box. Use this dialog box to set options for using Word to create Web pages.

Service Options

Click this to open the Service Options dialog box. Use this dialog box to set options for shared workspaces.

Compatibility options for

Compatibility options for

Select the document that these settings apply to. In the list, select the name of a document that is already open, or select All New Documents to make the setting apply to all documents that you will create.

Lay out this document as if created in

Select the word-processing program that you expect to be used for opening the document. The settings in the list of Layout options change according to the word-processing program that you select. To specify your own configuration of settings, select Custom.

Layout options

Lists options for laying out the document. Select the check boxes for the options you want.

Customize Ribbon

This option panel allows you to Choose from the various popular commands and even prepare keyboard shortcuts for them.

With Customizing the Ribbon you can the various tabs on the ribbon. You can even add a New Tab, New Group, Rename a Tab, etc.

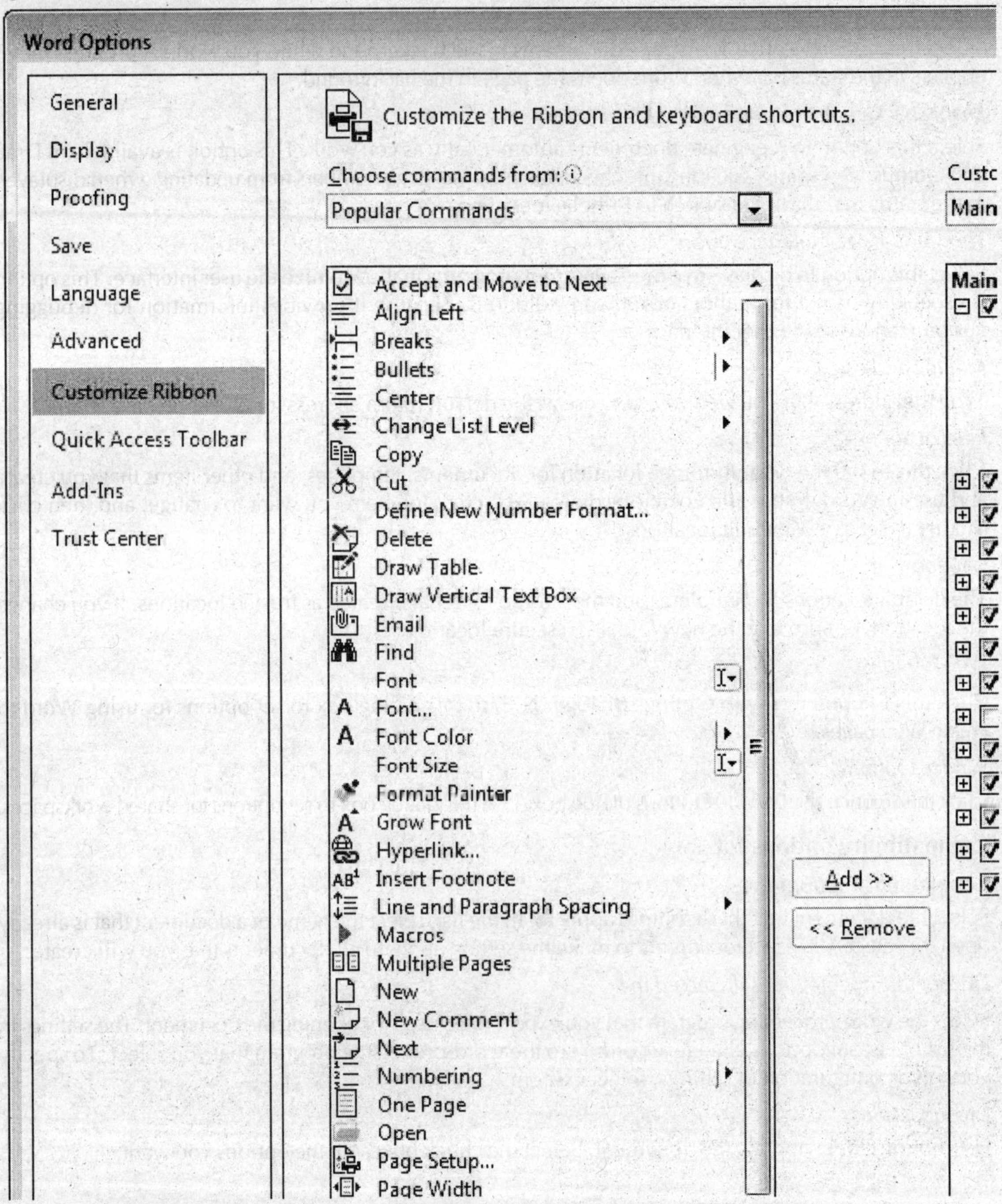

Quick Access Toolbar

Using the options available here, you can choose commands from the various popular commands to appear on the Quick Access Toolbar.

You can also opt for the Quick Access Toolbar to appear below the Ribbon.

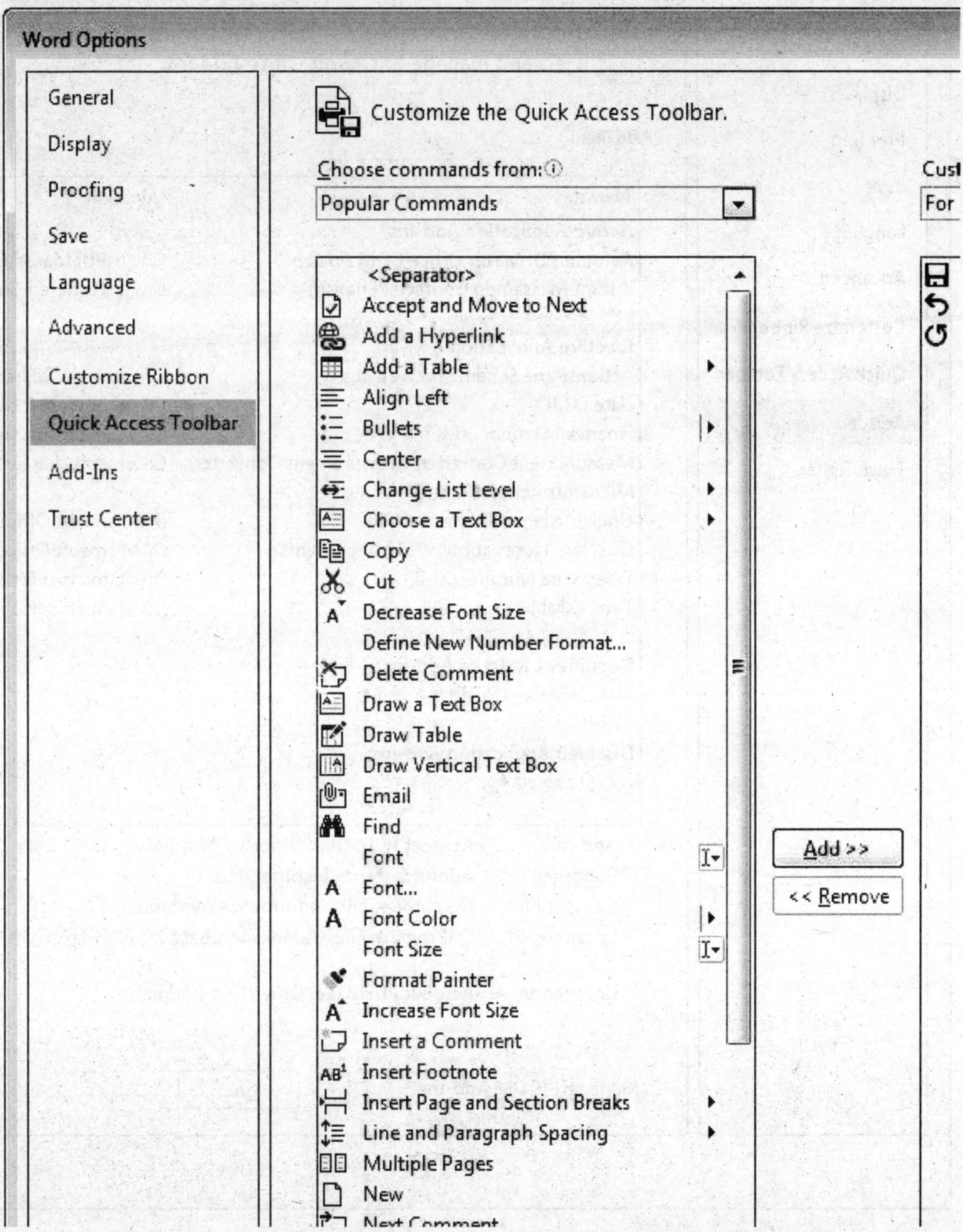

Add-Ins

This option allows you to View and manage Microsoft Office add-ins.

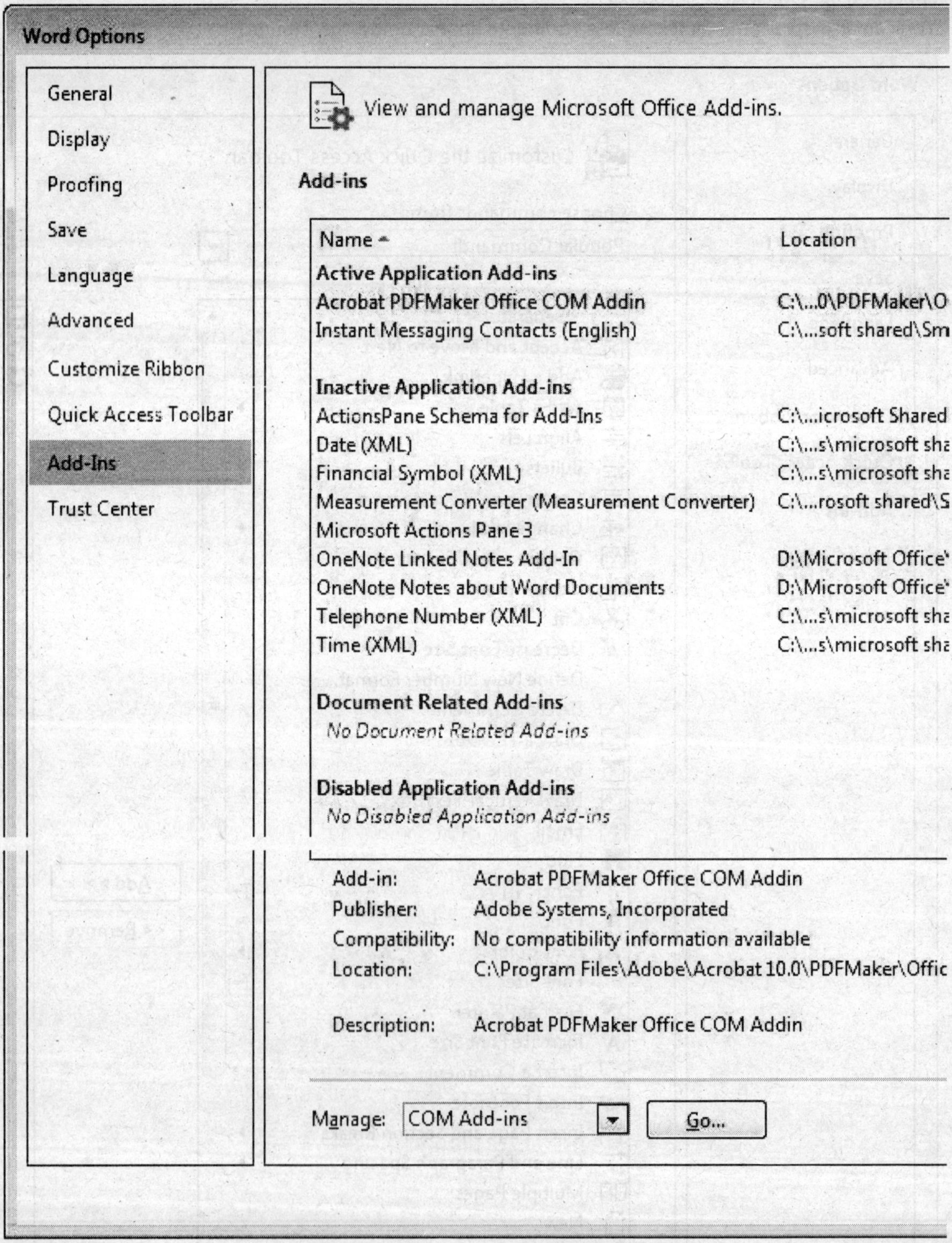

Trust Center

This allows you to Protect your privacy using the various options given in the dialog box.

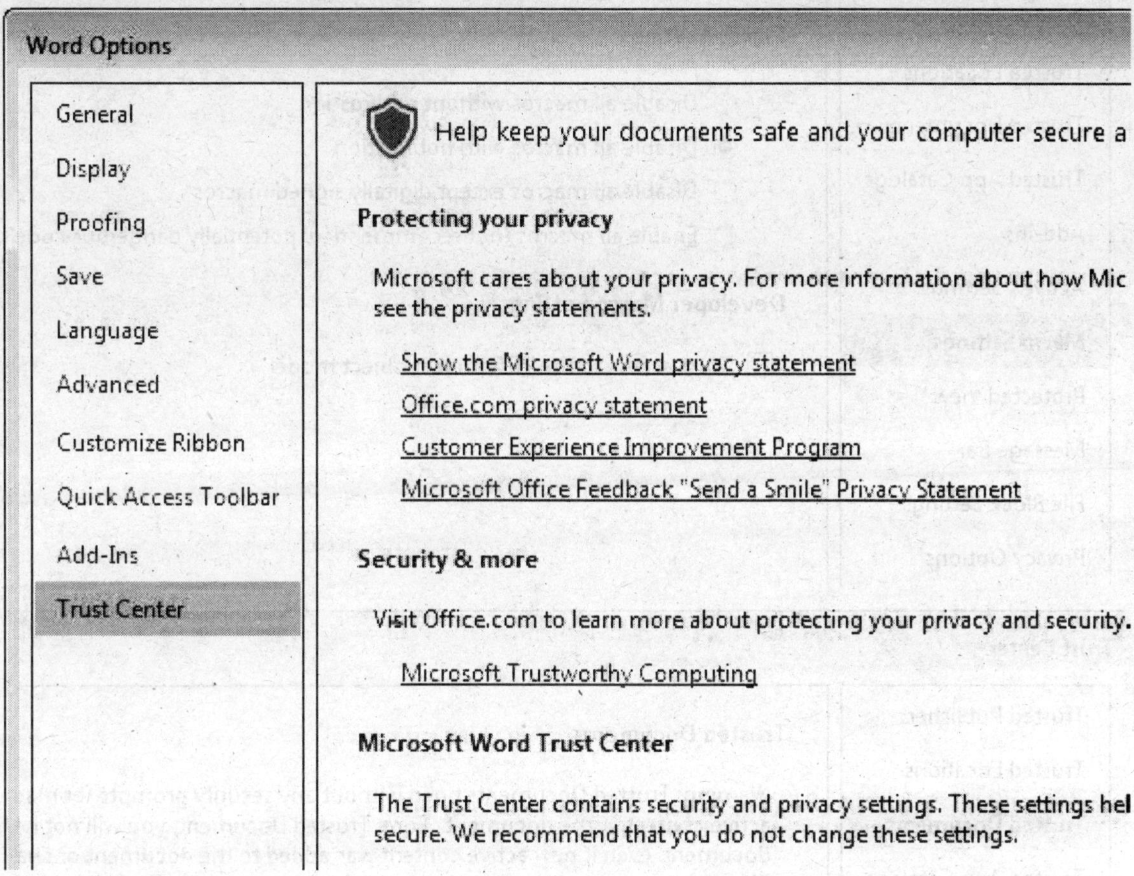

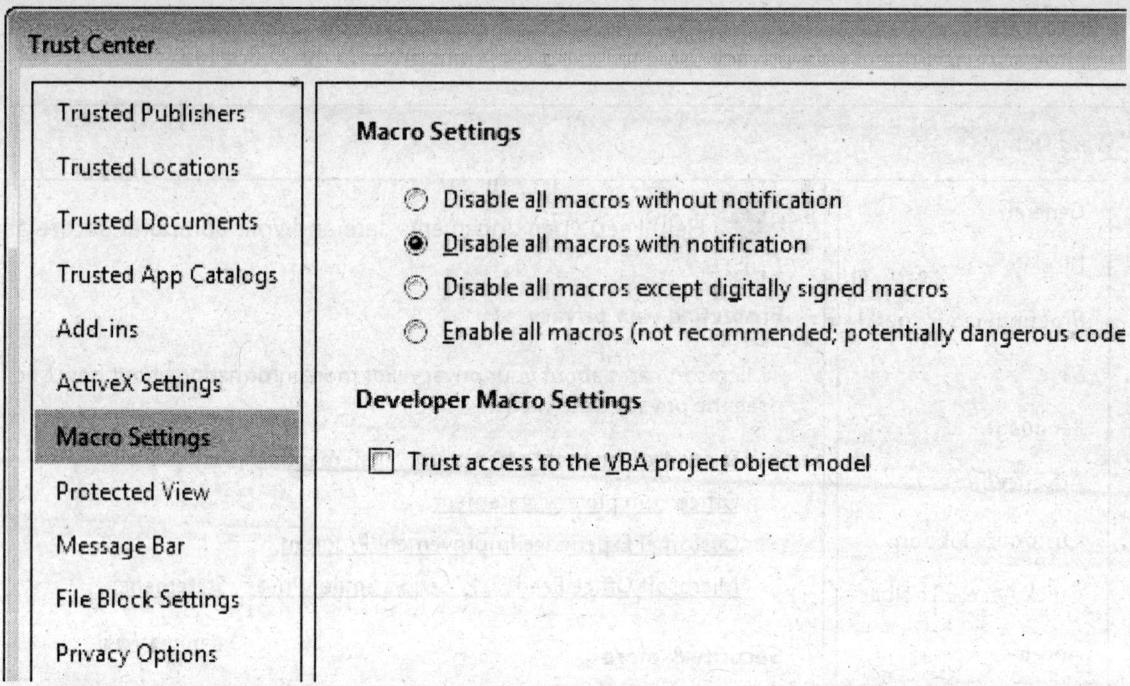
Trust Center
Trusted Publishers
Trusted Locations
Trusted Documents
Trusted App Catalogs
Add-ins
ActiveX Settings
Macro Settings
Protected View
Message Bar
File Block Settings
Privacy Options
Macro Settings
Disable all macros without notification
Disable all macros with notification
Disable all macros except digitally signed macros
Enable all macros (not recommended; potentially dangerous code
Developer Macro Settings
Trust access to the VBA project object model

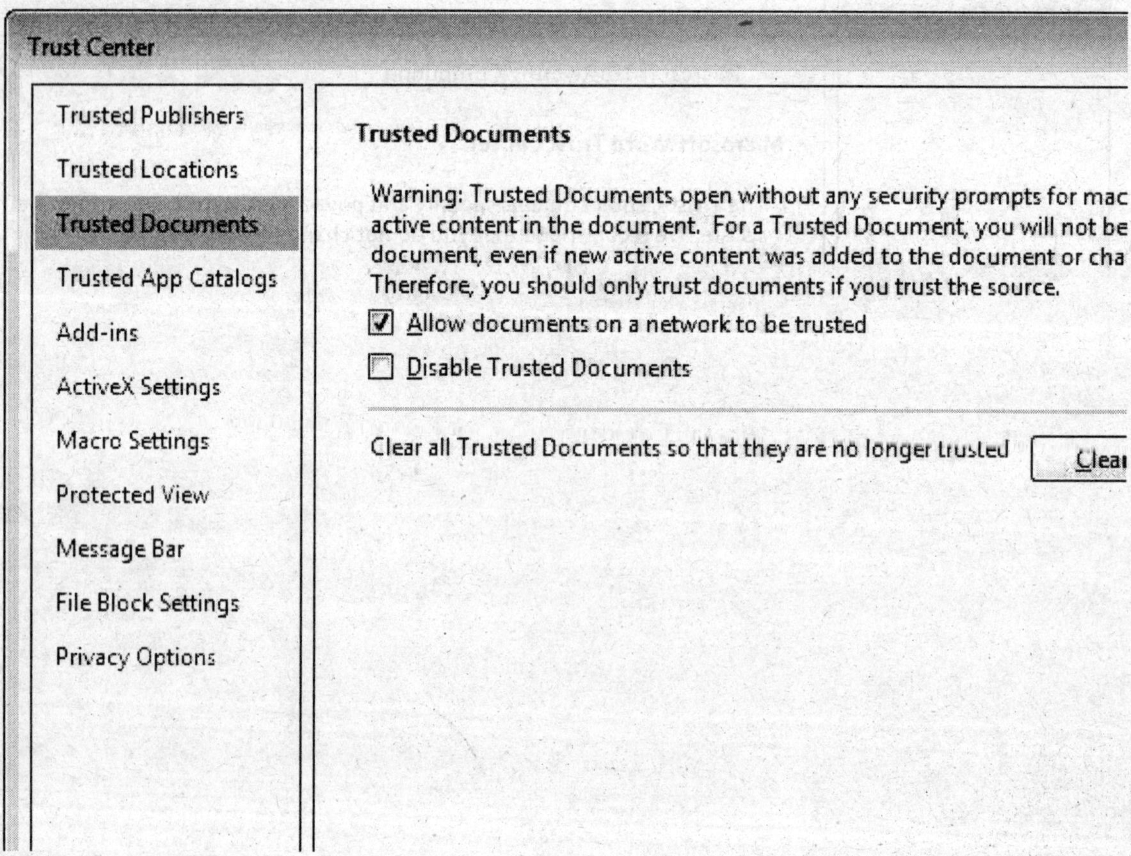
Trust Center
Trusted Publishers
Trusted Locations
Trusted Documents
Trusted App Catalogs
Add-ins
ActiveX Settings
Macro Settings
Protected View
Message Bar
File Block Settings
Privacy Options
Trusted Documents
Warning: Trusted Documents open without any security prompts for mac
active content in the document. For a Trusted Document, you will not be
document, even if new active content was added to the document or cha
Therefore, you should only trust documents if you trust the source.
Allow documents on a network to be trusted
Disable Trusted Documents
Clear all Trusted Documents so that they are no longer trusted
Clear

CHAPTER 5

MailMerging Documents and Creating Labels in Microsoft Word 2013

Introduction

MailMerge is one of the very important application of any word processing software. It has been given an important panel in the Word 2013. Word has indeed made it very easy to operate.

Using MailMerge in Word 2013

In MailMerge you have the variable data coming from a data source which can be either a database file, spreadsheet, or even a text file with fields marked in it. Then you have the document file whose text remains the same for all the subsequent merged files changing only the data which has been received from the source. So in fact you create multiple documents having the same text but having different fields depending upon the source.

Well, one can think of various usages of the MailMerge. The most important being sending the same letter to various parties. Sending the same invitation to various guests. Sending payment reminders to various creditors. Calling all the directors to the same board meeting. In all these cases, the text would remain more or less the same but the name and address of the receiver would change. You can even change the salutation too, for example, Dear Mr. so and so, picking the name from the data source.

MailMerge in Word is done in steps. Creating document (text), data source and then merging them before printing. Let us see how it is done. For your information, here I am creating a appreciation letter for the various members of the victories Indian Cricket Team. So, lets start.

1. Start Word 2013.
2. On the Panels menu, select Mailings.
3. From here on the Start Mail Merge, click at Step by Step Mail Merge Wizard.
4. As shown here, the first step is to select the document type.
5. Select Letters as shown here.
6. Click at Next to start document.
7. The second step as mentioned is to select the document.
8. You have the option of using the current document, starting from an existing document or from a template.
9. Step 3 asks you to type your letter.
10. We have written a letter to various people inviting them to the marriage.
11. As shown next the letter for the same has been type.
12. Now comes the part of selecting the recipients of the letter.
13. In the top portion of the Wizard, choose the Type a new list option and click at Create.
14. You would be given a blank dialog box to create a New Address Book. Here various options of filling the name, address, company's name, etc are given. Type the ones you want to use and ignore others. When you have types one, click at New Entry to go for the next entry.
15. Once you have typed all the entries, click at Ok. You would be asked to save the address list with a name.
16. Once again the same list would be shown to you for making the last minute correction, addition, deletion, etc. You can even change the sequence by sorting it.
17. In the next step, you would insert the field name at the place where it would be displayed. For this choose the

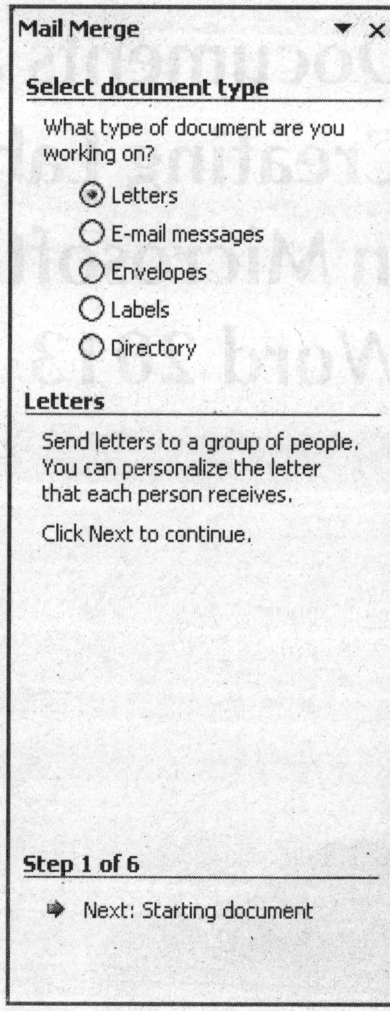

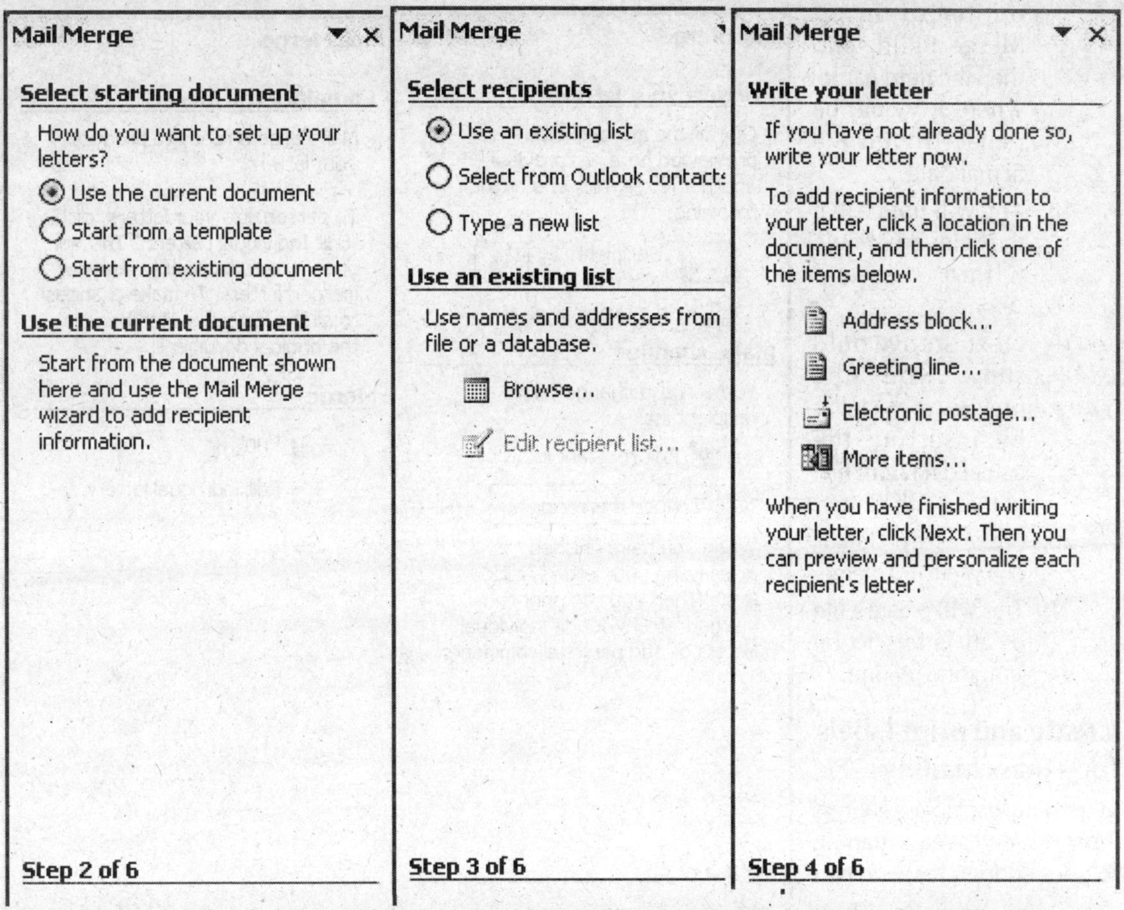
Mail Merge
Select starting document
How do you want to set up your letters?
Use the current document
Start from a template
Start from existing document
Use the current document
Start from the document shown here and use the Mail Merge wizard to add recipient information.
Step 2 of 6
Mail Merge
Select recipients
Use an existing list
Select from Outlook contacts
Type a new list
Use an existing list
Use names and addresses from file or a database.
Browse...
Edit recipient list...
Step 3 of 6
Mail Merge
Write your letter
If you have not already done so, write your letter now.
To add recipient information to your letter, click a location in the document, and then click one of the items below.
Address block...
Greeting line...
Electronic postage...
More items...
When you have finished writing your letter, click Next. Then you can preview and personalize each recipient's letter.
Step 4 of 6

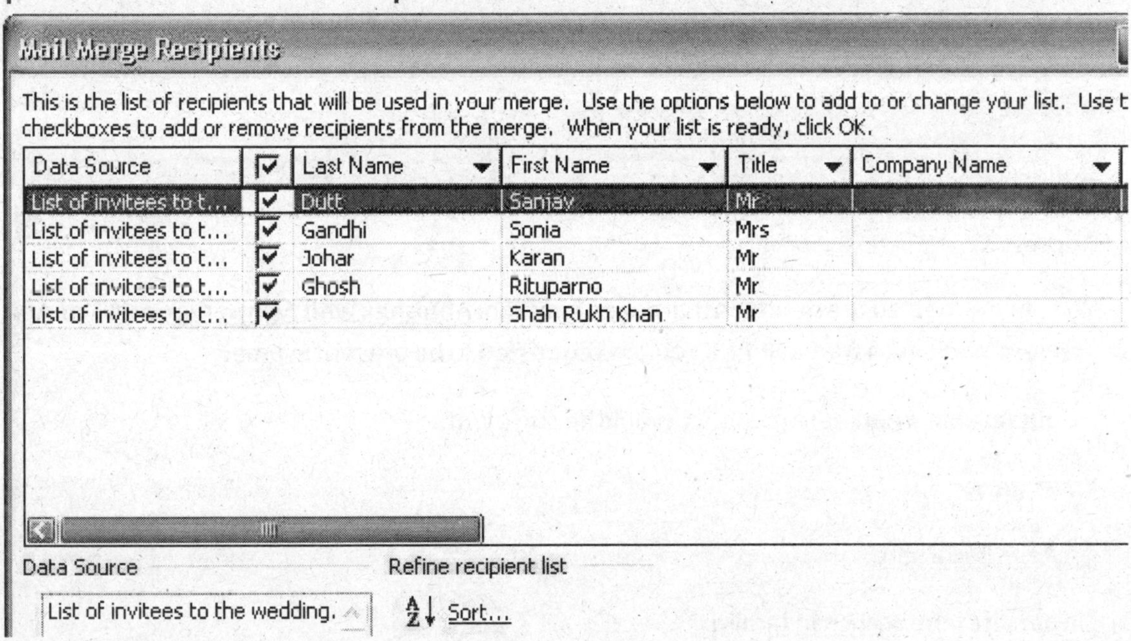
Mail Merge Recipients
This is the list of recipients that will be used in your merge. Use the options below to add to or change your list. Use t
checkboxes to add or remove recipients from the merge. When your list is ready, click OK.
Data Source
Last Name
First Name
Title
Company Name
List of invitees to t... Dutt Sanjay Mr
List of invitees to t... Gandhi Sonia Mrs
List of invitees to t... Johar Karan Mr
List of invitces to t... Ghosh Rituparno Mr
List of invitees to t... Shah Rukh Khan Mr
Data Source
Refine recipient list
List of invitees to the wedding.
Sort...

option of Insert Merge Field, and then the field name, where it would be replaced with the actual data.

18. You will notice that the fields are shown within < < and > >.
19. Next step would show you the preview of the letter by inserting the actual data from first entry into the letter.
20. Next step is to complete the merge.
21. This will create a file of all letters to be sent, one by one.

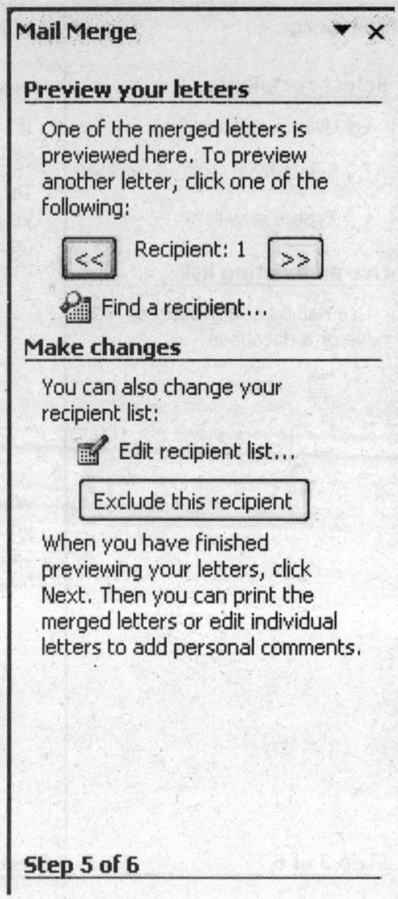

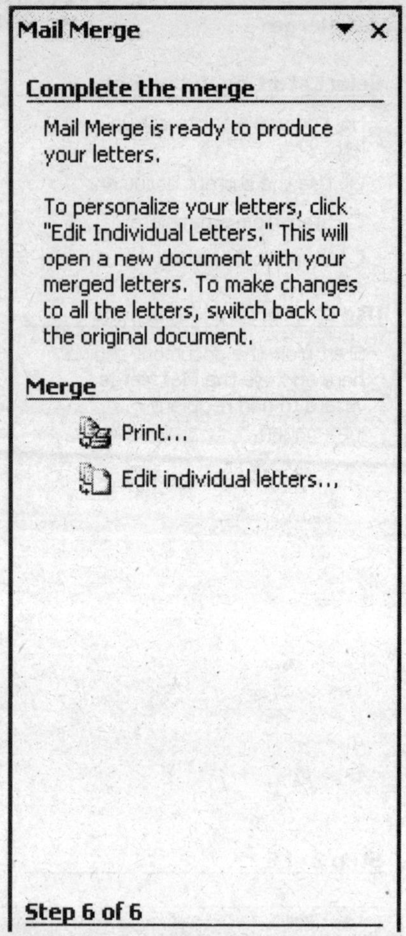

Create and print labels for a mass mailing

When you want to use address labels to send a mass mailing to your address list, you can

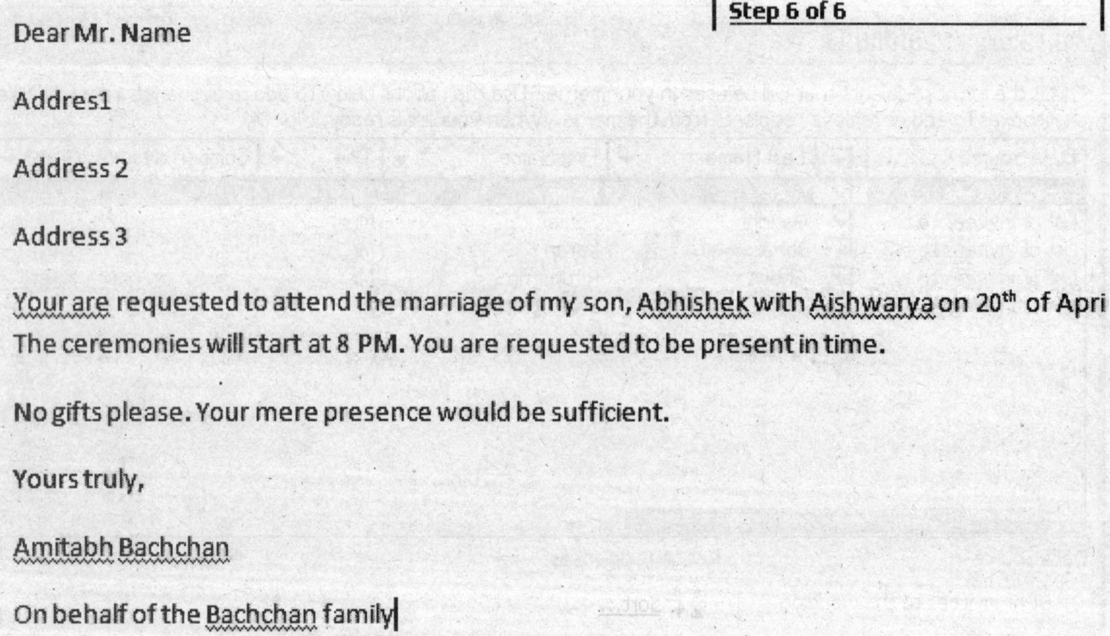

Dear Mr. Name

Addres1

Address 2

Address 3

Your are requested to attend the marriage of my son, Abhishek with Aishwarya on 20th of Apri

The ceremonies will start at 8 PM. You are requested to be present in time.

No gifts please. Your mere presence would be sufficient.

Yours truly,

Amitabh Bachchan

On behalf of the Bachchan family

Dear Mr. Sanjay Dutt

Mumbai

Your are requested to attend the marriage of my son, Abhishek with Aishwarya on 20th of April, The ceremonies will start at 8 PM. You are requested to be present in time.

No gifts please. Your mere presence would be sufficient.

Yours truly,

Amitabh Bachchan

On behalf of the Bachchan family

use mail merge to create a sheet of address labels. Each label contains an address from your list. The mail merge process entails the following overall steps:

Set up the labels

ou set up the layout of the labels one time, for all the labels in the mail merge. In a mail merge, the document that you use to do this is called the main document. In the label main document, you can also set up any content that you want repeated on each label, such as a company logo or your return address on shipping labels.

Connect the labels to your address list

Your address list is the data source that Microsoft Office Word uses in the mail merge. It is a file that contains the addresses to be printed on the labels.

Refine the list of recipients.

Word generates a label for each address in your mailing list. If you want to generate labels for only certain addresses in your mailing list, you can choose which addresses, or records, to include.

Add placeholders, called mail merge fields, to the labels.

When you perform the mail merge, the mail merge fields are filled with information from your address list.

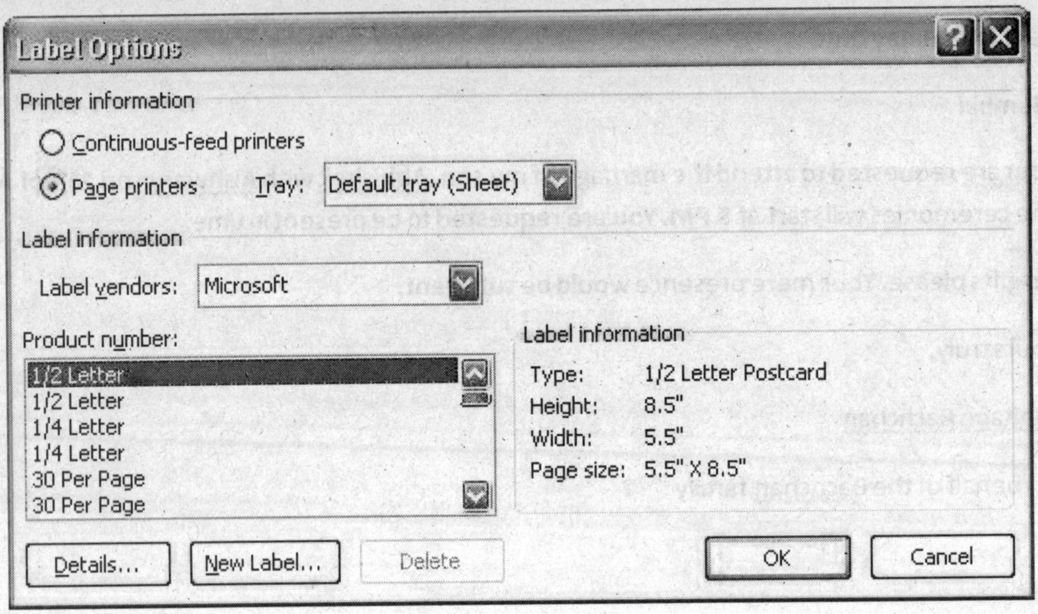

Preview, complete the merge, and print the labels. You can preview each label before you print the whole set

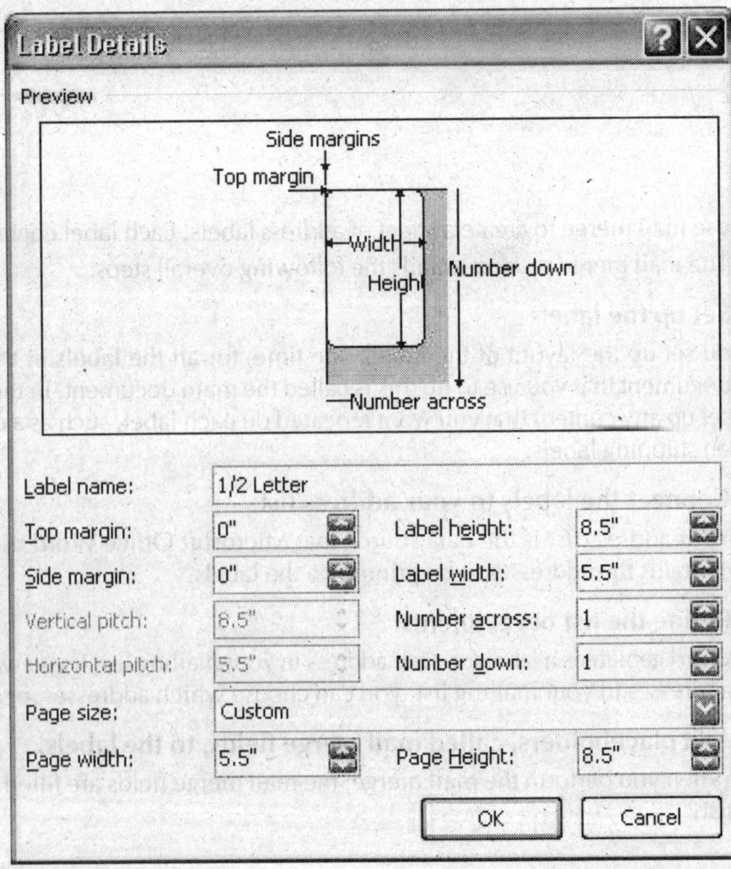

You use commands on the Mailings tab to perform a mail merge.

You can also perform a mail merge by using the Mail Merge task pane, which leads you step by step through the process. To use the task pane, in the Start Mail Merge group on the Mailings tab, click Start Mail Merge, and then click Step by Step Mail Merge Wizard. In Step 1 of the process, under Select document type, click Labels.

Set up the labels

Chances are that you already have a package of label sheets from one of the label sheet suppliers, such as Avery, AOne, or Formtec. Each sheet is a certain size and contains a certain number of labels with specific dimensions.

To set up the label main document, you need to match the dimensions of that document with the dimensions of the labels on the sheets that you have on hand.

Start Word.

1. A blank document opens by default. Leave it open. If you close it, the commands in the next step are not available.
2. On the Mailings tab, in the Start Mail Merge group, click Start Mail Merge.
3. Click Labels.

Resume a mail merge

If you need to stop working on a mail merge, you can save the label main document and resume the merge later. Word retains the data source and field information. If you were using the Mail Merge task pane, Word returns to your place in the task pane when you resume the merge.

When you are ready to resume the merge, open the document.

1. Word displays a message that asks you to confirm whether you want to open the document, which will run an SQL command.
2. Because this document is connected to a data source and you want to retrieve the data, click Yes. If you were opening a document that you did not realize was connected to a data source, you could click No to prevent potentially malicious access to data.
3. The text of the document, along with any fields that you inserted, appears.

4. Click the Mailings tab, and resume your work.

Resume a mail merge

If you need to stop working on a mail merge, you can save the label main document and resume the merge later. Word retains the data source and field information. If you were using the Mail Merge task pane, Word returns to your place in the task pane when you resume the merge.

1. When you are ready to resume the merge, open the document.
2. Word displays a message that asks you to confirm whether you want to open the document, which will run an SQL command.
3. Because this document is connected to a data source and you want to retrieve the data, click Yes. If you were opening a document that you did not realize was connected to a data source, you could click No to prevent potentially malicious access to data.
4. The text of the document, along with any fields that you inserted, appears.
5. Click the Mailings tab, and resume your work.

I am not showing the other steps, since they are very similar to the mailmerge of the letters.

CHAPTER 6

Working with Longer Documents in Microsoft Word 2013

Introduction

Working with long documents is cumbersome, particularly when several files created by several users need to be combined into one seamless report. For example, documents and reports such as Books, Annual Reports, Company Policies, are often the combined efforts of a team of people representing several departments. Each of these people create a separate file for their contribution to the report from which a final product is generated. When the files are bound into one large report, the need for page numbers, headers and footers, a table of contents, an index, and consistent formatting becomes apparent to the individual responsible for the final, printed version.

Create a Table of Contents

In all the books, in the beginning of the book, you will find a table of contents. It lists all the main topics in your document and notes on which page number each topic starts. Word helps you generate a table of contents for your document automatically. The easiest method for doing this is to assign one of Word's built-in heading styles (Heading 1 to Heading 9) to the headings you want to include in the table of contents. If you are not using Word's heading styles, you must assign a table of contents level to the styles you are using or mark text for inclusion in the table of contents.

Create a Table

1. Apply the built-in heading styles Heading 1 to Heading 9 to the headings in your document that you want to include in the table of contents.
2. Place the cursor in the document where you want the table of contents to appear. You may want to add a section or page break before your document text so the table of contents is on a separate page. You may also want to add a title for your page, such as "Table of Contents".
3. Click the Reference tab and select Table of Contents. The Table of Contents dialog box appears.
4. Select the Table of Contents tab if it is not already displayed.
5. From the Formats drop-down list, select the format that you want to apply to the table of

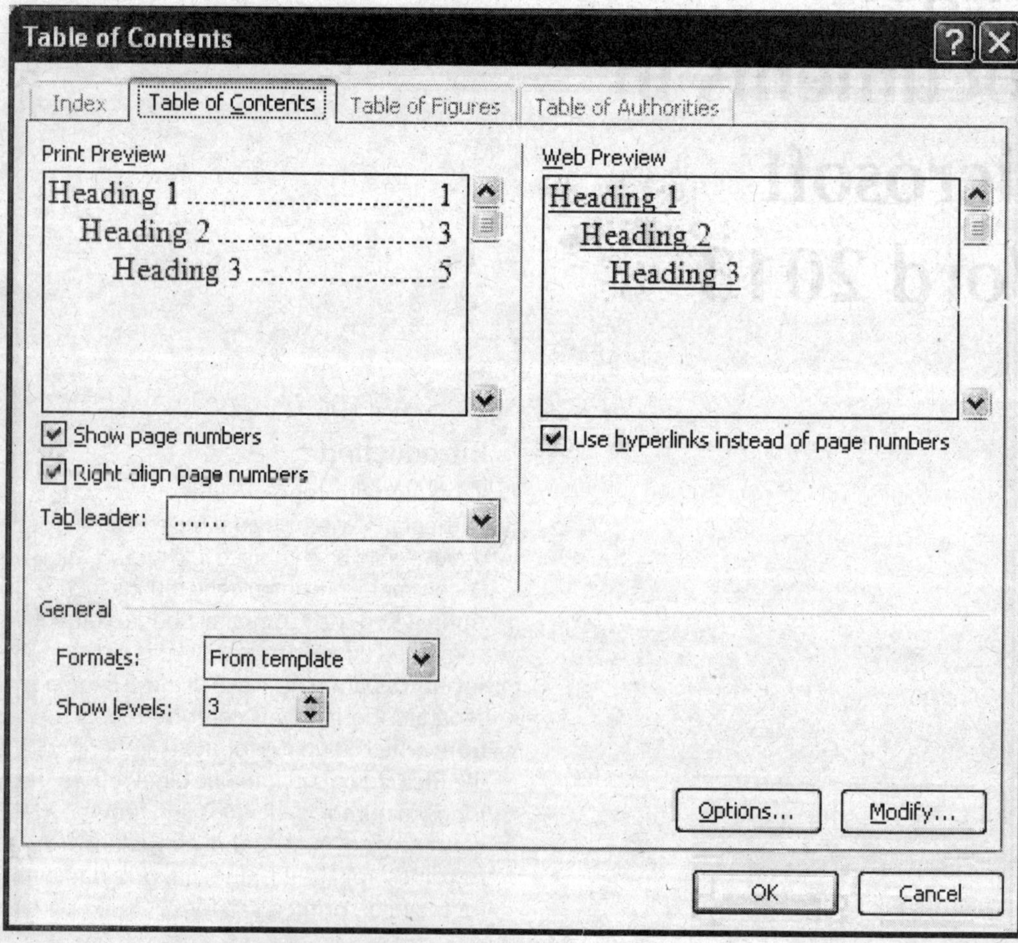

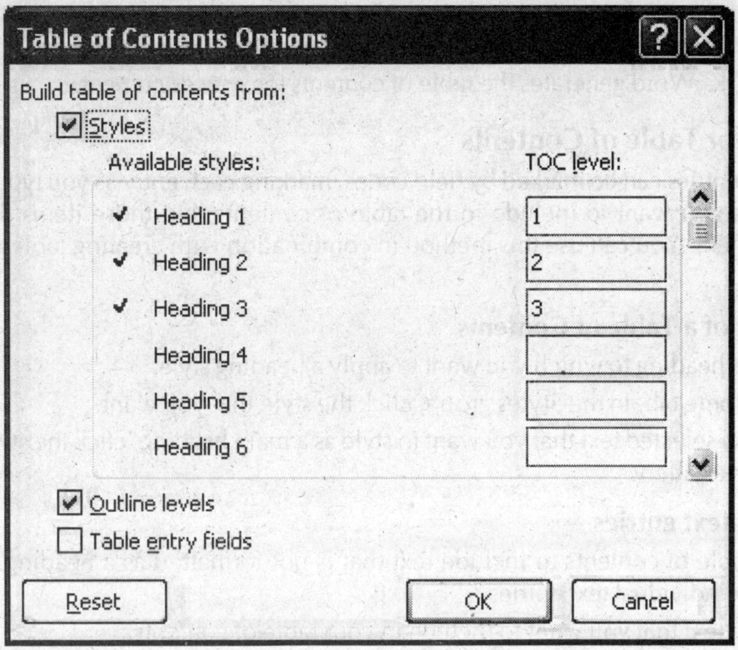

contents. As you click a format, a sample appears in the Print Preview window and in the Web Preview window.

6. If you want the page numbers to appear for each topic, click Show Page Numbers to enable that option. Click Right Align Page Numbers if you want the page numbers lined up on the right margin.
7. In the Show Levels box, enter the number of headings levels you want to appear in the table of contents, or use the up and down arrows to select the number.
8. From the Tab Leader drop-down list, select the repeat character (leader) you want to appear between the heading and the page number (it can be dots, dashes or underscores). Select None if you do not want any leaders.
9. If you want to change the format, choose Modify to open the Style dialog box. From the Styles box, select the heading level you want to change in the table of contents and then choose Modify to open the Modify Style dialog box. Choose Format to select the type

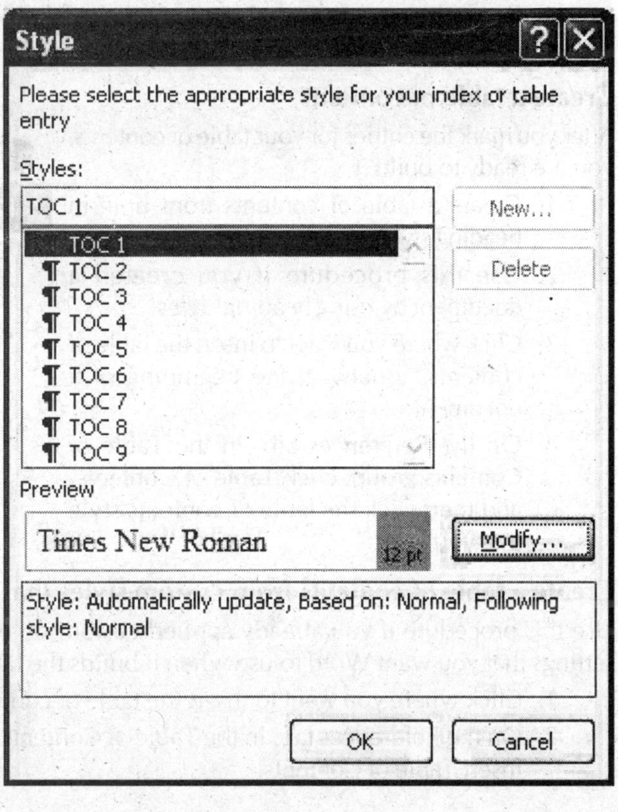

of format you want to specify and then select the formatting options you desire. Choose Ok to return to the Style dialog box, and then choose Apply.

10. Choose Ok. Word generates the table of contents for your document.

Marking Text for Table of Contents

Table of contents entries can be marked by field codes, marking each entry as you type. Use this method if you have items you want to include in the table of contents, but those items do not have styles associated with them. You can use this method in combination with creating tables of contents using styles.

Marking Entries of a Table of Contents

1. Select the heading to which you want to apply a heading style.
2. On the Home tab, in the Styles group, click the style that you want.

For example, if you selected text that you want to style as a main heading, click the style called Heading 1 in the Quick Style gallery.

Mark individual text entries

If you want the table of contents to include text that is not formatted as a heading, you can use this procedure to mark individual text entries.

1. Select the text that you want to include in your table of contents.
2. On the References tab, in the Table of Contents group, click Add Text.
3. Click the level that you want to label your selection, such as Level 1 for a main level display in the table of contents.
4. Repeat steps 1 through 3 until you have labeled all of the text that you want to appear in the table of contents.

Create a table of contents

After you mark the entries for your table of contents, you are ready to build it.

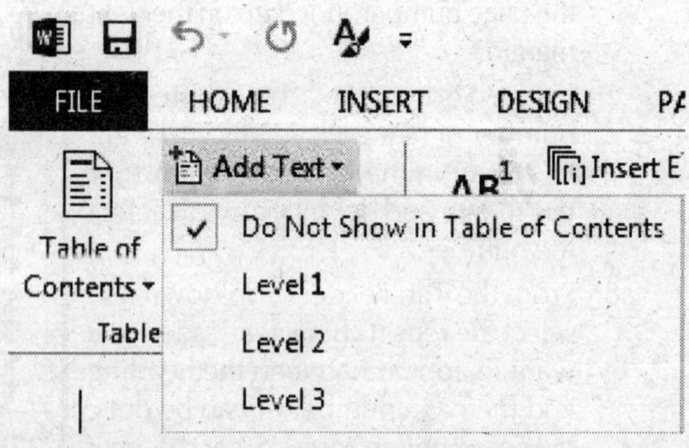

1. Create a table of contents from built-in heading styles
2. Use this procedure if you created a document by using heading styles.
3. Click where you want to insert the table of contents, usually at the beginning of a document.
4. On the References tab, in the Table of Contents group, click Table of Contents, and then click the table of contents style that you want.

Create a table of contents from custom styles that you applied

Use this procedure if you already applied custom styles to your headings. You can choose the style settings that you want Word to use when it builds the table of contents.

1. Click where you want to insert the table of contents.
2. On the References tab, in the Table of Contents group, click Table of Contents, and then click Insert Table of Contents.

3. Click Options.
4. Under Available styles, find the style that you applied to the headings in your document.
5. Under TOC level, next to the style name, type a number from 1 to 9 to indicate the level that you want the heading style to represent.

   If you want to use only custom styles, delete the TOC level numbers for the built-in styles, such as Heading 1.
6. Repeat step 4 and step 5 for each heading style that you want to include in the table of contents.
7. Click OK.
8. Choose a table of contents to fit the document type:
   - Printed document If you are creating a document that readers will read on a printed page, create a table of contents in which each entry lists both the heading and the page number where the heading appears. Readers can turn to the page that they want.
   - Online document For a document that readers will read online in Word, you can format the entries in the table of contents as hyperlinks, so that readers can go to a heading by clicking its entry in the table of contents.
9. To use one of the available designs, click a design in the Formats box.
10. Select any other table of contents options that you want.

Update the table of contents

If you added or removed headings or other table of contents entries in your document, you can quickly update the table of contents.

1. On the References tab, in the Table of Contents group, click Update Table.
2. Click Update page numbers only or Update entire table.

Delete a table of contents

1. On the References tab, in the Table of Contents group, click Table of Contents.
2. Click Remove Table of Contents.

Create an Index

An index lists the terms and topics that are discussed in a document, along with the pages that they appear on. To create an index, you mark the index entries by providing the name of the main entry and the cross-reference in your document, and then you build the index.

About index entries

You can create an index entry:

- For an Individual word, phrase, or symbol
- For a topic that spans a range of pages
- That refers to another entry, such as "Transportation. See Bicycles"

When you select text and mark it as an index entry, Microsoft Office Word adds a special XE (Index Entry) field that includes the marked main entry and any cross-reference information that you choose to include.

After you mark all the index entries, you choose an index design and build the finished index. Word collects the index entries, sorts them alphabetically, references their page numbers, finds and removes duplicate entries from the same page, and displays the index in the document.

Mark index entries and create an index

To create an index, you mark the entries, select a design, and then build the index.

To mark index entries, do one of the following:

- Mark words or phrases
- Mark entries for text that spans a range of pages

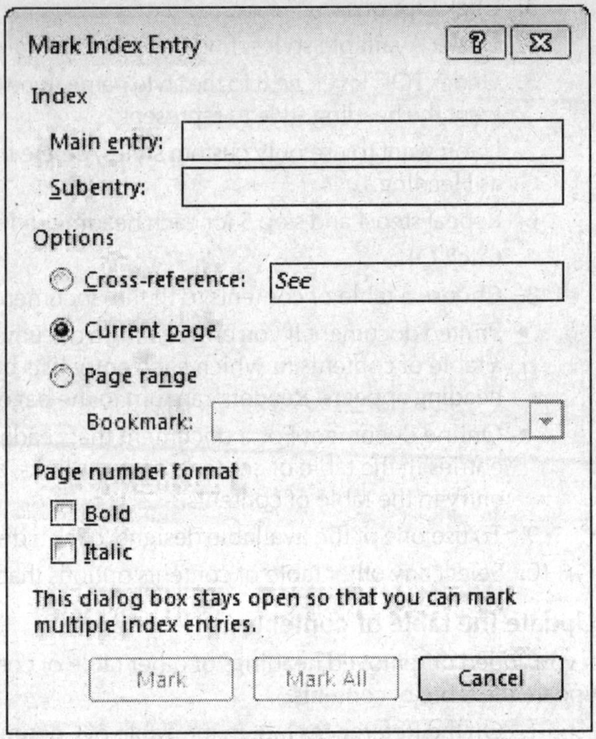

Mark words or phrases

1. To use existing text as an index entry, select the text. To enter your own text as an index entry, click where you want to insert the index entry.
2. On the References tab, in the Index group, click Mark Entry.
3. To create the main index entry that uses your own text, type or edit the text in the Main entry box.
4. If you want, you can customize the entry by creating a subentry , a third-level entry, or a cross-reference to another entry:
   - To create a subentry, type the text in the Subentry box.
   - To include a third-level entry, type the subentry text followed by a colon (:), and then type the text of the third-level entry.
   - To create a cross-reference to another entry, click Cross-reference under Options, and then type the text for the other entry in the box.
5. To format the page numbers that will appear in the index, select the Bold check box or the Italic check box below Page number format.
6. To format the text for the index, select the text in the Main entry or Subentry box, right-click, and then click Font. Select the formatting options that you want to use.
7. To mark the index entry, click Mark. To mark all occurrences of this text in the document, click Mark All.
8. To mark additional index entries, select the text, click in the Mark Index Entry dialog box, and then repeat step 3 through step 6.

Mark entries for text that spans a range of pages

1. Select the range of text that you want the index entry to refer to.
2. On the Insert tab, in the Links group, click Bookmark.
3. In the Bookmark name box, type a name, and then click Add.
4. In the document, click at the end of the text that you marked with a bookmark.
5. On the References tab, in the Index group, click Mark Entry.
6. In the Main entry box, type the index entry for the marked text.

   To format the page numbers that will appear in the index, select the Bold check box or the Italic check box below Page number format.

   To format the text for the index, select the text in the Main entry or Subentry box, right-click, and then click Font. Select the formatting options that you want to use.

7. Under Options, click Page range.
8. In the Bookmark box, type or select the bookmark name that you typed in step 3, and then click Mark.

Create the index

1. After you mark the entries, you are ready to select an index design and insert the index into your document.
2. Click where you want to add the index.
3. On the References tab, in the Index group, click Create Index, and then click Insert Index.
4. Do one of the following:
   - Click a design in the Formats box to use one of the available index designs.
   - Design a custom index layout:
5. In the Formats box, click From template, and then click Modify.
6. In the Style dialog box, click the index style that you want to change, and then click Modify.
7. Under Formatting, select the options that you want.
8. To add the style changes to your template , click All documents based on the template.
9. Click OK twice.

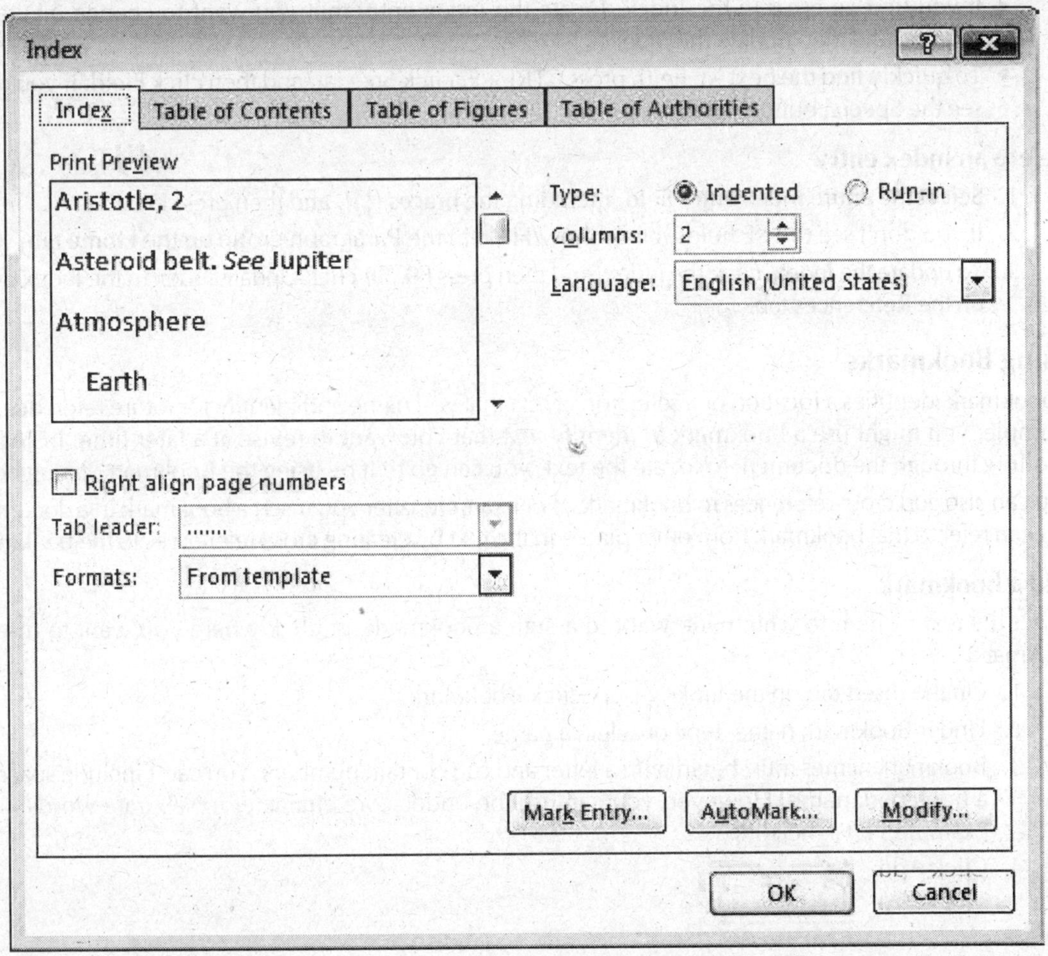

10. Select any other index options that you want.

Notes

- To update the index, click the index, and then press F9. Or click Update Index in the Index group on the References tab.
- If you find an error in the index, locate the index entry that you want to change, make the change, and then update the index.
- If you create an index in a master document , expand the subdocuments before you insert or update the index.

Edit or format an index entry

1. If you don't see the XE fields, click Show/Hide in the Paragraph group on the Home tab.
2. Find the XE field for the entry that you want to change, for example, { XE "Callisto" \t "See Moons" }.
3. To edit or format an index entry, change the text inside the quotation marks.
4. To update the index, click the index, and then press F9. Or click Update Index in the Index group on the References tab.
   Notes

- If you find an error in the index, locate the index entry that you want to change, make the change, and then update the index.
- To quickly find the next XE field, press CTRL + F, click Special, and then click Field. If you don't see the Special button, click More.

Delete an index entry

1. Select the entire index entry field, including the braces ({}), and then press DELETE.
2. If you don't see the XE fields, click Show/Hide in the Paragraph group on the Home tab.
3. To update the index, click the index, and then press F9. Or click Update Index in the Index group on the References tab.

Using Bookmarks

A bookmark identifies a location or a selection of text that you name and identify for future reference. For example, you might use a bookmark to identify text that you want to revise at a later time. Instead of scrolling through the document to locate the text, you can go to it by using the Bookmark dialog box. You can also add cross references to bookmarks. For example, after you insert a bookmark in a document, you can refer to that bookmark from other places in the text by creating cross-references to the bookmark.

Add a bookmark

Select the text or item to which you want to assign a bookmark, or click where you want to insert a bookmark.

1. On the Insert tab, in the Links group, click Bookmark.
2. Under Bookmark name, type or select a name.
3. Bookmark names must begin with a letter and can contain numbers. You can't include spaces in a bookmark name. However, you can use the underscore character to separate words — for example, "First_heading."
4. Click Add.

Change a bookmark

When you add a bookmark to a block of text, Microsoft Office Word surrounds the text with square brackets. When you change a bookmarked item, make sure that you change the text or graphics inside the brackets.

1. Display bookmark brackets
2. Click the Microsoft Office Button , and then click Word Options.
3. Click Advanced, and then select the Show bookmarks check box under Show document content.
4. Click OK.
5. If you assign a bookmark to an item, the bookmark appears in brackets ([...]) on the screen. If you assign a bookmark to a location, the bookmark appears as an I-beam. The brackets are not printed.

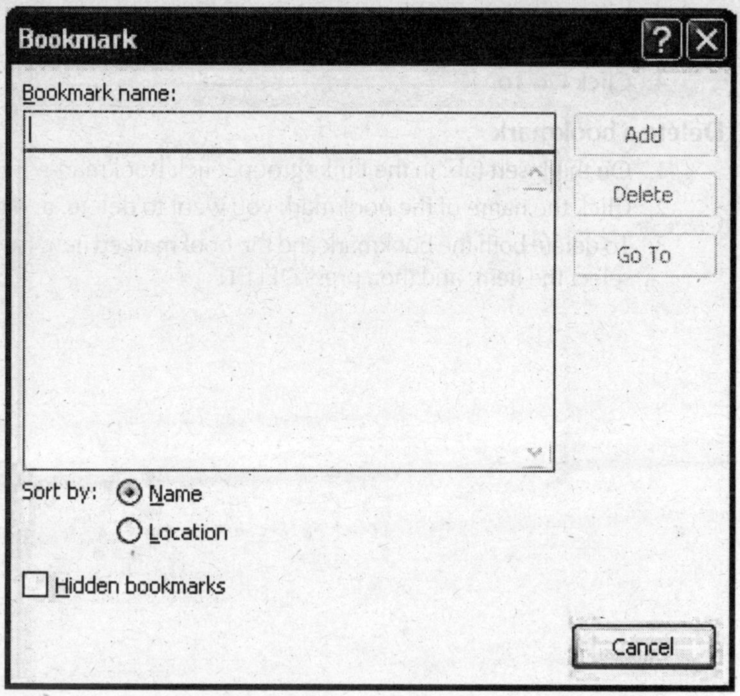

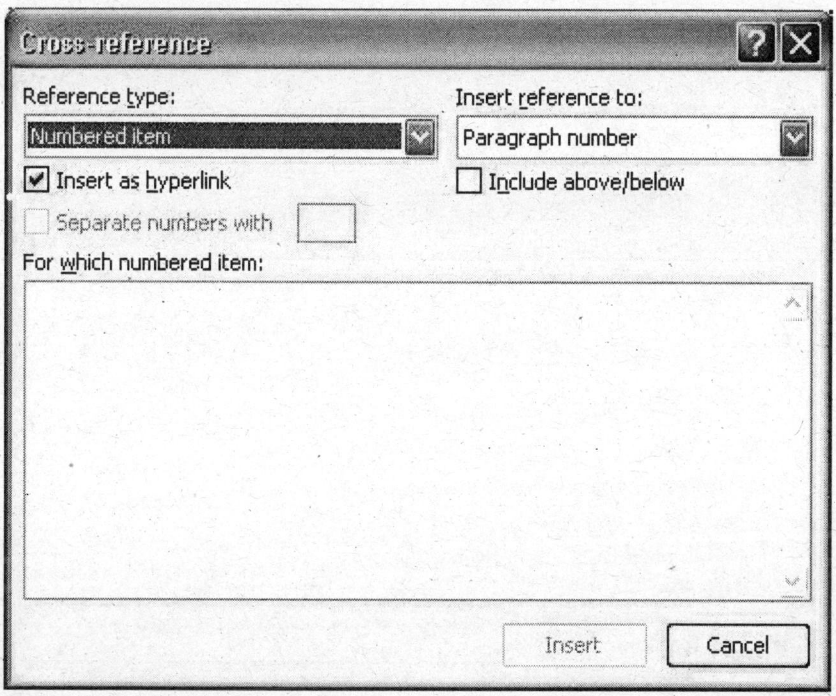

Go to a specific bookmark

1. On the Insert tab, in the Links group, click Bookmark.
2. Click either Name or Location to sort the list of bookmarks in the document.
3. Click the name of the bookmark that you want to go to.
4. Click Go To.

Delete a bookmark

1. On the Insert tab, in the Links group, click Bookmark.
2. Click the name of the bookmark you want to delete, and then click Delete.
3. To delete both the bookmark and the bookmarked item (such as a block of text or other element), select the item, and then press DELETE.

CHAPTER 7

Creating Tables in Microsoft Word 2013

Introduction

Tables are an integral parts of Word. They help you in setting the text in tabular form which used to be set by the use of Tabs in the older versions of word processors and even on typewriters. Although in tables, you still use tabs but they are more easy to format and use. Besides, they give a cleaner and professional look.

Creating a Table

A table can be created either of the two methods. You can create the table structure before you enter any text, or you can convert text you have already created to a table. There is an easy way to create the structure for a simple table and a way to create a more complex table.

To create the structure for a simple table

1. Position the insertion point at the location for the table.
2. Click the Insert Tab on the Standard toolbar.
3. Drag across, the number of columns and down, the number of rows you want

   An unformatted table appears

or you can follow the following alternate method.

1. Position curosr at the location for the table.
2. From the Insert tab, choose Table and Insert Table.
3. In the Insert Table dialog box, specify the columns and rows, in this case we have chosen a table of 3 x 3.
4. Click Ok.

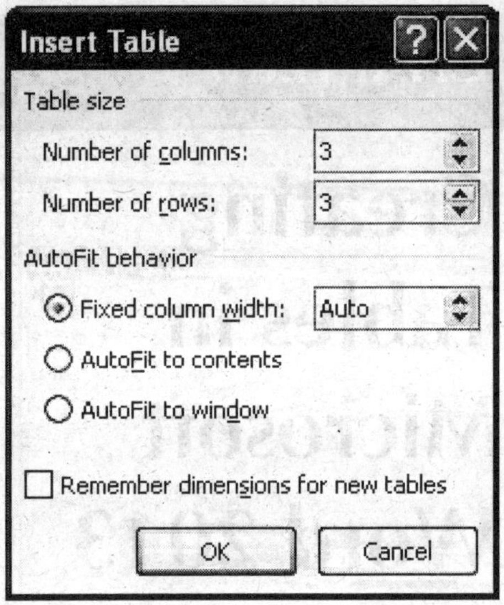

At this stage you should not bother about the other features of the dialog box. Now that the table in available you would like to enter the data into it.

Entering Data in a Table

Data can be typed directly into the cells or it can be moved or copied from other cells.

To Enter Data in a Table

1. Click in a cell with the mouse and type the data required to be typed. As you type, the cursor wraps within the cell and the entire row will become taller if it needs to accommodate multiple lines of text.
2. Press Tab to move to the cell to the right, and type text in the next cell.
3. Continue pressing tab after you finish each cell.
4. When you finish entering text in the last cell of the table, press Tab to create a new row, if required.

In our case following the letter of the earlier chapter, we will create the table for the number of calls made, etc. So in the given cells just type the required text and once that is done you can proceed further.

Once you have typed the above data, your table will look like the one shown here, in the part of the document, Bill.

One look at the table, you can see that something is missing. Somehow the table is not looking presentable. What it needs is the alignment of the text.

Aligning Data in a Table

For aligning of the data, you can use either of the following:

To Align Data Vertically or Horizontally Within Cells

1. Select the cells you want to align.

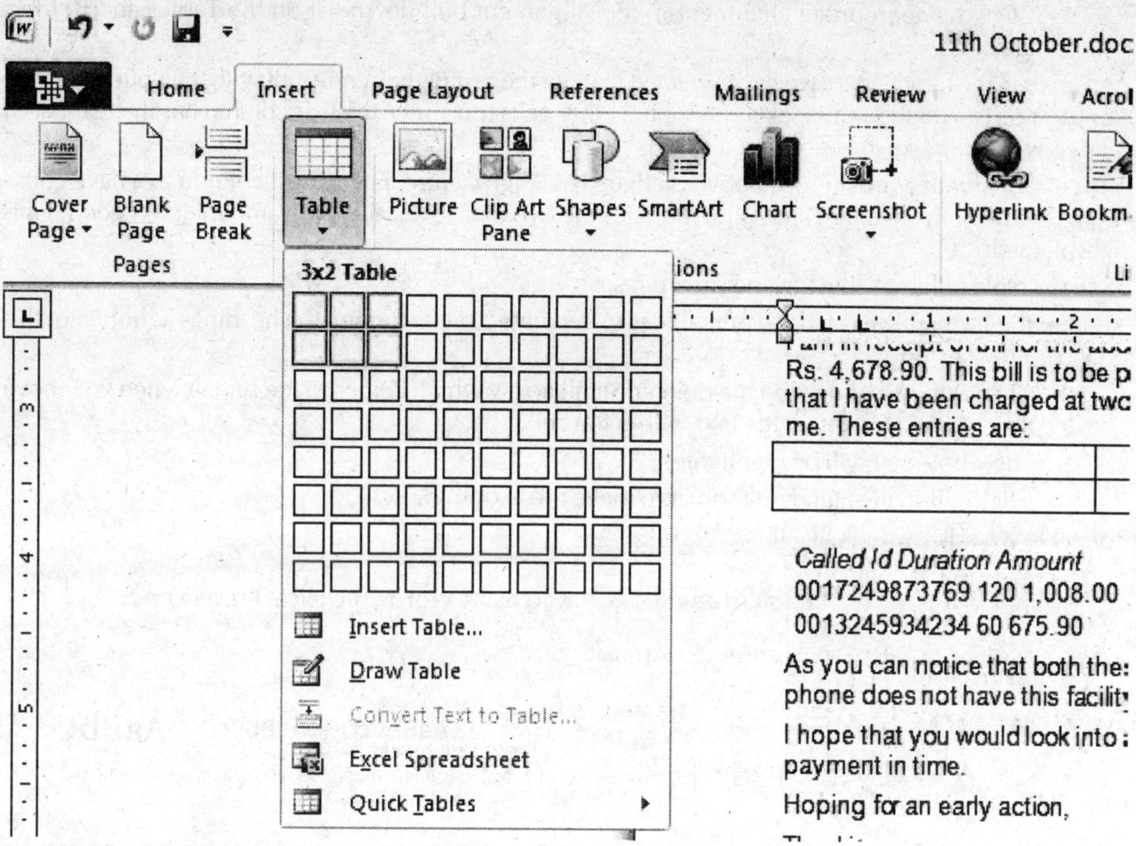

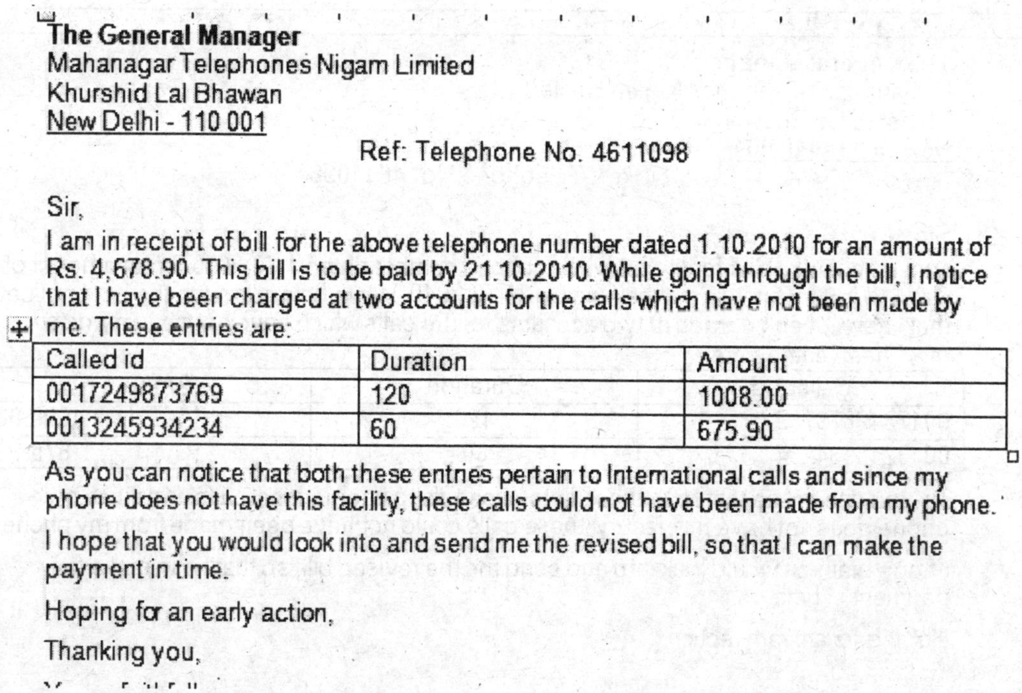

The General Manager
Mahanagar Telephones Nigam Limited
Khurshid Lal Bhawan
New Delhi - 110 001

Ref: Telephone No. 4611098

Sir,

I am in receipt of bill for the above telephone number dated 1.10.2010 for an amount of Rs. 4,678.90. This bill is to be paid by 21.10.2010. While going through the bill, I notice that I have been charged at two accounts for the calls which have not been made by me. These entries are:

Called id	Duration	Amount
0017249873769	120	1008.00
0013245934234	60	675.90

As you can notice that both these entries pertain to International calls and since my phone does not have this facility, these calls could not have been made from my phone.

I hope that you would look into and send me the revised bill, so that I can make the payment in time.

Hoping for an early action,

Thanking you,

2. Click the appropriate alignment in the Alignment pull-down list on the Tables and Borders toolbar.

As shown in the figure next , we have selected to align the text of the centre cell with the option of Align Centre. You can do the similar exercise for the other cells too. Since the first column has the text based matter, we would like to keep it left aligned.

The centre column as mentioned above is aligned as Align Centre. For the last column, we have chose Align Centre for the heading and Align Right for the two data rows, since the amount looks good if it is right aligned.

Now the table will look like the one shown next.

Another thing which we can do to our table is to decorate a bit by turning the headings as **bold**. For this do the following:

1. Click at the heading with the pointed small arrow which comes to the screen when you move the cursor to the left of the text within the cell.
2. The whole cell will be highlighted.
3. Click at B in the Standard toolbar to make the text Bold.

The table would now look like this.

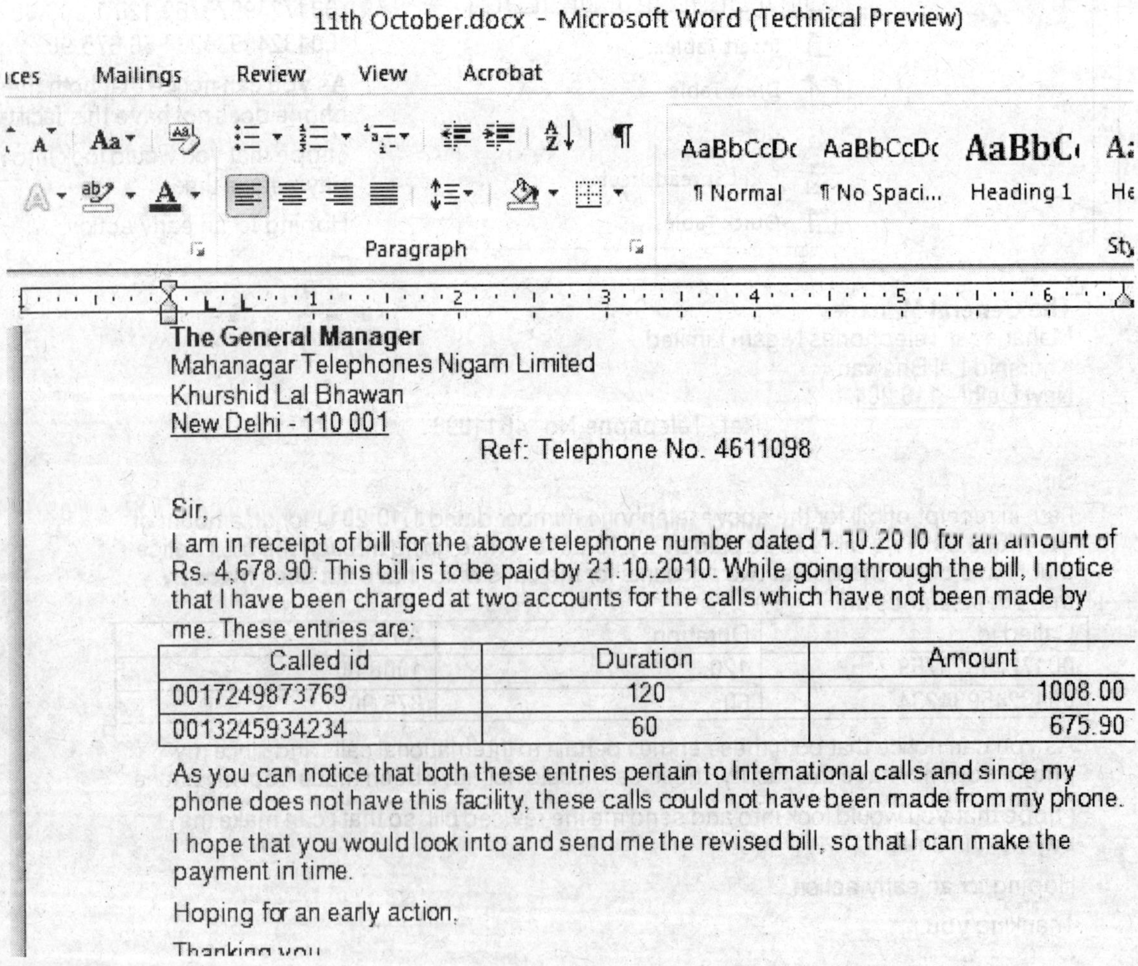

The General Manager
Mahanagar Telephones Nigam Limited
Khurshid Lal Bhawan
New Delhi - 110 001

Ref: Telephone No. 4611098

Sir,
I am in receipt of bill for the above telephone number dated 1.10.20 l0 for an amount of Rs. 4,678.90. This bill is to be paid by 21.10.2010. While going through the bill, I notice that I have been charged at two accounts for the calls which have not been made by me. These entries are:

Called id	Duration	Amount
0017249873769	120	1008.00
0013245934234	60	675.90

As you can notice that both these entries pertain to International calls and since my phone does not have this facility, these calls could not have been made from my phone.

I hope that you would look into and send me the revised bill, so that I can make the payment in time.

Hoping for an early action,

Thanking you

It would not be a good idea to give the total of the amount column. Since we do not have the extra row for the total of the amount, we would be adding a row to the table. For this we read the following.

Inserting Rows and Columns

You can add rows and columns to any portion of your table on all the sides using the following options.

To insert a row

1. Click in a cell at the location for the new blank row.
2. From the Table menu, choose Insert and then choose Rows Below from the Insert submenu.

Using this option we will add a new row to our table in document Bill.

To insert a column

1. Position the mouse pointer at the top of the column at the location for the new column. A large down-arrow appears.
2. Click while the down-arrow is visible to select the column.
3. From the Layout tab, choose Insert above or Insert below as per your requirements to add row above or below the current row.

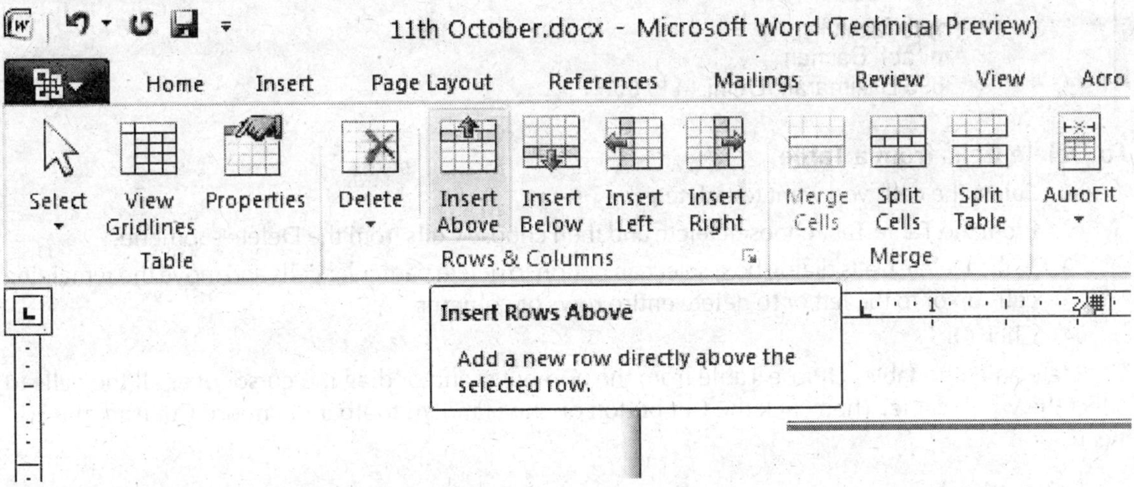

To insert multiple columns or rows, select the number of existing columns or rows corresponding to the number that you want to insert before you choose an option from the insert submenu. If there are not enough existing columns or rows where you want to do the insertion, do multiple Insert operations.

Using the above method we will add a new column to our table in document Bill. So now we have added a new row and a new column. Thus, our new table looks like the one shown on the next page.

Using the methods mentioned earlier, you can type in the cell under the heading Duration, the heading which you want to type, i.e., Total Amount.

This way out table will now look like the one shown next.

Now we proceed ahead to find out the total of the column named amount and place it in the right most cell.

Deleting Data from a Table

To delete data from a table, you can clear the contents of a cell by selecting text and deleting it, but you can also delete cells, rows, and columns.

New Delhi - 110 001

Ref: Telephone No. 4611098

Sir,

I am in receipt of bill for the above telephone number dated 1.10.2010 for an amount of Rs. 4,678.90. This bill is to be paid by 21.10.2010. While going through the bill, I notice that I have been charged at two accounts for the calls which have not been made by me. These entries are:

Called id	Duration	Amount
0017249873769	120	1008.00
0013245934234	60	675.90

As you can notice that both these entries pertain to International calls and since my phone does not have this facility, these calls could not have been made from my phone.

I hope that you would look into and send me the revised bill, so that I can make the payment in time.

Hoping for an early action,

Thanking you,

Yours faithfully,
Amitabh Bachan
3695 Ballimaran, Delhi - 110 006

To Delete Cells from a Table

1. Select the cells you want to delete.
2. From the Table Tab, choose Delete and then choose Cells from the Delete submenu.
3. In the Delete Cells dialog box, select an option to delete particular cells and move the remaining cells up or to the left or to delete entire rows or columns.
4. Click Ok.

To delete an entire table, choose Table from the pop-out menu or drag the cursor over all the cells to select the whole table. Then click the Cut button on the Standard toolbar or choose Cut from the Edit menu.

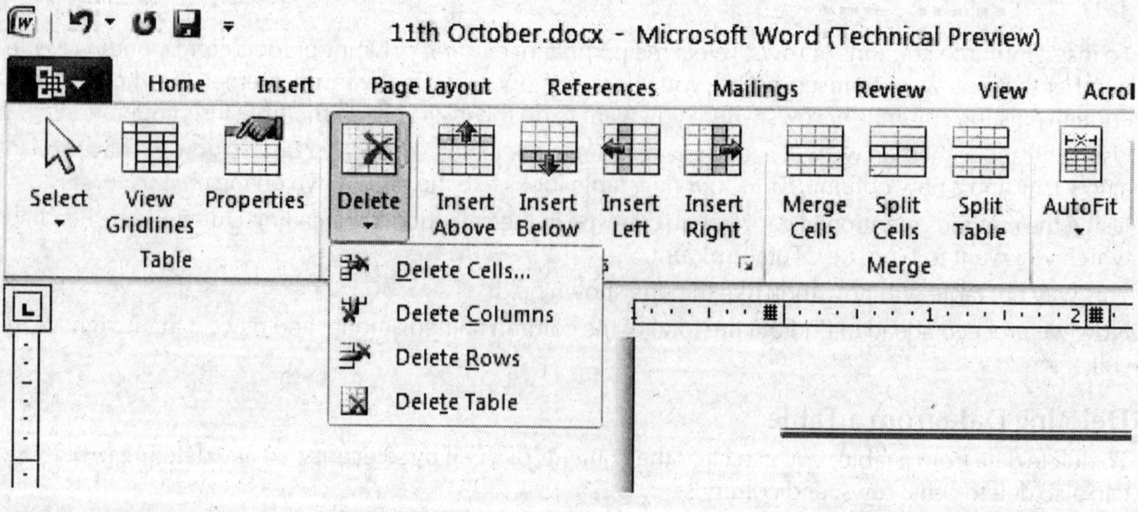

Borders and Shading

By using Borders you can draw lines around the cells and fill them with shades using the command Shading.

To Automatically Format a Table with Template

1. Click anywhere in the table to select it.
2. From the Table Tools, choose Design tab.
3. In the Table Styles, choose the style you want for your table. You can click at right arrow to see more designs or click at More to see the dialog box of the built-in designs of the table.
4. Choose the one you want and it will be applied to your table.
5. You can modify the style by choosing the Modify Table Style option.

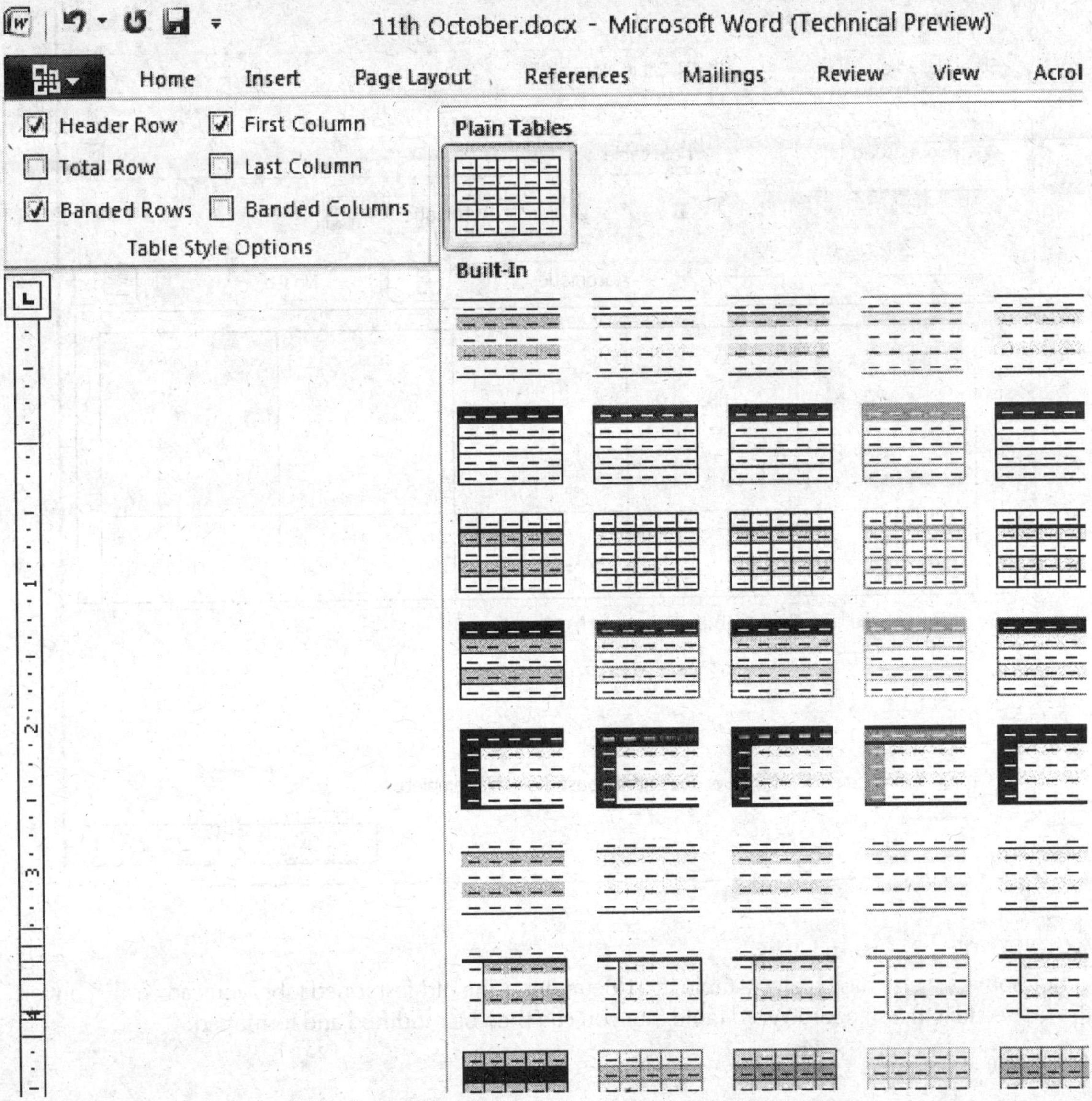

To Manually set Borders and Shading

1. Select the cells for which you want to modify the borders or add shading.
2. On the Tables and Borders toolbar, select line style and weight from the drop-down lists.
3. Click the Border tool, and use the options on the drop-down palette to apply borders to the top, bottom, left, right, inside, or outside of the selected cells.
4. To apply shading to the selected cells, select a shading option from the Shading drop-down list.

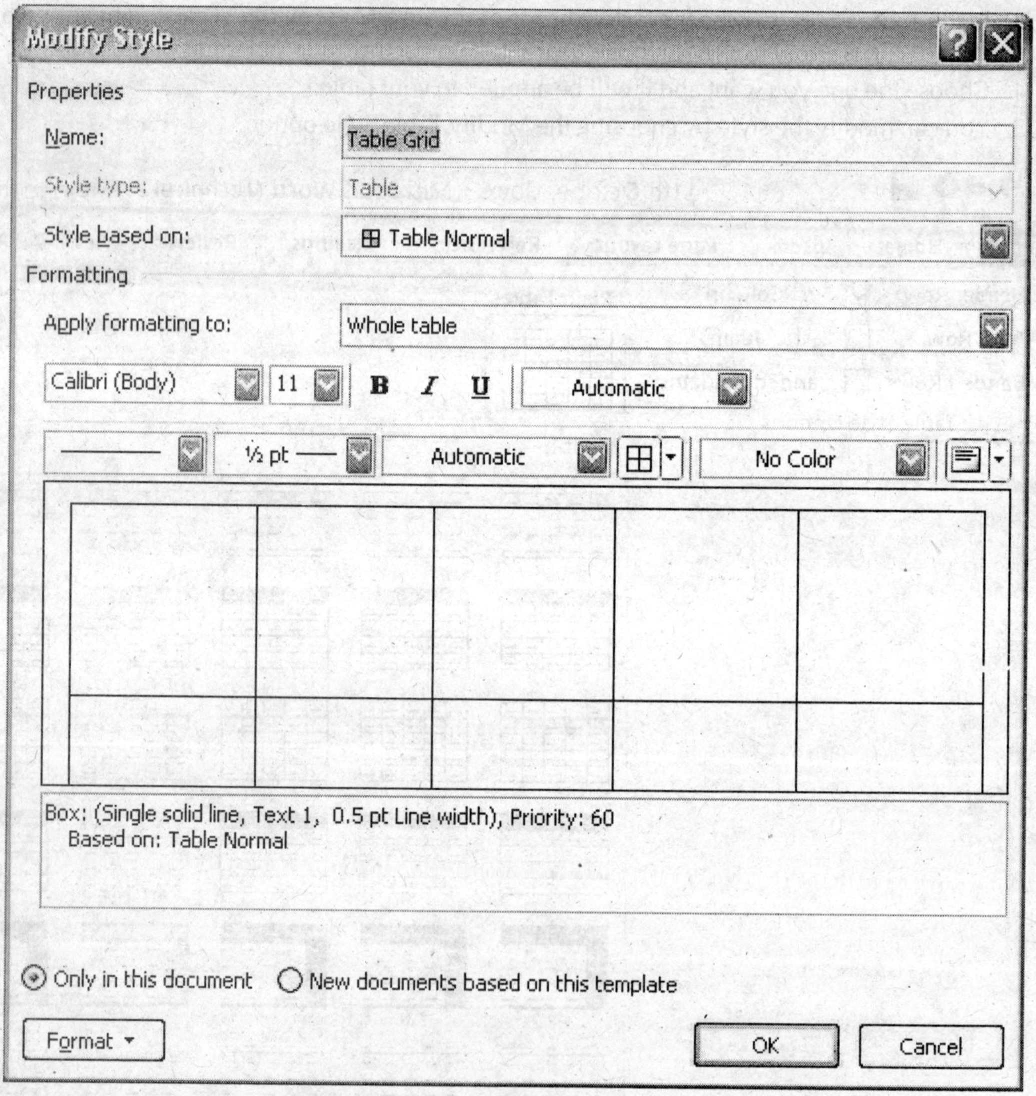

Converting Text to a Table

When someone else has created a table in a document using old-fashioned tabs, you can easily convert the tabbed text to a standard Word table that you can then be modified and formatted.

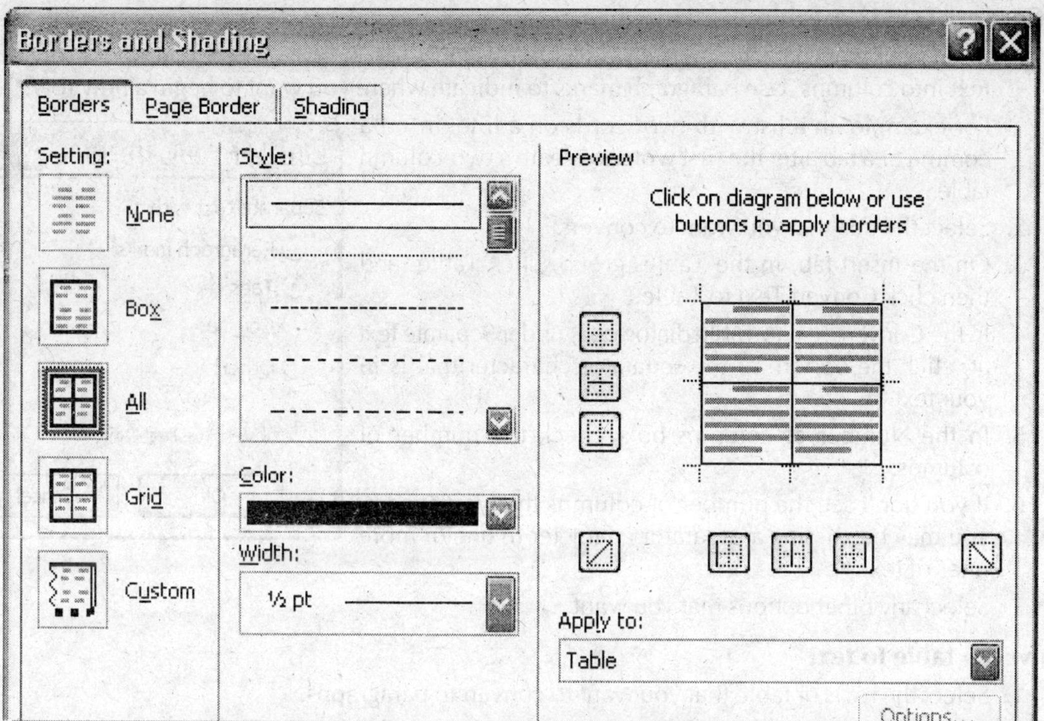
Borders and Shading
Borders
Page Border
Shading
Setting:
None
Box
All
Grid
Custom
Style:
Color:
Width:
½ pt
Preview
Click on diagram below or use buttons to apply borders
Apply to:
Table
Options...

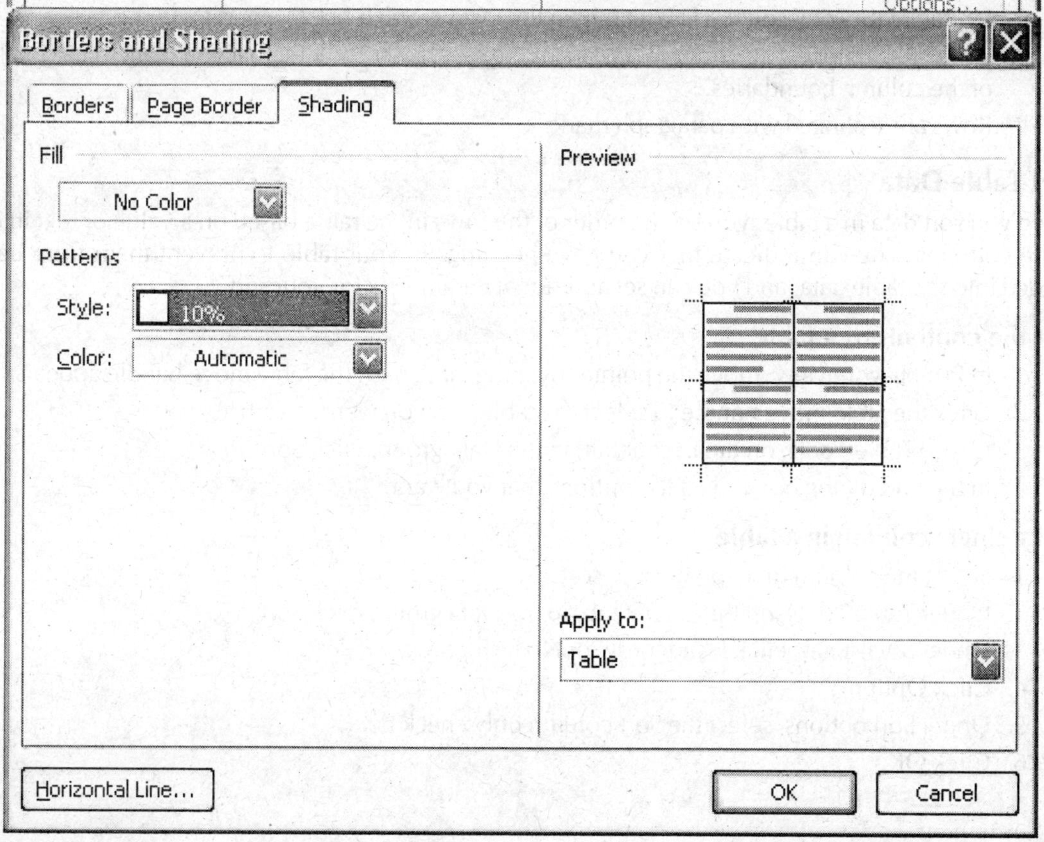
Borders and Shading
Borders
Page Border
Shading
Fill
No Color
Patterns
Style:
10%
Color:
Automatic
Preview
Apply to:
Table
Horizontal Line...
OK
Cancel

To Convert Text to a Table

1. Insert separator characters — such as commas or tabs — to indicate where you want to divide the text into columns. Use paragraph marks to indicate where you want to begin a new row.

   For example, in a list with two words on a line, insert a comma or a tab after the first word to create a two-column table.

2. Select the text that you want to convert.
3. On the Insert tab, in the Tables group, click Table, and then click Convert Text to Table.
4. In the Convert Text to Table dialog box, under Separate text at, click the option for the separator character that is in your text.
5. In the Number of columns box, check the number of columns.
6. If you don't see the number of columns that you expect, you may be missing a separator character in one or more lines of text.
7. Select any other options that you want.

Convert a table to text

1. Select the rows or table that you want to convert to paragraphs.
2. Under Table Tools, on the Layout tab, in the Data group, click Convert to Text.
3. Under Separate text at, click the option for the separator character that you want to use in place of the column boundaries.
4. Rows are separated with paragraph marks.

Sort Table Data

When you sort data in a table, you set the order of the rows in the table based on a value or text in one of the columns. You can indicate that you have headings in your table to prevent them from being melded into the table data, and you can set additional parameters for your sort.

Sort the contents of a table

1. In Print Layout view, move the pointer over the table until the table move handle appears.
2. Click the table move handle to select the table that you want to sort.
3. Under Table Tools, on the Layout tab, in the Data group, click Sort.
4. In the Sort dialog box, select the options that you want.

Sort a single column in a table

1. Select the column that you want to sort.
2. Under Table Tools, on the Layout tab, in the Data group, click Sort.
3. Under My list has, click Header row or No header row.
4. Click Options.
5. Under Sort options, select the Sort column only check box.
6. Click OK.

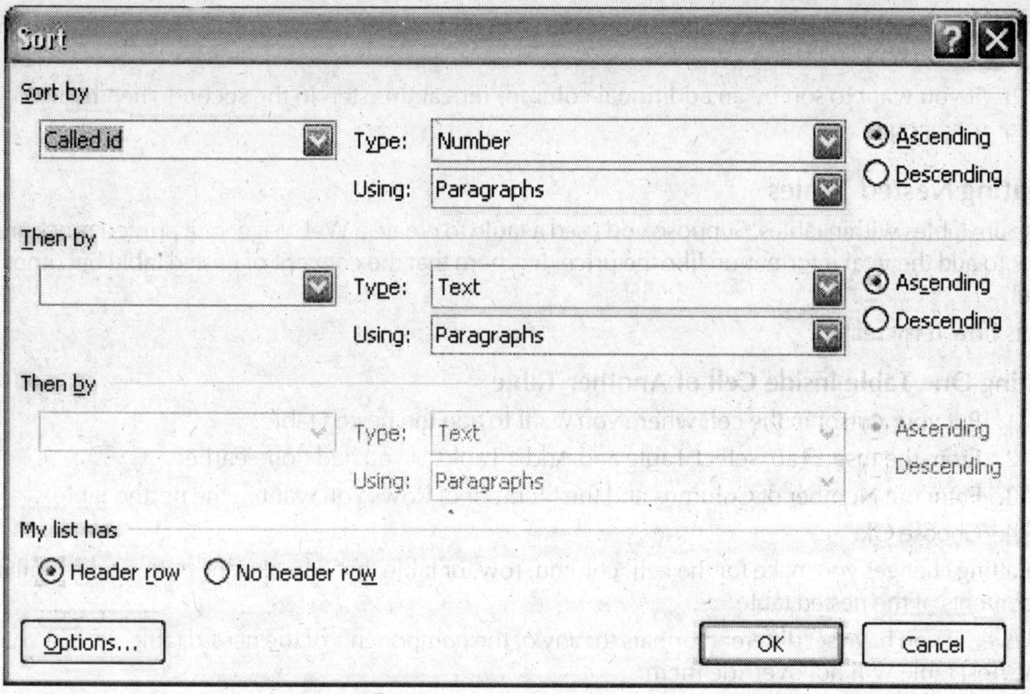

Sort by more than one word or field inside a table column

To sort the data in a table that is based on the contents of a column that includes more than one word, you must first use characters to separate the data — including data in the header row. For example, if the cells in a column contain both last and first names, you can use commas to separate the names.

1. Select the column that you want to sort.
2. Under Table Tools, on the Layout tab, in the Data group, click Sort.
3. Under My list has, click Header row or No header row.
4. Click Options.
5. Under Separate fields at, click the type of character that separates the words or fields that you want to sort, and then click OK.
6. Under Sort by, in the Using list, select which word or field you want to sort by.
7. In the first Then by list, enter the column that contains the data

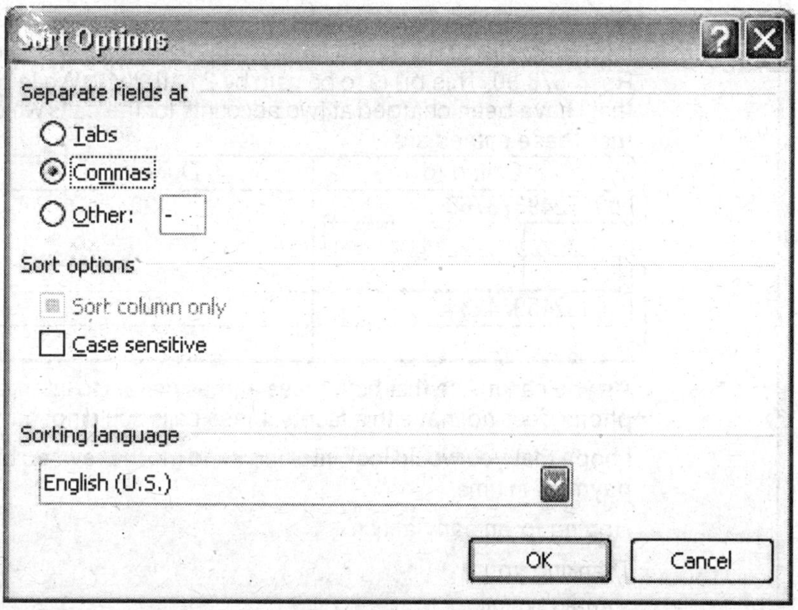

that you want to sort by, and then in the Using list, select which word or field you want to sort by.

8. If you want to sort by an additional column, repeat this step in the second Then by list.
9. Click OK.

Creating Nested Tables

These are tables within tables. Suppose you used a table to create a Web page, or a printed brochure and forgot to add the vital information like the price. It is here that the concept of nested table becomes very useful.

This is how it is created.

Nesting One Table Inside Cell of Another Table

1. Put your cursor in the cell where you want to add the nested table.
2. From the Insert Tab, select Table and Add a Table as you had done earlier.
3. Enter the Number of Columns and the Number of Rows you want in the nested table.
4. Choose Ok.

Formatting changes you make for the cell, column, row, or table that contains the nested table will affect the contents of the nested table.

However, if you have set different formats for any of the components of the nested table, format changes to the host table will not override them.

To,

The General Manager

Mahanagar Telephones Nigam Limited

Khurshid Lal Bhawan

New Delhi - 110 001

Ref: Telephone No. 4611098

Sir,

I am in receipt of bill for the above telephone number dated 1.10.2010 for an amount of Rs. 4,678.90. This bill is to be paid by 21.10.2010. While going through the bill, I notice that I have been charged at two accounts for the calls which have not been made by me. These entries are:

<table>
<tr><th>Called id</th><th>Duration</th><th>Amount</th></tr>
<tr><td>0017249873769</td><td>120</td><td>1008.00</td></tr>
<tr><td><table><tr><td></td><td></td><td></td></tr><tr><td></td><td></td><td></td></tr></table></td><td></td><td></td></tr>
<tr><td>0013245934234</td><td>60</td><td>675.90</td></tr>
<tr><td></td><td></td><td></td></tr>
</table>

As you can notice that both these entries pertain to International calls and since my phone does not have this facility, these calls could not have been made from my phone.

I hope that you would look into and send me the revised bill, so that I can make the payment in time.

Hoping for an early action,

Thanking you,

Yours faithfully

Calculations in a Table

Word is capable of handling simple calculations in a table. If you find you need to perform many complicated formulas, you should consider using Excel 2007 and importing or embedding a worksheet into your document. For simple calculations, you can use a Word table.

Performing Calculations

1. Click in the cell where you want the results of the calculations to appear.
2. Open the Layout menu and select Formula. The Formula dialog box appears.
3. Word tries to anticipate your needs by entering a formula for you. If you do not want to use that formula, delete it and enter your own formula or choose a function from the Paste Function drop-down list (click on this with the Help question mark to see a button that opens a list of function definitions).

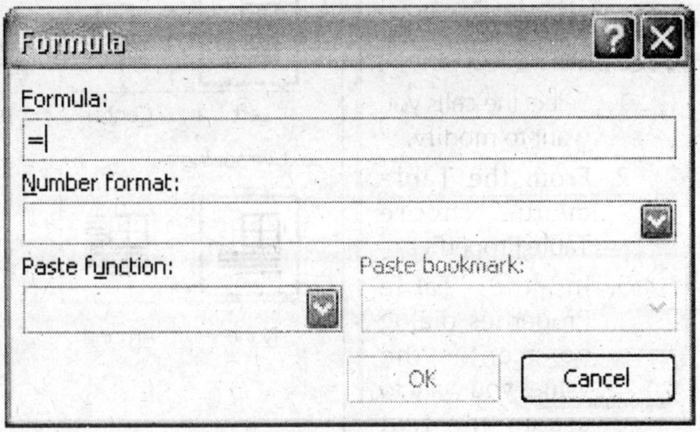

4. To reference the contents of a table cell, type the cell addresses in the parenthesis in the formula. Each cell has an address, which is a combination of its column name and its row number. The first column on the left is A, the second is B, and so on. The first row is 1, second row is 2, and so on. Therefore, the address (or cell reference) of the cell in the second row down and second column across is B2. Formulas must begin with an equal sign (=). A formula might be =B1+B2; a function might be =SUM(B1,B2).
5. From the Number Format drop-down list, select a format for the numbers (currency, percentage, and so on).
6. Choose Ok and the result will appear in the selected cell.

Merging Cells

You can merge two or more adjacent cells to create column or row headings.

To merge cells

1. Select the adjacent cells to be merged.
2. Click the Merge Cells button on the Table Layout option.

To split merged cells back into their original individual cells, click the merged cell and click the Split cells button on the Tables and Borders toolbar.

Drawing a More Complex Table

You can change different aspects of the structure to create a more complex table.

To Move a Line

Click the line and drag it to the new position

To Equalize Cell Heights or Widths

1. Click outside the table to clear the tool selection.
2. Click and drag through the cells you want to adjust.

3. Click either the Distribute Rows Evenly button or the Distribute Columns Evenly button on the Layout option of the toolbar.

To Set Row Height or Column Width Precisely

1. Select the cells you want to modify.
2. From the Table menu, choose Table Properties.
3. In the Table Properties dialog box, enter the values you want to use in the text boxes on the Row, Column, or Cell tab or use the arrows to choose predefined values.
4. Click Ok.

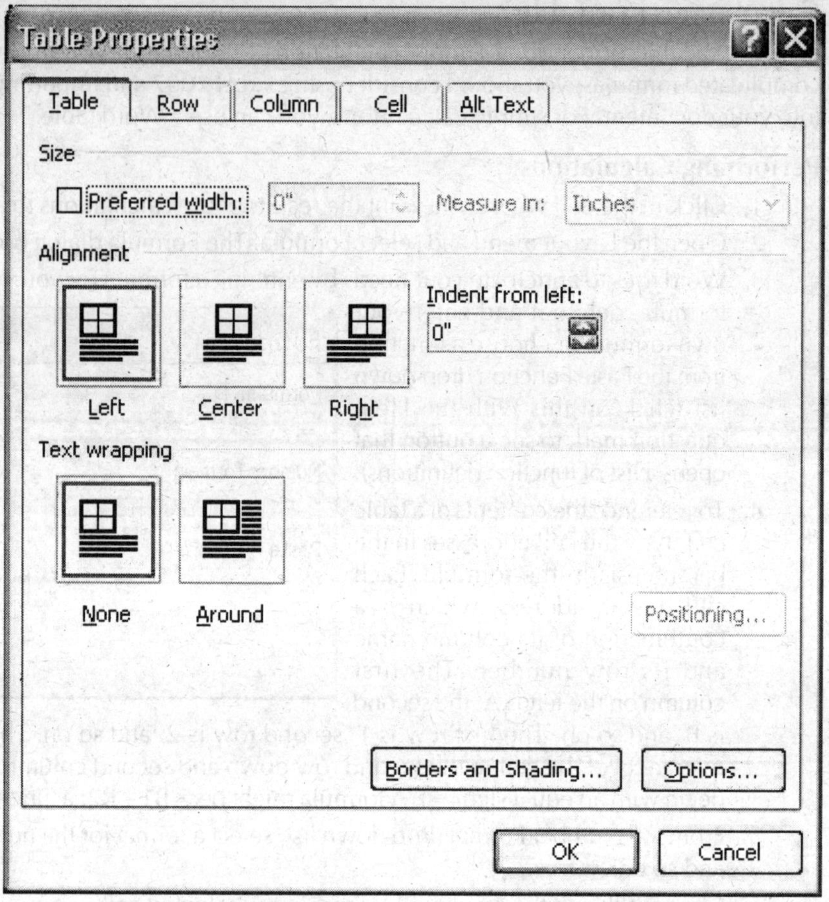

CHAPTER 8

Working with Graphics and Charts in Microsoft Word 2013

Introduction

It is not that the Word 2013 is only text and tables. It has options for working with Graphics too. You can import various graphics, which have been created using the other programs. These graphics could have been created using Windows Paint, Microsoft PowerPoint, CorelDRAW, AutoCAD etc. It has its own set of Clip Arts too, which can be used to enhance your word document.

Adding a Graphic

To add a graphic to the word document do the following:

1. Place the cursor where you want to insert the graphic.
2. Click at Picture in the Insert menu.
3. Select the folder where the graphic is stored from the Look in drop-down list.
4. The Files of Type drop-down list is automatically set to display. All Pictures, but you can select the specific type of graphic file you want to appear in the list.
5. Select the name of the file you want to use from the listed files, enter the name in the File Name text box or highlight the file. Click the down arrow next to Views on the toolbar and then select Preview to see a preview of the selected file.
6. Click any of the following options from the Insert drop-down list.
   - **Insert**. Inserts the picture at your cursor position in the document.
   - **Link to File**. By default, Word embeds pictures in the document, which adds to the size of the file. Choose this option to reduce the size of the file by linking to it. One benefit of linking is that the graphic in the document updates immediately if any changes are made to the original file.
   - **Insert and Link**. Inserts the picture into the document and links to the source file so the picture is immediately updated if the original graphic is changed.
7. Choose Insert to add the graphic image to your document.

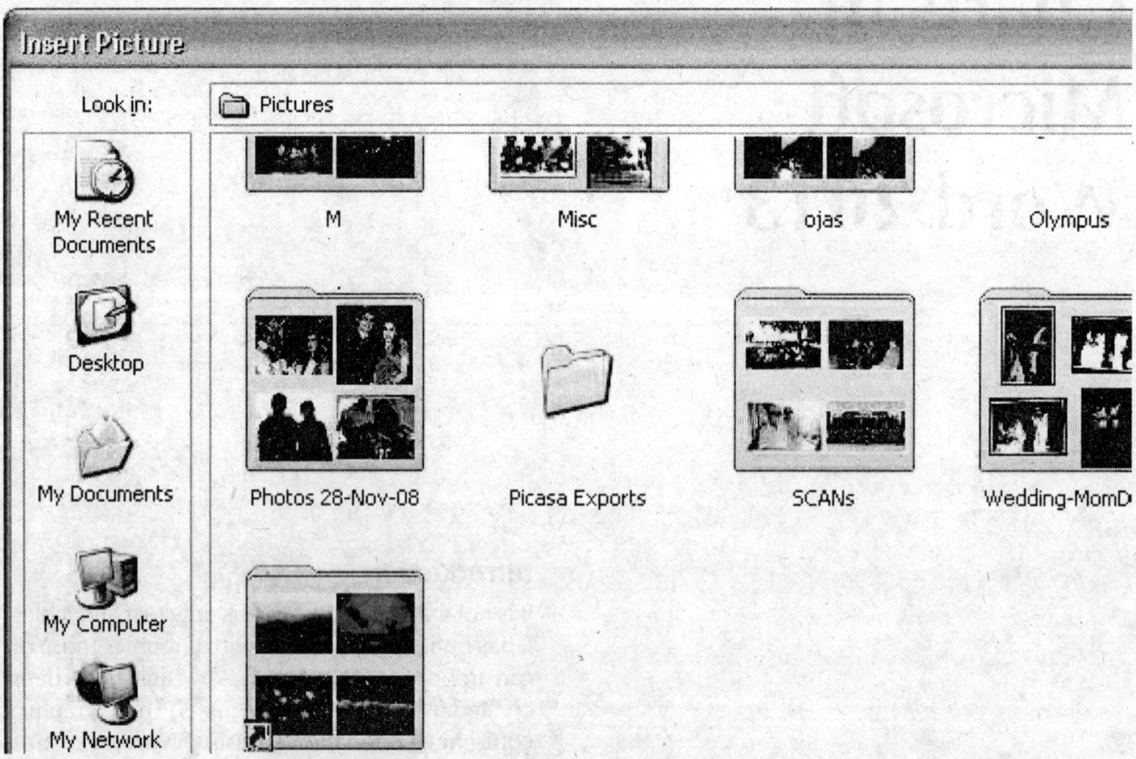

Insert Clip Art

Word comes with a library of Clip Art, which is comprised of drawings and pictures you use to add

To,

The General Manager
Mahanagar Telephones Nigam Limited
Khurshid Lal Bhawan
<u>New Delhi - 110 001</u>

Ref: Telephone No. 4611098

Sir,

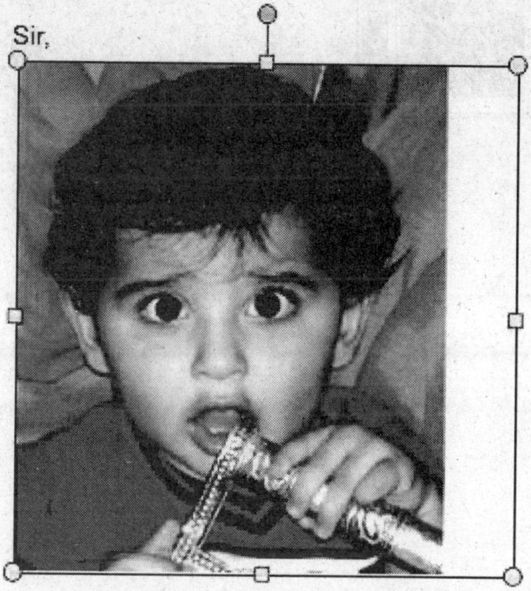

I am in receipt of bill for the above telephone number dated 1.10.2010 for an amount of Rs. 4,678.90. This bill is to be paid by 21.10.2010. While going through the bill, I notice that I have been charged at two accounts for the calls which have not been made by me. These entries are:

Called id	Duration	Amount
0017249873769	120	1008.00
0013245934234	60	675.90

appeal and interest to your documents. Adding clip art to the documents is easy and can be the added element that draws attention to your document versus someone else's in a competitive market.

Add Clip Art to a Document

1. Place your cursor where you want to put the clip art picture or drawing in your document.
2. Open the Insert tab and choose Clip Art to open the Insert Clip Art dialog box.
3. The Microsoft Office Clip Organizer tab is displayed on the Task Pane which when selected, shows a set of clip art categories.
4. Clip a category picture to display the clips in that category. When you point to one of the clips, the graphic format and categories of that clip appear as a pop-up.
5. Clip once on the clip to see a menu.
6. Choose Insert Clip to insert the clip in your document.

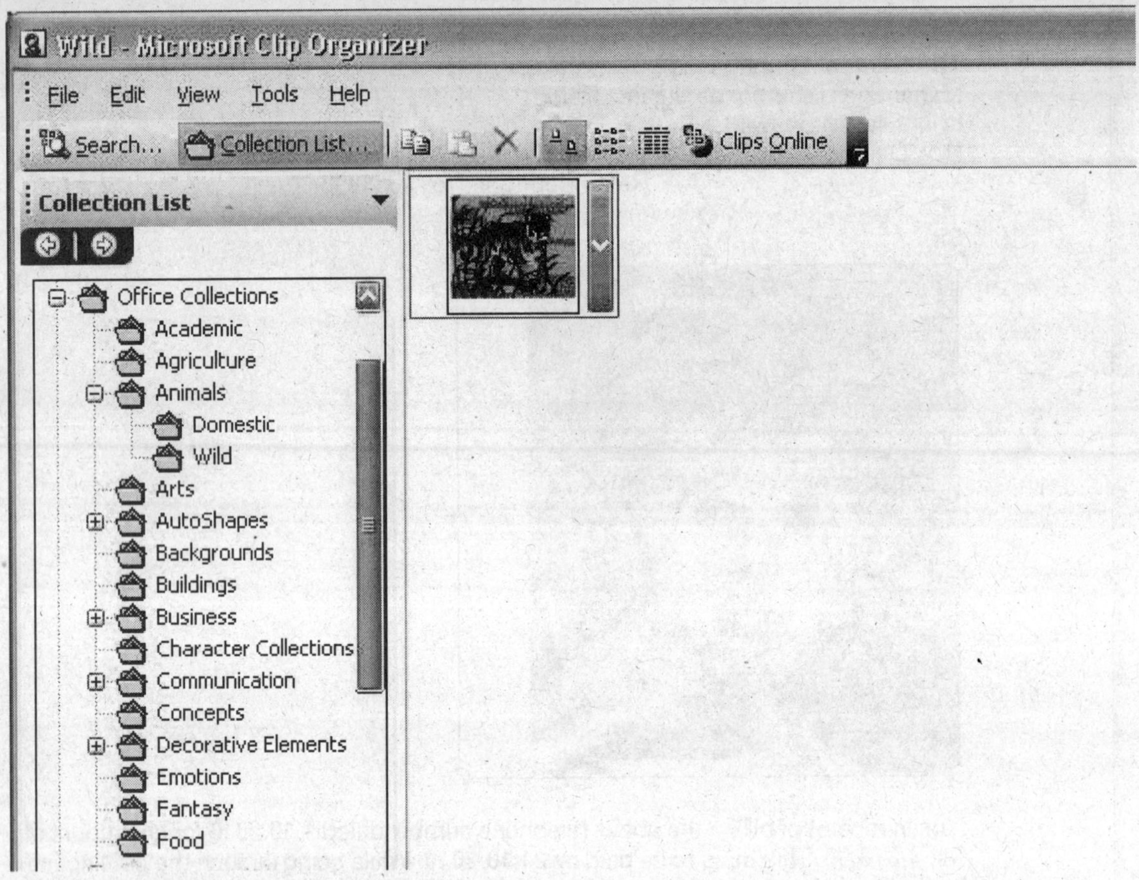

To,

The General Manager
Mahanagar Telephones Nigam Limited
Khurshid Lal Bhawan
New Delhi - 110 001

Ref: Telephone No. 4611098

Sir,

I am in receipt of bill for the above telephone number dated 1.10.2010 for an amount of Rs. 4,678.90. This bill is to be paid by 21.10.2010. While going through the bill, I notice that I have been charged at two accounts for the calls which have not been made by me. These entries are:

Crop a Graphic

You can crop (trim) a graphic to ease out the excess matter from the original graphic.

1. Select the graphic and choose Crop tool on the Picture toolbar.
2. Position the mouse pointer over the handle on the side you want to cop and drag toward the center of the image and portion of the picture you wanted to trim disappears.
3. Release the mouse button.

Sizing the Graphic

1. Select the graphic and right-click the graphic and select Size from the pop-menu.
2. To keep the image in proportion (maintaining the ration between the width and height), click Lock Aspect Ratio to replace a check mark there.
3. Under Size and rotate, change the Height or Width measurement (the other dimension automatically adjusts when you press Tab to keep the graphic in proportion if you locked the aspect ratio). Or, to use percentages instead of exact dimensions, change the Height or Width percentage in the Scale area.
4. Choose OK to apply your modifications to the image.

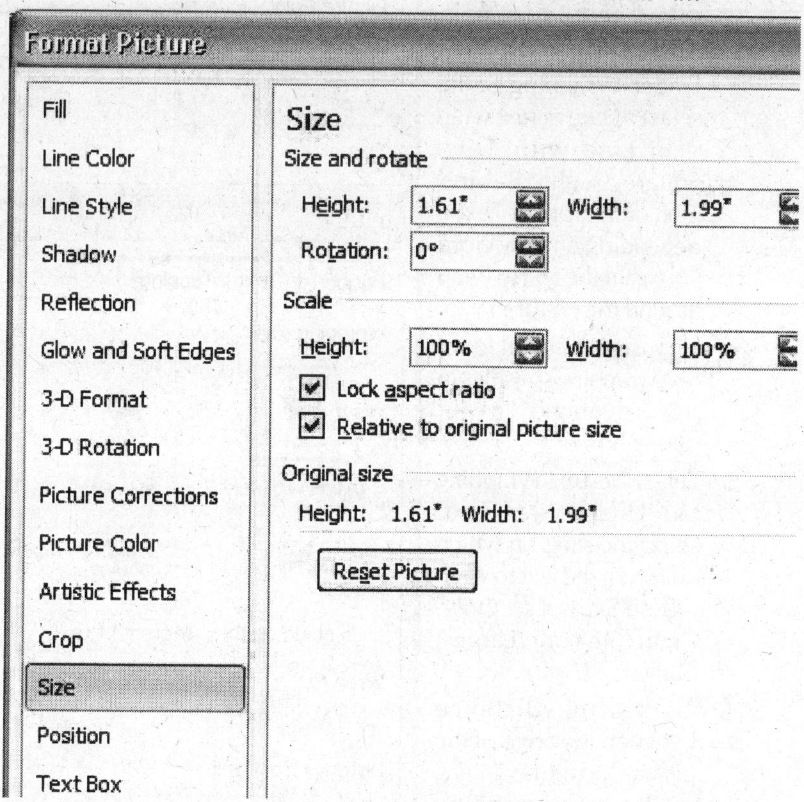

Crop a Picture Using the Format Picture Dialog box

1. Select the image and right click at Format Picture to get a dialog box.
2. Enter the exact measurement (in inches) of the amount you want to crop from the Left, Right, Top or Bottom of the picture.
3. Choose OK to apply your modifications of the image.

Wrap Text around Graphics

A graphic causes a break in your text. The text immediately after the graphic does not start until the next line after the picture, leaving whitespace to the left or right of the graphic. It also leaves space on the top of the bottom or the graphic. This is a called text wrap and is Word's default setting for wrapping text around a picture.

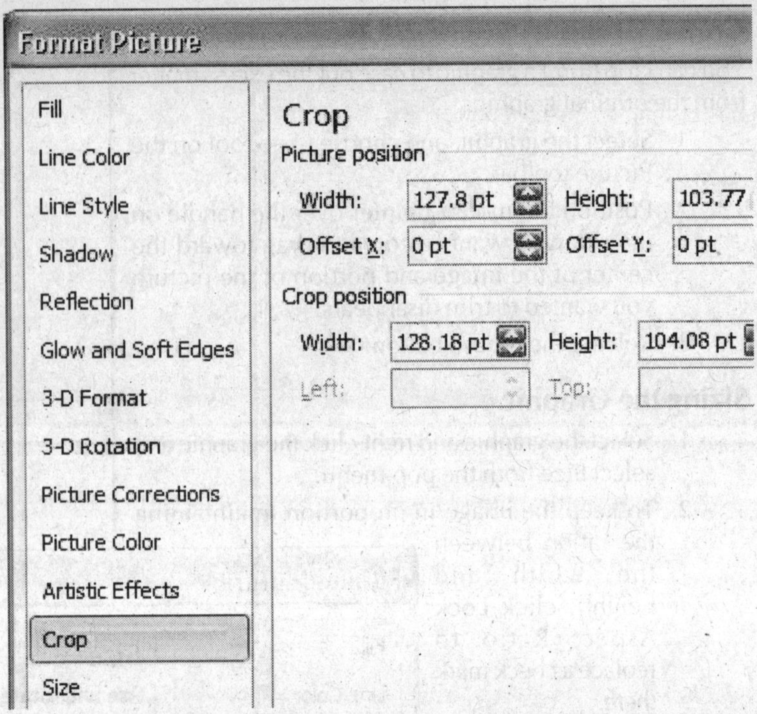

Set Text Wrap Options

1. Select the image.
2. Open the Format bar and select Text wrap from Arrange option.
3. Under Wrapping Style, select a style of text wrap – In Line with Text, Square, Tight, Behind Text or In Front of Text – depending on how close you want the text to wrap around the picture.
4. Choose Advanced to set text wrapping specifies in the Advanced Layout dialog box.
5. Select the Text Wrapping tab. Under Wrap Text, select the sides on which you want the text to wrap – Both Sides, Left Only, Right Only or Largest Only.
6. To set the distance between the edge of the picture and the beginning of the text wrapping around it, enter the distance in the Top, Bottom, Left and Right boxes under Distance from Text.
7. Choose OK to close the Advanced Layout dialog box.
8. Choose OK to close the Format Picture dialog box.

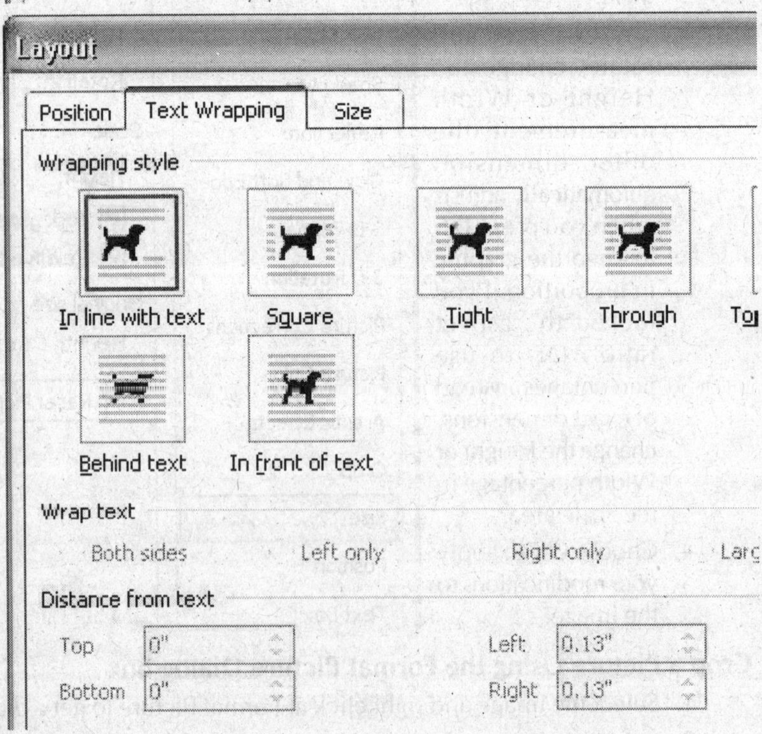

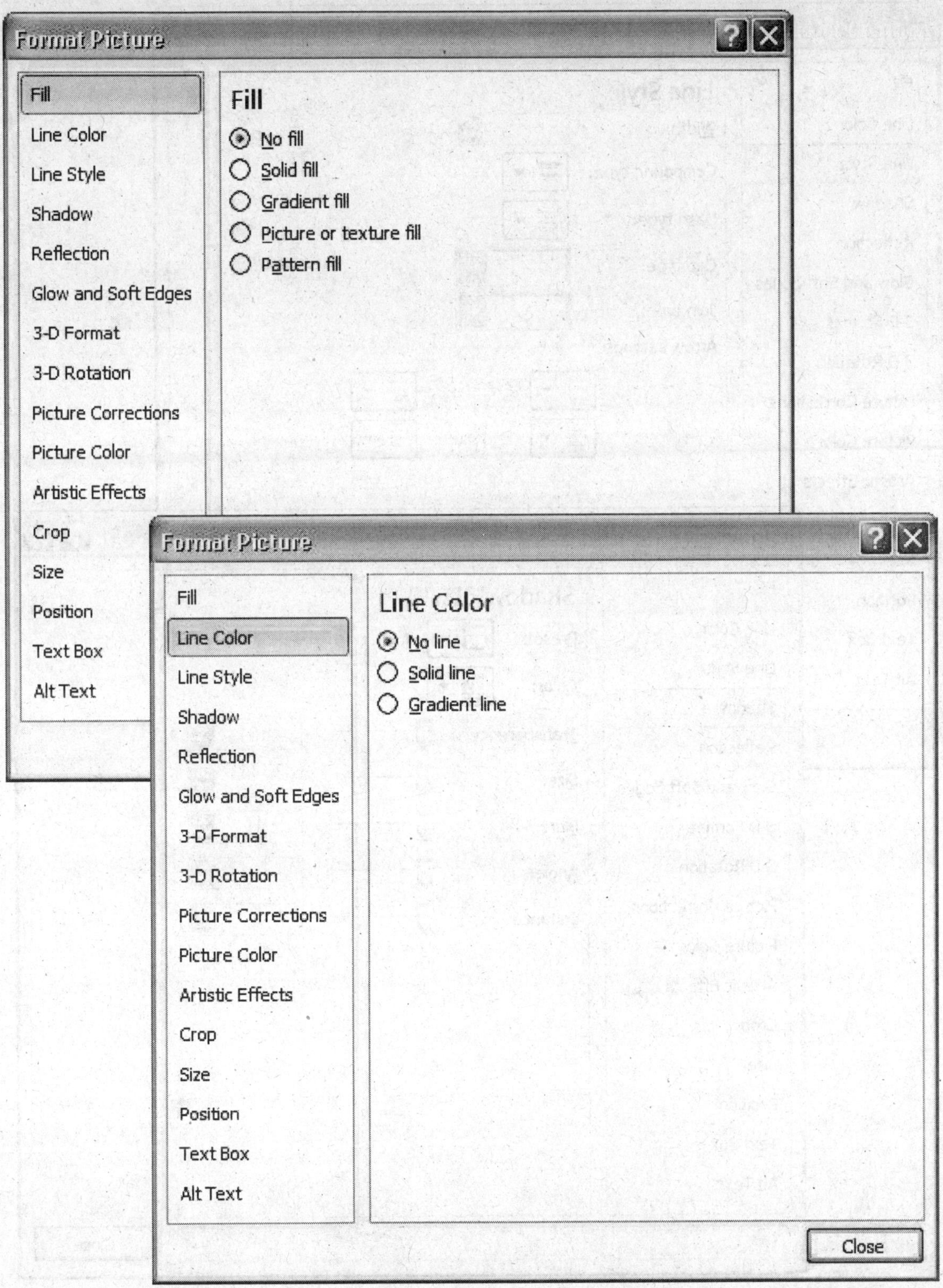
Format Picture
Fill
Line Color
Line Style
Shadow
Reflection
Glow and Soft Edges
3-D Format
3-D Rotation
Picture Corrections
Picture Color
Artistic Effects
Crop
Size
Position
Text Box
Alt Text
Fill
No fill
Solid fill
Gradient fill
Picture or texture fill
Pattern fill
Format Picture
Fill
Line Color
Line Style
Shadow
Reflection
Glow and Soft Edges
3-D Format
3-D Rotation
Picture Corrections
Picture Color
Artistic Effects
Crop
Size
Position
Text Box
Alt Text
Line Color
No line
Solid line
Gradient line
Close

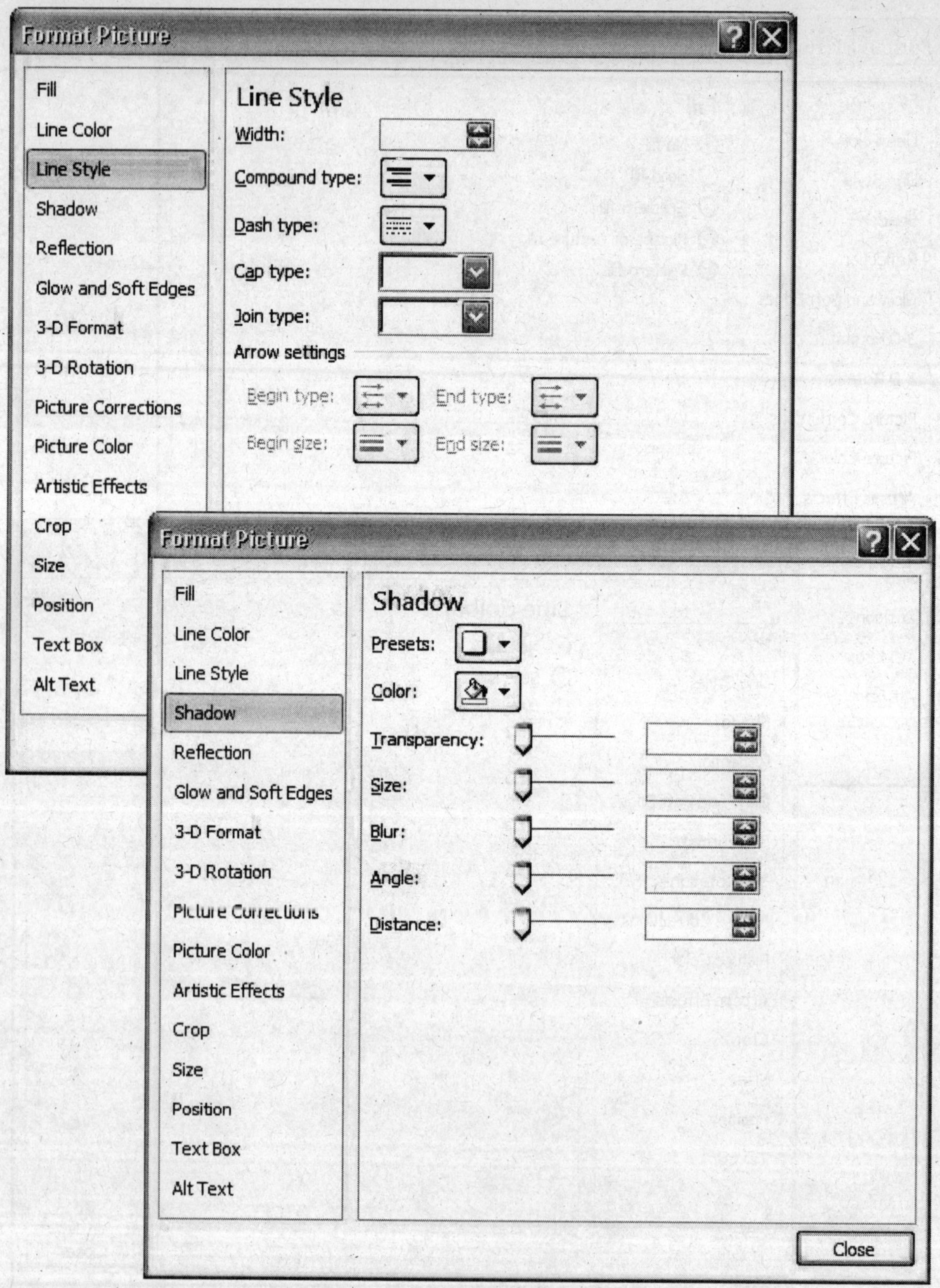
Format Picture
Fill
Line Color
Line Style
Shadow
Reflection
Glow and Soft Edges
3-D Format
3-D Rotation
Picture Corrections
Picture Color
Artistic Effects
Crop
Size
Position
Text Box
Alt Text
Line Style
Width:
Compound type:
Dash type:
Cap type:
Join type:
Arrow settings
Begin type:
End type:
Begin size:
End size:
Format Picture
Fill
Line Color
Line Style
Shadow
Reflection
Glow and Soft Edges
3-D Format
3-D Rotation
Picture Corrections
Picture Color
Artistic Effects
Crop
Size
Position
Text Box
Alt Text
Shadow
Presets:
Color:
Transparency:
Size:
Blur:
Angle:
Distance:
Close

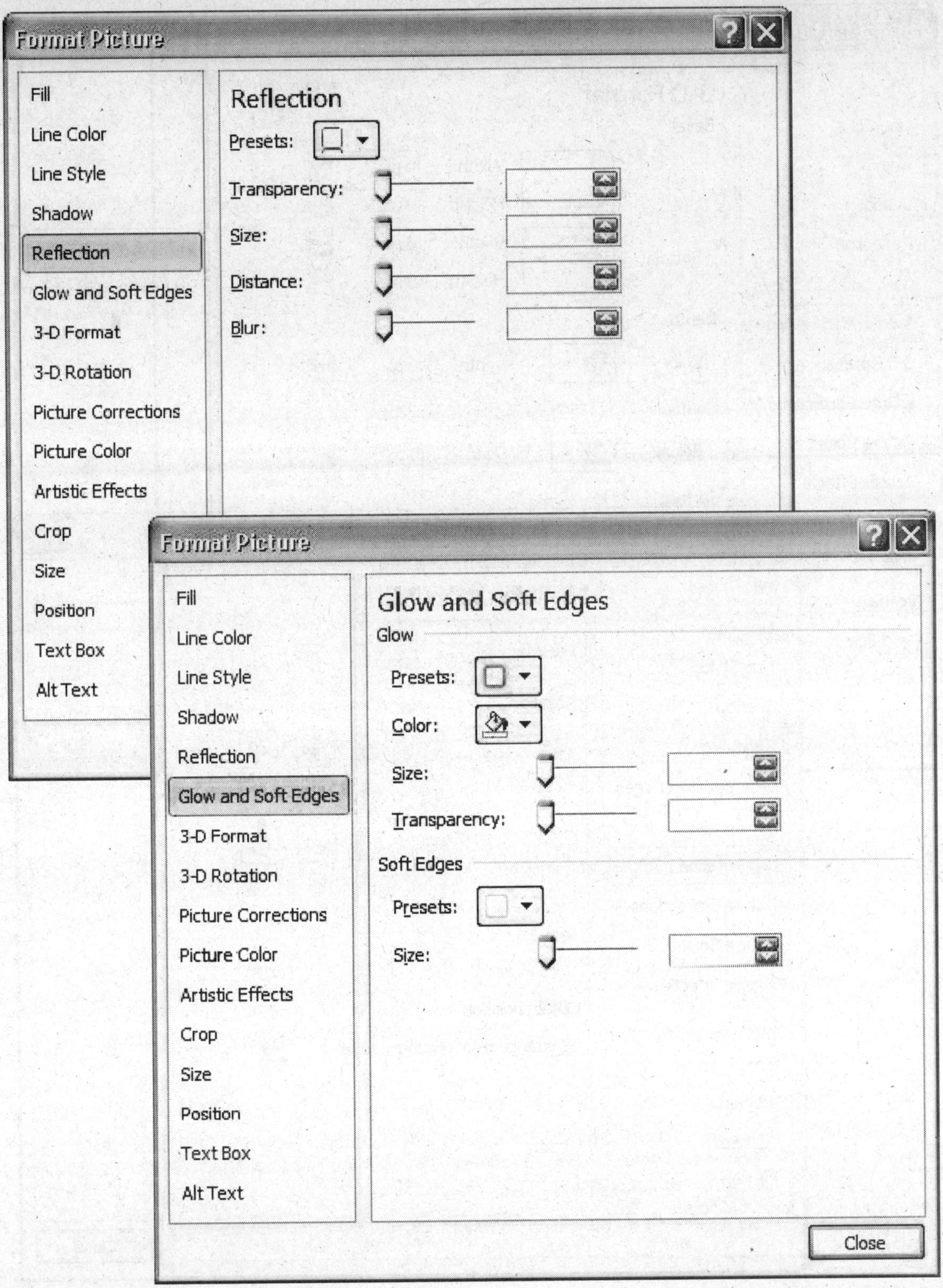
Format Picture
Fill
Line Color
Line Style
Shadow
Reflection
Glow and Soft Edges
3-D Format
3-D Rotation
Picture Corrections
Picture Color
Artistic Effects
Crop
Size
Position
Text Box
Alt Text
Reflection
Presets:
Transparency:
Size:
Distance:
Blur:
Format Picture
Fill
Line Color
Line Style
Shadow
Reflection
Glow and Soft Edges
3-D Format
3-D Rotation
Picture Corrections
Picture Color
Artistic Effects
Crop
Size
Position
Text Box
Alt Text
Glow and Soft Edges
Glow
Presets:
Color:
Size:
Transparency:
Soft Edges
Presets:
Size:
Close

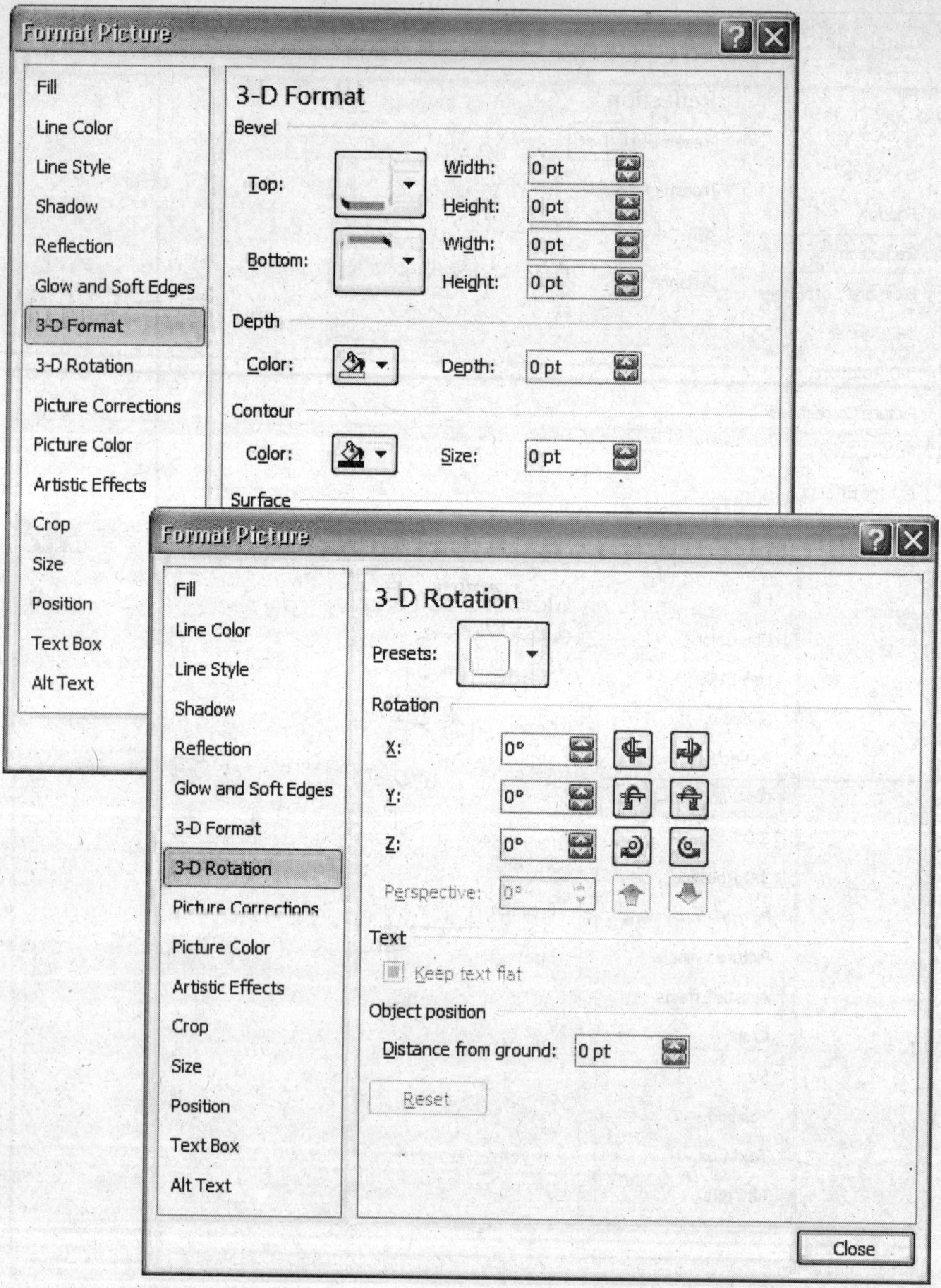
Format Picture
Fill
Line Color
Line Style
Shadow
Reflection
Glow and Soft Edges
3-D Format
3-D Rotation
Picture Corrections
Picture Color
Artistic Effects
Crop
Size
Position
Text Box
Alt Text
3-D Format
Bevel
Top:
Width: 0 pt
Height: 0 pt
Bottom:
Width: 0 pt
Height: 0 pt
Depth
Color:
Depth: 0 pt
Contour
Color:
Size: 0 pt
Surface
Format Picture
Fill
Line Color
Line Style
Shadow
Reflection
Glow and Soft Edges
3-D Format
3-D Rotation
Picture Corrections
Picture Color
Artistic Effects
Crop
Size
Position
Text Box
Alt Text
3-D Rotation
Presets:
Rotation
X: 0°
Y: 0°
Z: 0°
Perspective: 0°
Text
Keep text flat
Object position
Distance from ground: 0 pt
Reset
Close

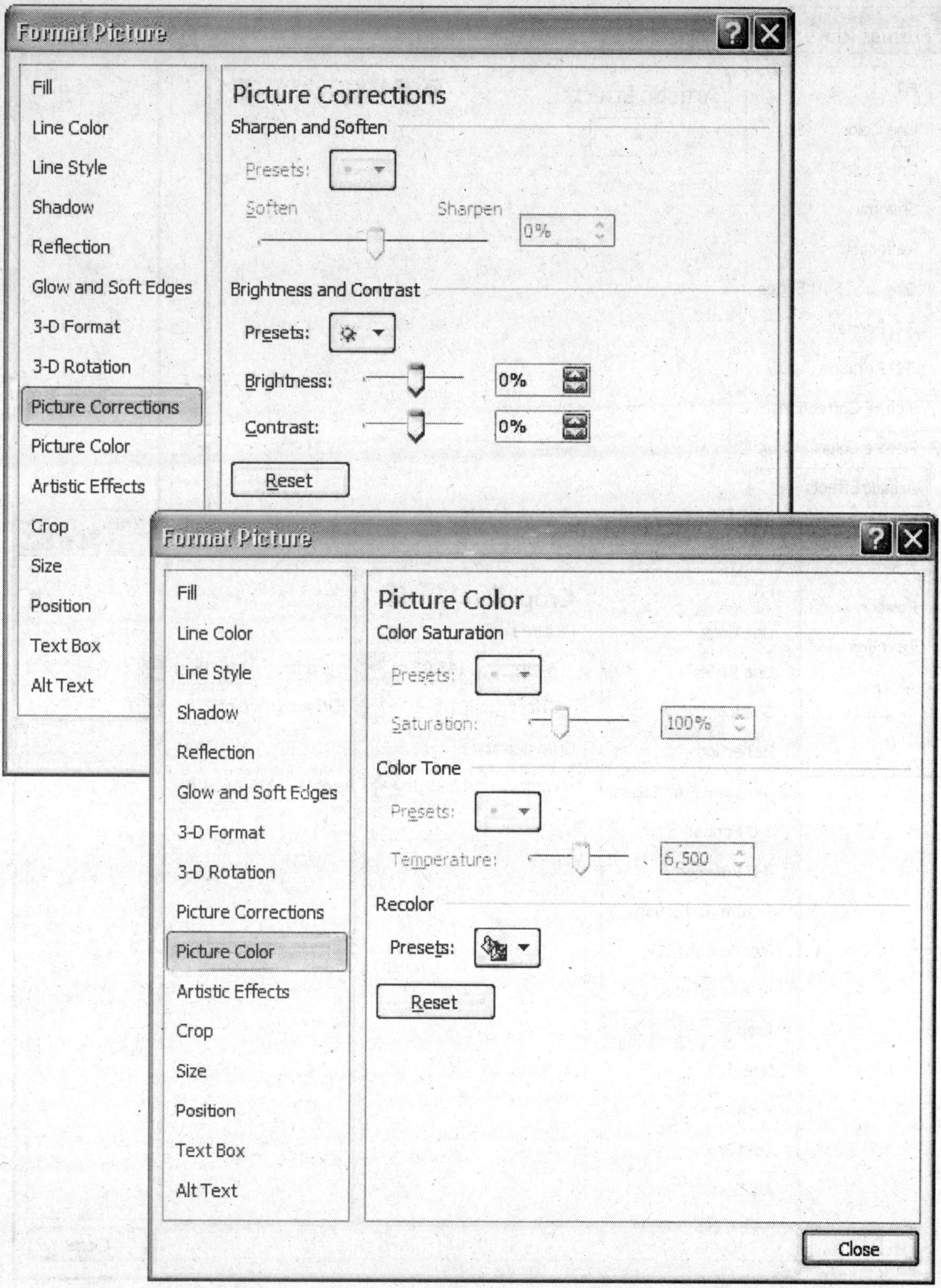
Format Picture
Fill
Line Color
Line Style
Shadow
Reflection
Glow and Soft Edges
3-D Format
3-D Rotation
Picture Corrections
Picture Color
Artistic Effects
Crop
Size
Position
Text Box
Alt Text
Picture Corrections
Sharpen and Soften
Presets:
Soften
Sharpen
0%
Brightness and Contrast
Presets:
Brightness:
0%
Contrast:
0%
Reset
Format Picture
Fill
Line Color
Line Style
Shadow
Reflection
Glow and Soft Edges
3-D Format
3-D Rotation
Picture Corrections
Picture Color
Artistic Effects
Crop
Size
Position
Text Box
Alt Text
Picture Color
Color Saturation
Presets:
Saturation:
100%
Color Tone
Presets:
Temperature:
6,500
Recolor
Presets:
Reset
Close

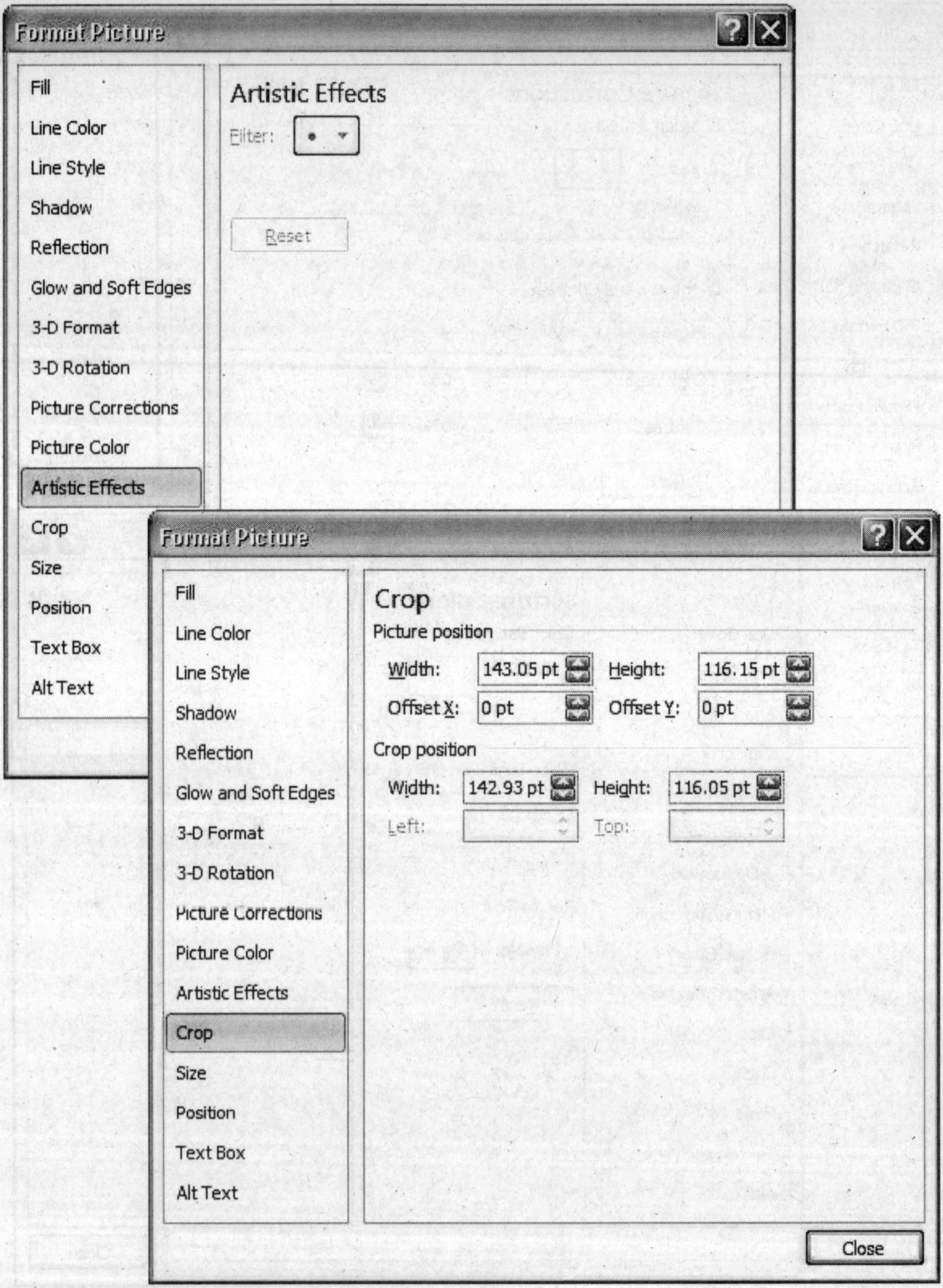
Format Picture
Fill
Line Color
Line Style
Shadow
Reflection
Glow and Soft Edges
3-D Format
3-D Rotation
Picture Corrections
Picture Color
Artistic Effects
Crop
Size
Position
Text Box
Alt Text
Artistic Effects
Filter:
Reset
Format Picture
Fill
Line Color
Line Style
Shadow
Reflection
Glow and Soft Edges
3-D Format
3-D Rotation
Picture Corrections
Picture Color
Artistic Effects
Crop
Size
Position
Text Box
Alt Text
Crop
Picture position
Width: 143.05 pt
Height: 116.15 pt
Offset X: 0 pt
Offset Y: 0 pt
Crop position
Width: 142.93 pt
Height: 116.05 pt
Left:
Top:
Close

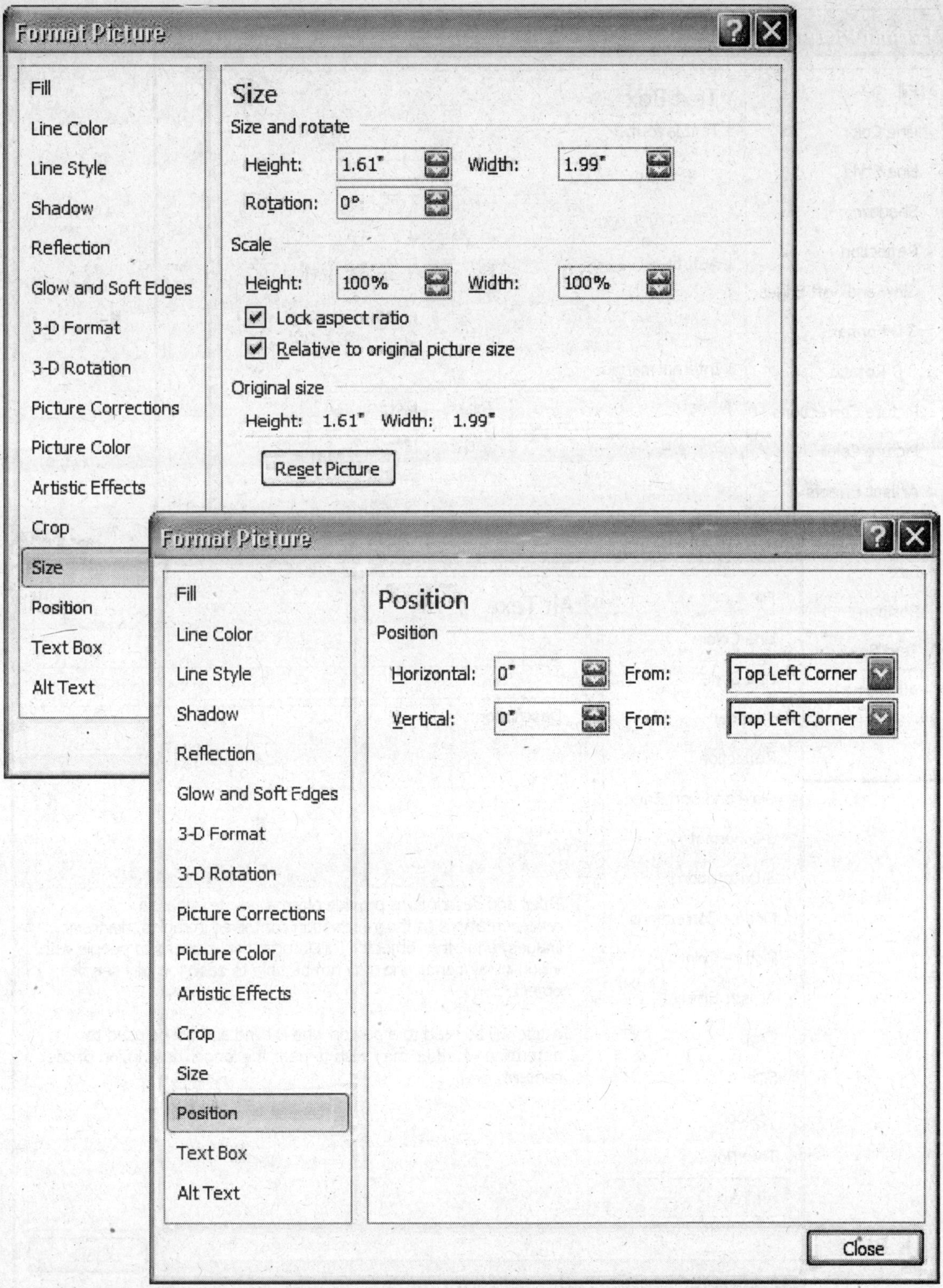
Format Picture
Fill
Line Color
Line Style
Shadow
Reflection
Glow and Soft Edges
3-D Format
3-D Rotation
Picture Corrections
Picture Color
Artistic Effects
Crop
Size
Position
Text Box
Alt Text
Size
Size and rotate
Height: 1.61"
Width: 1.99"
Rotation: 0°
Scale
Height: 100%
Width: 100%
Lock aspect ratio
Relative to original picture size
Original size
Height: 1.61" Width: 1.99"
Reset Picture
Format Picture
Position
Position
Horizontal: 0"
From: Top Left Corner
Vertical: 0"
From: Top Left Corner
Close

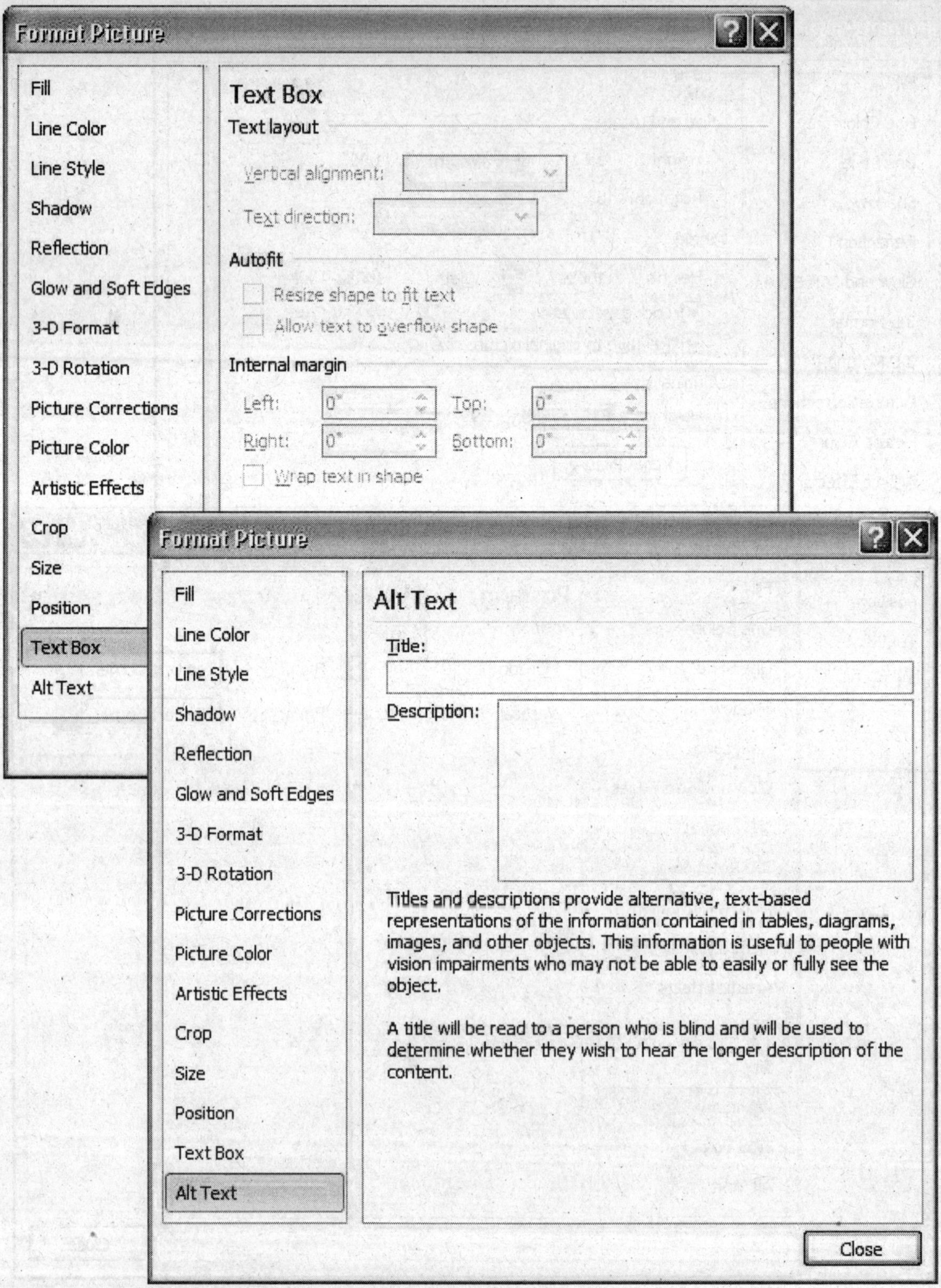
Format Picture
Fill
Line Color
Line Style
Shadow
Reflection
Glow and Soft Edges
3-D Format
3-D Rotation
Picture Corrections
Picture Color
Artistic Effects
Crop
Size
Position
Text Box
Alt Text
Text Box
Text layout
Vertical alignment:
Text direction:
Autofit
Resize shape to fit text
Allow text to overflow shape
Internal margin
Left: 0"
Top: 0"
Right: 0"
Bottom: 0"
Wrap text in shape
Format Picture
Fill
Line Color
Line Style
Shadow
Reflection
Glow and Soft Edges
3-D Format
3-D Rotation
Picture Corrections
Picture Color
Artistic Effects
Crop
Size
Position
Text Box
Alt Text
Alt Text
Title:
Description:
Titles and descriptions provide alternative, text-based representations of the information contained in tables, diagrams, images, and other objects. This information is useful to people with vision impairments who may not be able to easily or fully see the object.
A title will be read to a person who is blind and will be used to determine whether they wish to hear the longer description of the content.
Close

Insert a Symbol

The symbols will depend upon the fonts that you are using in your computer some of the popular fonts with symbols are: Symbol, Wingdings, Zaph Dingbats, Monotype Sorts, etc. You can insert symbols from these fonts into your document.

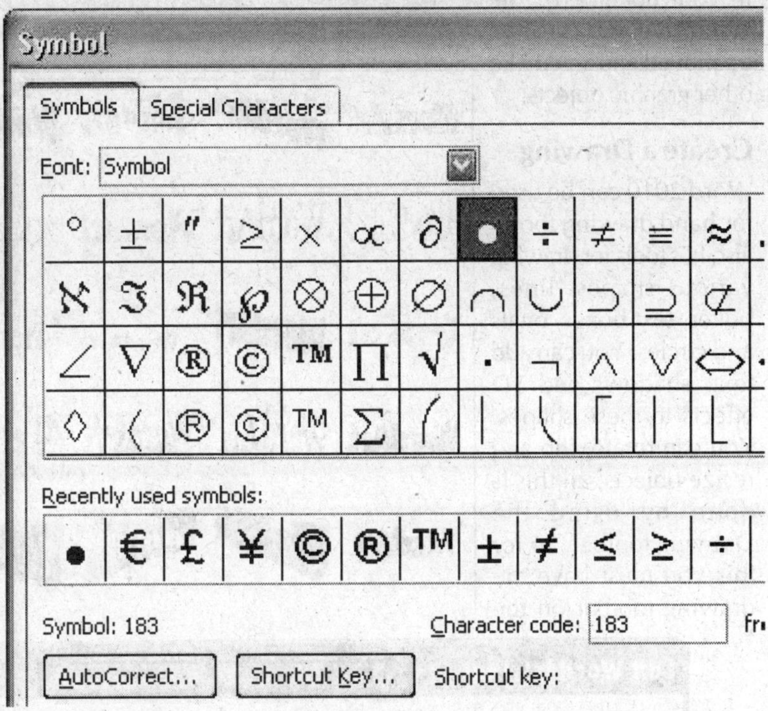

1. Place cursor where you want the symbol to appear.
2. Open the Insert tab and choose Symbol to open the Symbol dialog box. Click the Symbols tab if it is not already on top.
3. From the Font drop-down list, select the symbol set you want to use Choose (normal text) to see the list for the current font, which includes letters with diacritical marks, currency symbols, the paragraph symbol, the registered mark, the trademark symbol, the copyright symbol and so on. Using various fonts you can even get mathematical symbols, arrows, pointing hands, snowflakes, bullets and more.
4. Look through the grid of symbols for the one you want. Click a symbol square to see an enlarged view of the symbol.
5. To insert the selected symbol in your document, choose Insert or double-click the symbol.
6. Choose Close to close the dialog box after you insert one or more symbols. Choose Cancel to close the dialog box without inserting a symbol.

Insert a WordArt object

WordArt is an independent program available with Word 2010. It allows you to decorate your text with preset shapes. With WordArt objects, your text can be curved, twisted and even rotated. WordArt can be accessed while in Word by choosing Insert WordArt on the Drawing toolbar or by opening the Insert menu and selecting Picture and then WordArt.

The WordArt window appears. This has the various shapes of the text with WordArt written in all types of shapes as shown above.

1. Select the WordArt effect you want from the WordArt Gallery dialog box. Choose OK.
2. When the Edit WordArt Text dialog box appears, replace the "Your Text Here" in the Text box with your own text.
3. Choose a Font from the drop-down list and choose a Size. If you want bold or italic type, click the appropriate buttons.
4. The WordArt object appears in your document, with sizing handles around it to show it is still selected. Word also displays the Word Art toolbar.

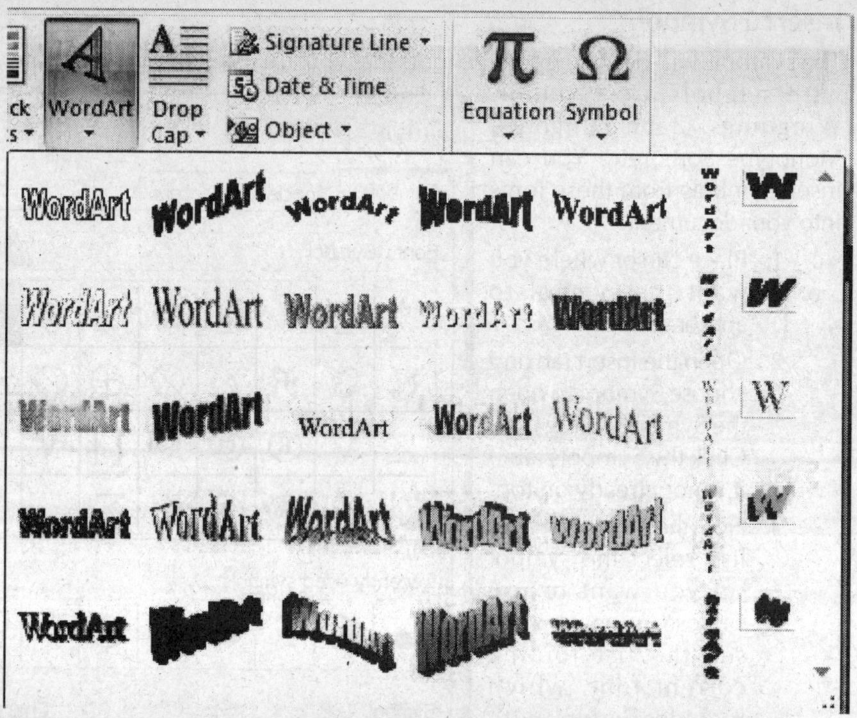

Deselect the WordArt by clicking somewhere else in your document. The WordArt object can then be moved and sized like other graphic objects.

Create a Drawing

Word 2010 can be used for hand drawing too. It also has tools for drawing various shapes, lines, boxes, text boxes, ovals and circles. You can add text, shadows and 3D effects to these shapes. You can rotate, flip and resize objects, all this is done by using the Drawing toolbar. So for this you must have the drawing toolbar on the

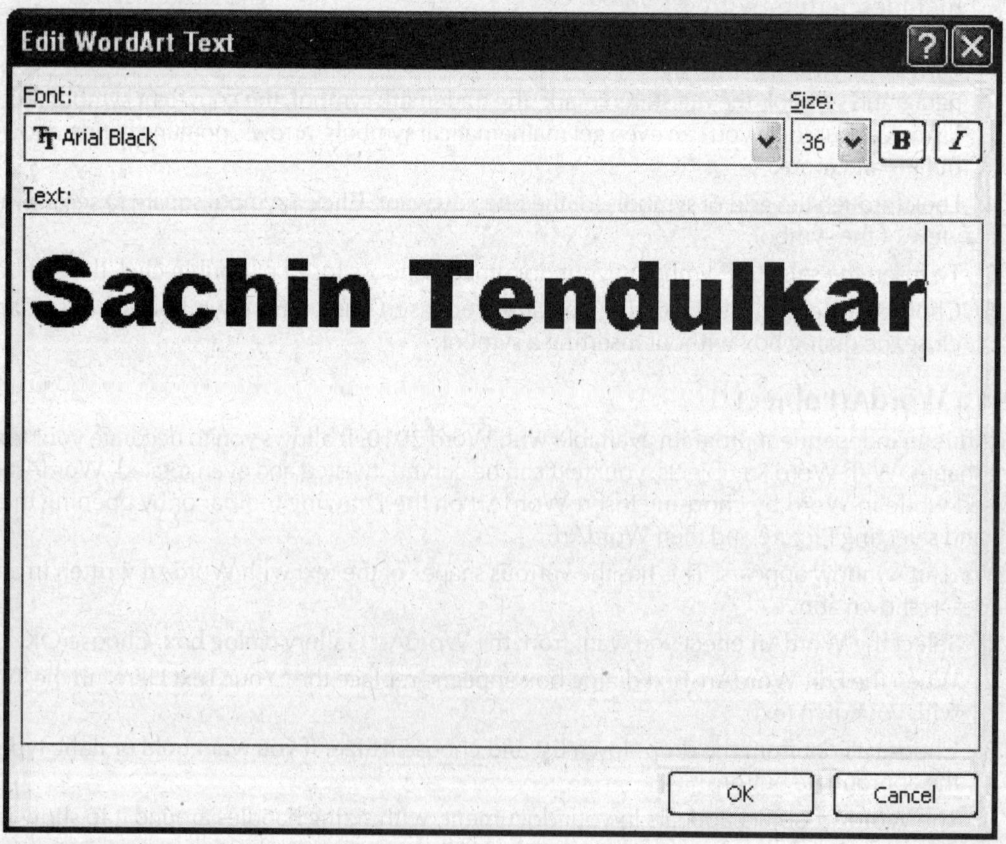

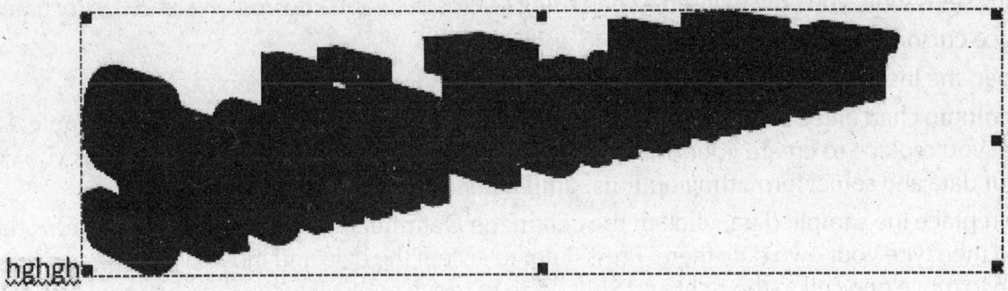

screen. To create drawing objects such as Lines, Arrows, Rectangles, Ovals, Text boxes, 3D Shapes, select the object or tool on the Drawing toolbar.

Various tools available on the toolbar are:

Draw	Displays a menu of drawing commands
Select Objects	Selects drawing objects
Free Rotate	Rotates objects to any angle
AutoShapes	Displays a pop-up menu of different shapes
Line	Draws straight lines
Arrow	Draws arrows
Rectangle	Draws ovals and circles
Ovals	Draws ovals and circles
Text Box	Created a box to place text anywhere on the page without putting it inside another shape
Insert WordArt	Lets you create a WordArt object in your document.
Insert Clip Art	Lets you select a piece of clip art to insert in your document.
Fill Color	Applies fill colors or attributes to selected objects
Line Color	Applies color or patterns to selected lines or outlines
Font Color	Applies colour to selected to selected text
Line Style	Applies a line thickness or style to a selected line or outline
Dash Style	Applies a dashed line style to a selected line or outline
Arrow Style	Applies an arrow style or direction to a selected line or arrow
Shadow	Applies a shadow to a selected object
3D	Applies a three-dimensional (3D) setting to a selected object.

Working with Charts

Charts and graphs are another options of presenting your data in the form of pie chart and column graphs. Often, reports such as a annual report contain charts illustrating data such as sales and profits. Word does not create charts but uses a program called Microsoft Graph, which is installed by default.

Create a Graph

The following steps show you how to insert a chart using Microsoft Graph into your Word 2010 document.

1. Place cursor where you want the chart to appear.
2. Open the Insert menu and select Chart to insert Chart into the document.
3. A column chart and a Datasheet window appears. The Datasheet of Excel contains sample data that you replace to create your own graph. The chart is transformed automatically as you add your data and select formatting options, until it becomes the chart you want.
4. To replace the sample data, click in the cell in the Datasheet where you want to put new data and then type your own data there. Press Enter to accept the data and move down the row; press Tab to move one cell to the right and Shift + Tab to move one cell to the left (the arrow keys also help you have navigate in the Datasheet). Choose View Datasheet on the Standard toolbar to close the Datasheet.
5. Click the down arrow next to the Chart Type button on the Standard toolbar to select a chart from the types shown. Then click the picture of the type of chart you want to create.
6. Click outside the border around the graph to return to the Word document.

The sample data that appears in the Datasheet when you start a new chart is always the same. It serves as

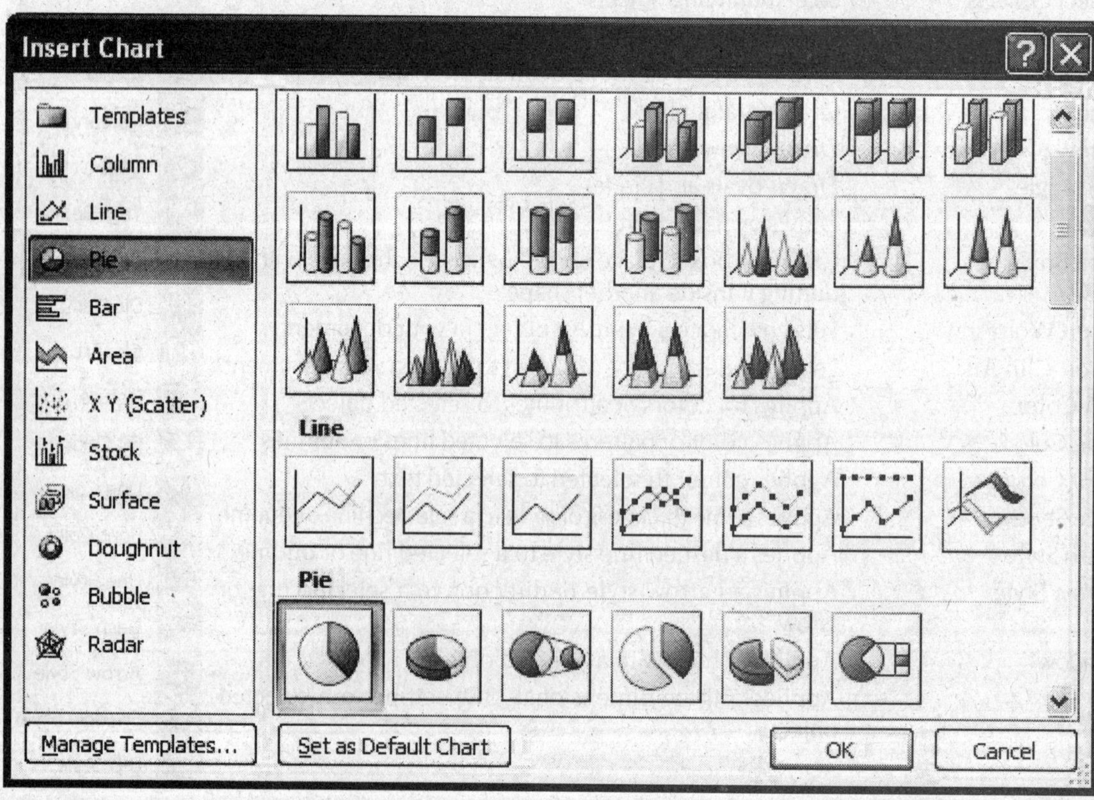

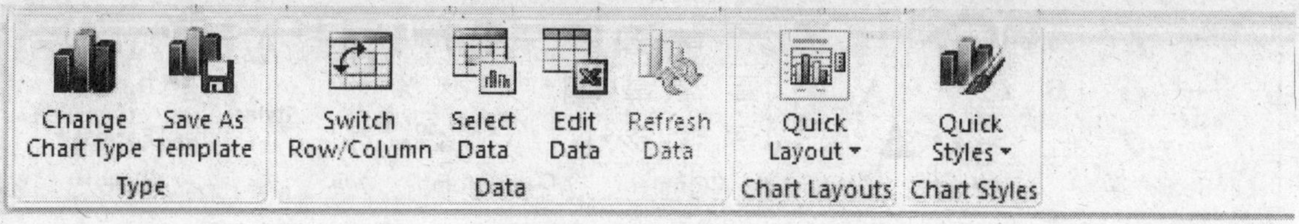

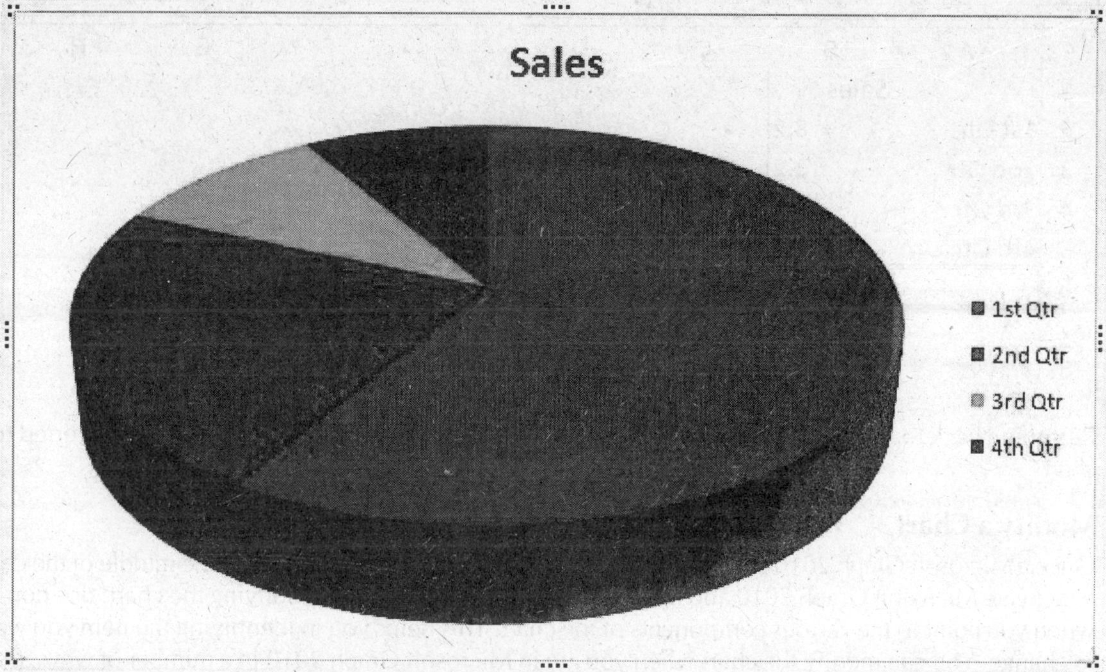

an aid that helps you enter the data in the right places. Be sure to delete any of the sample data that remains after you have entered you own information.

Create a Chart from a Table

Data that exists in a table (such as sales and profit data) can act as the data for the chart. If you have the data you need for a chart in a Word table, there is no need to enter the data again in the Datasheet. Instead, start the chart with the following steps.

1. Create the table in Word. Put text labels in the cells in the top row and in the left column. Put numbers in the other cells.
2. Select at the cells in the table (click in the table to put your insertions point there and then open the Table menu, choose Select and then select Table from the submenu) unless your table includes a row and a column of totals. In that case, select all the cells expect those total rows or columns.
3. Open the Insert menu and select Picture and then select the Create Chart from the Picture sub-menu.
4. Choose OK. The data from your table appears in the Datasheet.
5. Choose Chart Type on the Standard toolbar and then select a chart type.
6. Click outside the graph area to return to your Word document.

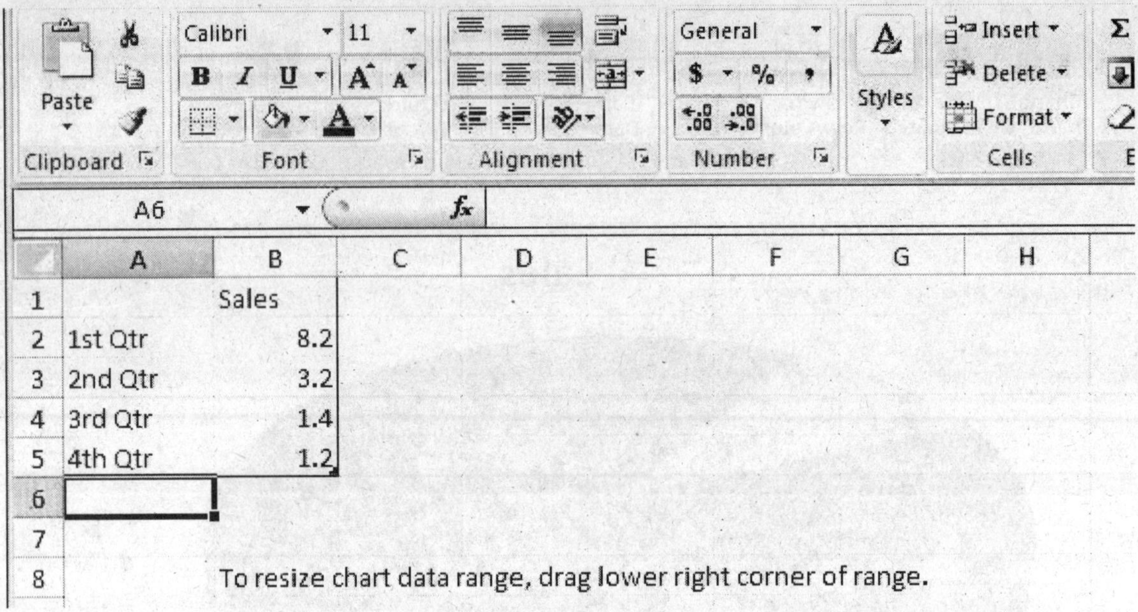

Returning back to your file named Bill, you see a table there too. This table can also be converted to a chart.

Modify a Chart

Once a Microsoft Graph 2010 chart is embedded in your document, double-click the middle of the chart to activate Microsoft Graph 2010 and modify the chart. To help you in modifying the chart, tips pop up when you point to the various components of the chart. This helps you in identifying the item you want to change. You can modify the chart when you are in Microsoft Graph 2010 in a number of ways, from chancing the data to altering its appearance.

The following list gives you some suggestions on how you can modify your chart.

- To edit the data, open the Datasheet by choosing View Datasheet on the Standard toolbar. Replace data by clicking in the cell and typing the new value or label. Press Enter or move the insertion point to the next cell to accept the change.
- To change the chart type, open the Chart menu and select Chart Type to open the Chart Type dialog box. From the Chart Type list, select the type of chart you want. Then make a selection from the Chart Sub Type options and choose OK.

To change the color of bars, lines or areas, double-click on the item to open the Format Data Series dialog box. For pie chart slices, click once on the pie and then double-click the slice you want to change to open the format Data Point dialog box. Set the line style and color on the appropriate options. Then choose OK to apply them to the chart.

To change the number format (how the number appear) of the chart values, double-click the number on the values axis (Y-axis) to open the Format Axis dialog box and then select the Number tab. Choose a number format (such as currency or percentage) from the Category box. The options vary with each category, so you may have to specify number of decimal places, symbols, appearance of negative numbers, use of a thousand separator, data and time formats and so on. Choose OK.

To set the interval between the numbers or specify the minimum or maximum values, double-click the numbers on the value axis (Y-axis) to open the Format Axis dialog box and then select the Scale tab.

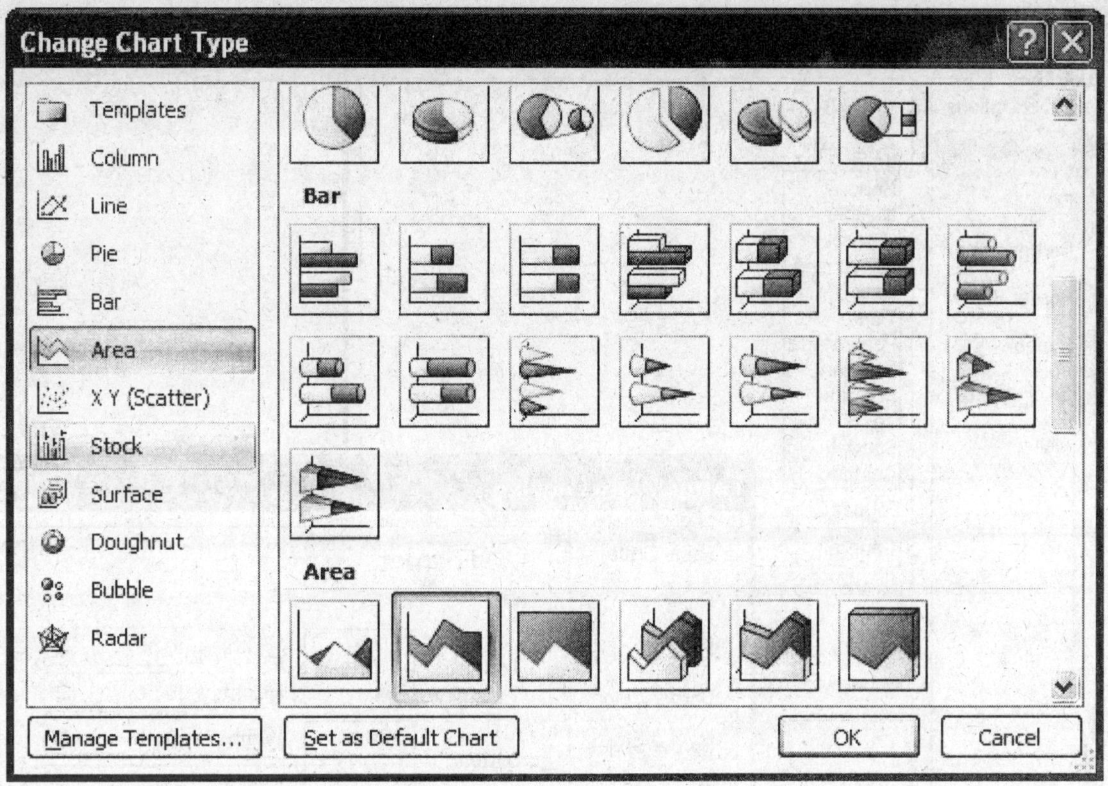

Change the Major Unit number to specify the interval between numbers, which also sets the spacing between the gridlines (lines that act as a reference to help you evaluate data in relation to the axes). Enter values in the Minimum and Maximum boxes to change those values. Choose OK.

To add titles to the value and category axes, click open the Chart menu and select Chart Options on the menu to open the Chart Options dialog box. Select the Titles tab and enter the title text in the Category (X) Axis or Value (Y) Axis box. Click in the hart Title box and enter a title for entire chart. Click OK.

When you complete your modifications, click outside the graph border to return to your Word document. Move the graph by pointing in the middle of it and dragging it to a new position on the page. Change the size of the chart by selecting it and then dragging one of the handles (small hollow boxes surrounding the chart) toward or away from the center of the graph. After you click outside the graph, it acts like any graphic inserted into a word document.

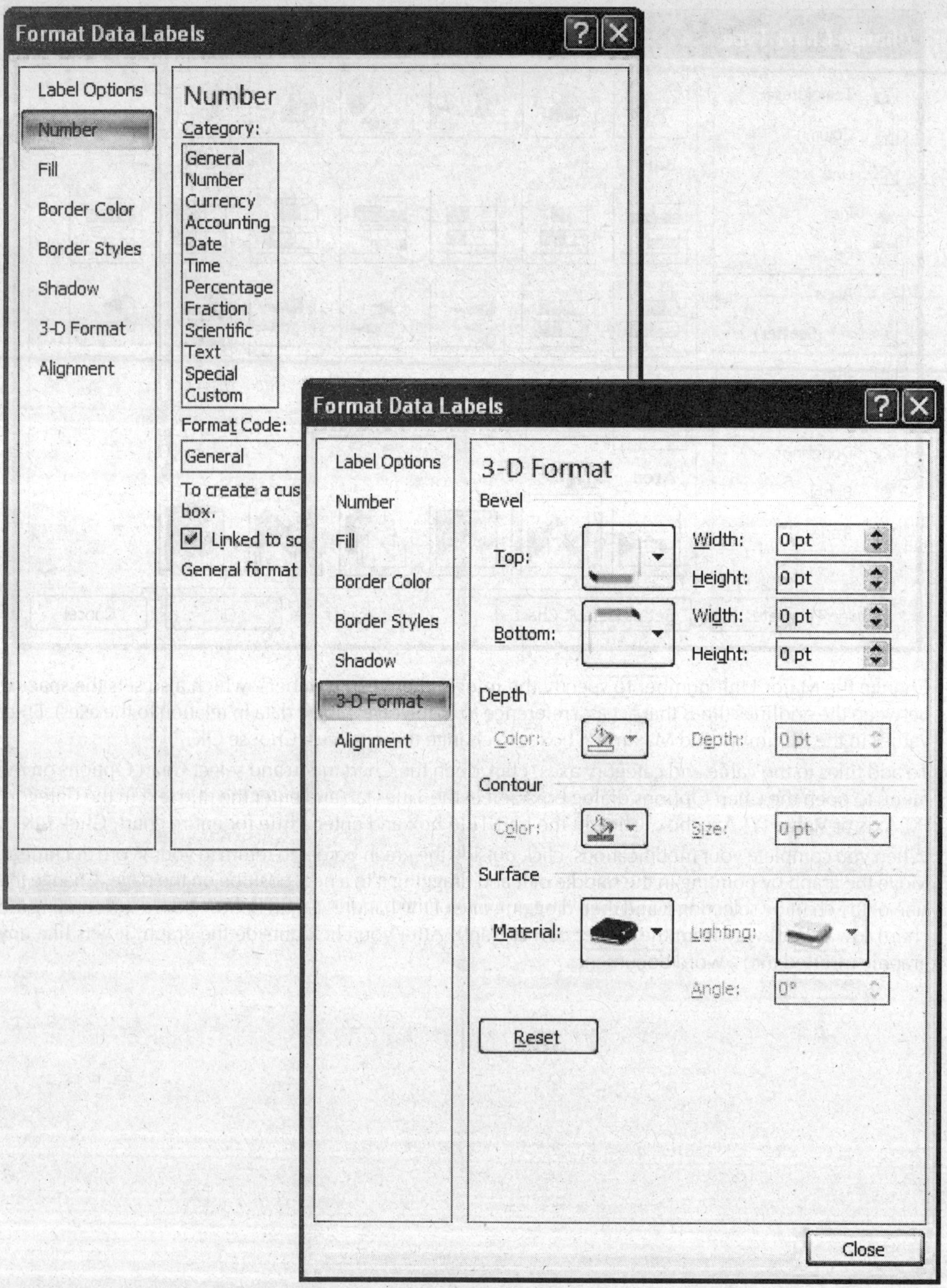
Format Data Labels
Label Options
Number
Fill
Border Color
Border Styles
Shadow
3-D Format
Alignment
Number
Category:
General
Number
Currency
Accounting
Date
Time
Percentage
Fraction
Scientific
Text
Special
Custom
Format Code:
General
Linked to so
General format
Format Data Labels
3-D Format
Bevel
Top:
Width:
0 pt
Height:
0 pt
Bottom:
Width:
0 pt
Height:
0 pt
Depth
Color:
Depth:
0 pt
Contour
Color:
Size:
0 pt
Surface
Material:
Lighting:
Angle:
0°
Reset
Close

CHAPTER 9

Additional Commands of Microsoft Word 2013

Introduction

It is not that the Word 2013 is only text and tables. It has options for working with Graphics too. You can import various graphics, which have been created using the other programs. These graphics could have been created using Windows Paint, Microsoft PowerPoint, CorelDRAW, AutoCAD etc. It has its own set of Clip Arts too, which can be used to enhance your word document.

Break, insert

Insert a section break

You can use section breaks to change the layout or formatting of a page or pages in your document. For example, you can lay out part of a single-column page as two columns. You can separate the chapters in your document so that the page numbering for each chapter begins at 1. You can also create a different header or footer for a section of your document.

In Microsoft Office Word 2013, you can choose many page layouts from the gallery of new page designs. For example, you can add a single-column page that has a two-column section by clicking that page layout option in the gallery of New Page designs.

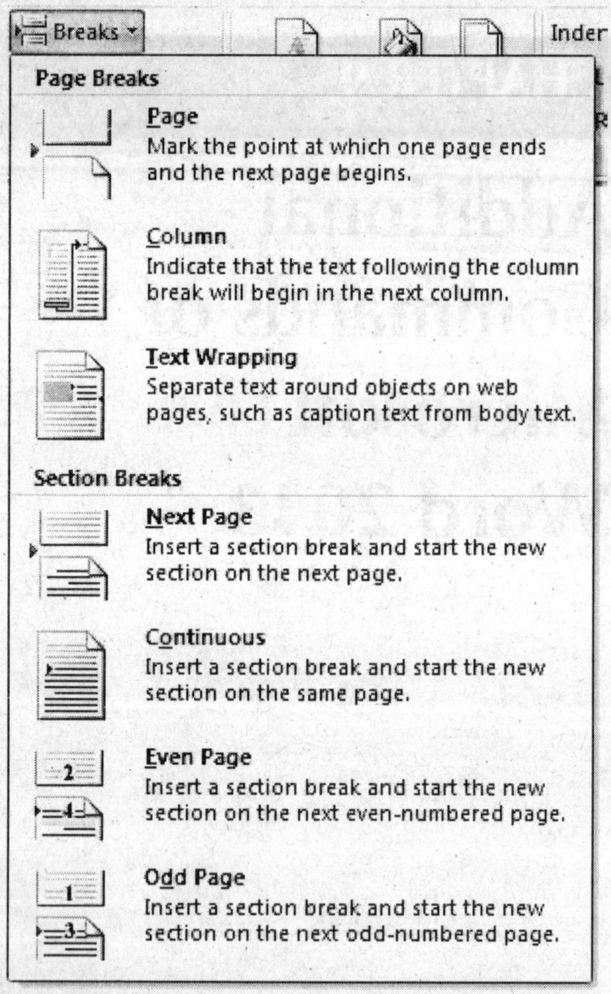

Types of section breaks that you can insert

Section breaks are used to create layout or formatting changes in a portion of a document. You can change the following formats for individual sections:

- Margins
- Paper size or orientation
- Paper source for a printer
- Page borders
- Vertical alignment of text on a page
- Headers and footers
- Columns
- Page numbering
- Line numbering
- Footnotes and endnotes

Notes

- A section break controls the section formatting of the text that precedes it. When you delete a section break, you also delete the section formatting for the text before the break. That text becomes part of the following section, and it assumes the formatting of that section. For example, if you separate the chapters of a document by using section breaks and then you delete the section break at the beginning of Chapter 2, Chapter 1 and Chapter 2 are in the same section and assume the formatting that previously was used only by Chapter 2.
- The section break that controls the formatting of the last part of your document is not shown as part of the document. To change the document formatting, click in the last paragraph of the document.

The Next Page command inserts a section break and starts the new section on the next page. This type of section break is especially useful for starting new chapters in a document.

The Continuous command inserts a section break and starts the new section on the same page. A continuous section break is useful for creating a formatting change, such as a different number of columns, on a page. The Even Page or Odd Page command inserts a section break and starts the new section on the next even-numbered or odd-numbered page. If you want document chapters always to begin on an odd page or on an even page, use the Odd page or Even page section break option.

Change the document layout or formatting

1. Click where you want to make a formatting change.

   You might want to select a portion of the document around which to insert a pair of section breaks.
2. On the Page Layout tab, in the Page Setup group, click Breaks.

   In the Section Breaks group, click the section break type that fits the type of formatting change that you want to make.
3. For example, if you're separating a document into chapters, you might want each chapter to start on an odd page. Click Odd Page in the Section Breaks group.

Remove changes of the document layout

A section break defines where a formatting change occurs in the document. When you delete a section break, you also delete the section formatting for the text before the break. That text becomes part of the following section, and it assumes the formatting of that section.

Make sure that you're in Draft view so that you can see the double dotted line section break.

1. Select the section break that you want to delete.
2. Press DELETE.

Bullets and Numbers

It is used to put numbers and bullets in the text. You can choose the bullet of your own and even in numbers you can choose the style.

Create a bulleted or numbered list

You can quickly add bullets or numbers to existing lines of text, or Word can automatically create lists as you type.

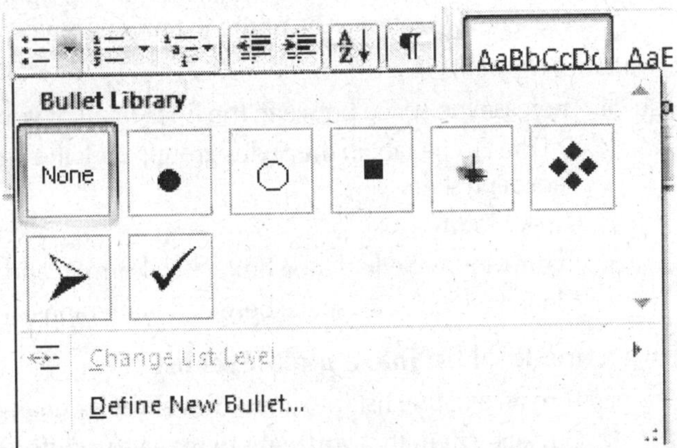

By default, if you start a paragraph with an asterisk or a number 1., Word recognizes that you are trying to start a bulleted or numbered list. If you don't want your text turned into a list, you can click the AutoCorrect Options button that appears.

Lists: One level or many levels

Make a list with just one level, or make a multilevel list to show lists within a list.

When you create a bulleted or numbered list, you can do any of the following:

- Use the convenient Bullet and Numbering libraries Use the default bullet and numbering formats for lists, customize the lists, or select other formats from the Bullet and Numbering libraries.
- Format bullets or numbers Format bullets or numbers differently from the text in a list. For example, click a number and change the number color for the entire list, without making changes to the text in the list.

- Use pictures or symbols Create a picture bulleted list to add visual interest to a document or a Web page.

Create a one-level bulleted or numbered list

Word can automatically create bulleted and numbered lists as you type, or you can quickly add bullets or numbers to existing lines of text.

Type a bulleted or numbered list

1. Type * (asterisk) to start a bulleted list or 1. to start a numbered list, and then press SPACEBAR or the TAB key.
2. Type any text that you want.
3. Press ENTER to add the next list item.

   Word automatically inserts the next bullet or number.
4. [illegible]h the list, press ENTER twice, or press BACKSPACE to delete the last bullet or number in the list.

If bullets and numbering do not begin automatically

1. Click the Microsoft Office Button , and then click Word Options.
2. Click Proofing.
3. Click AutoCorrect Options, and then click the AutoFormat As You Type tab.
4. Under Apply as you type, select the Automatic bulleted lists check box and the Automatic numbered lists check box.

Add bullets or numbering to a list

1. Select the items that you want to add bullets or numbering to.
2. On the Home tab, in the Paragraph group, click Bullets or Numbering.

Notes

- You can find different bullet styles and numbering formats by clicking the arrow next to Bullets or Numbering on the Home tab, in the Paragraph group.
- You can move an entire list to the left or the right. Click a bullet or number in the list, and drag it to a new location. The entire list moves as you drag. The numbering levels do not change.

Spread out the items in a list

You can increase the space between the lines in all of your lists by clearing a check box.

1. On the Home tab, in the Styles group, click the arrow next to Styles, and then right click the List Paragraph style.
2. Click Modify.
3. In the Modify Style dialog box, click Format, and then click Paragraph.
4. Clear the Don't add space between paragraphs of the same style check box.

Turn a one-level list into a multilevel list

You can turn an existing list into a multilevel list by changing the hierarchical level of items in the list.

1. Click any item that you want to move to a different level.
2. On the Home tab, in the Paragraph group, click the arrow next to Bullets or Numbering, click Change List Level, and then click the level that you want.

Choose a multilevel list style from the gallery

You can apply a gallery style to any multilevel list.

1. Click an item in the list.
2. On the Home tab, in the Paragraph group, click the arrow next to Multilevel List.
3. Click the multilevel list style that you want.

Change Case

Using this option you can change the case of the selected text. You can choose the option of having it all CAPS or in all lowercase. **Sentence case** will make only the first character Caps and the rest of the sentence in lower case. **Title case** will make all the title words start with a capital letter. **Toggle case** will make the Capital letter lower and lower letter as Capital, i.e., reverse the case. So choose the option which you want and click at the proper selection and see the result.

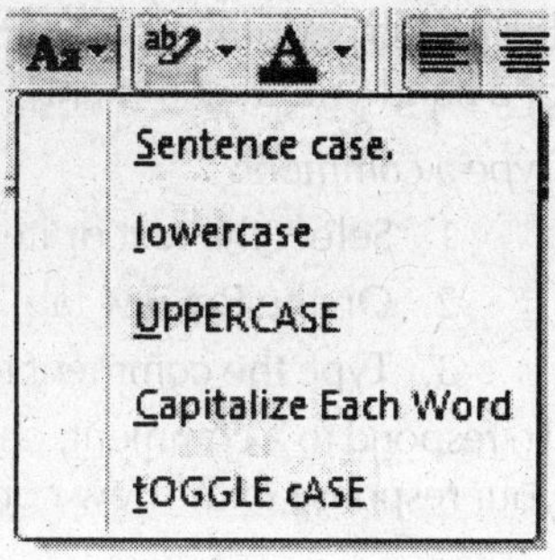

Columns

This command is used to make your text run into different columns. You can choose the number of columns you want to have in your text. You can make your text look like a newspaper having 5 columns.

1. Select the text which you want to divide into columns.
2. Select **Columns** from **Page Layout** tab to get **Columns** dialog box as shown next.
3. Choose your options and click Ok.

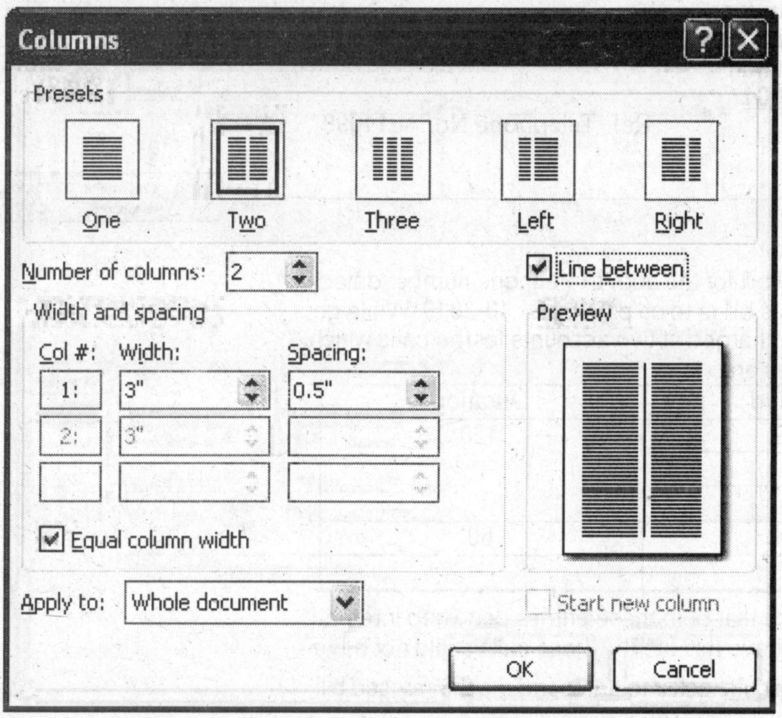

Comment, Insert

You can insert a comment inside balloons that appear in the document margins. You can also hide comments from view.

If you don't want comments to appear in your document during a review, you must clear your document of comments by deleting them. To find out whether comments remain in your document, click Show Markup on the Review tab in the Tracking group.

Insert a comment

You can type a comment. On a Tablet PC (Tablet PC: A computer that runs Microsoft Windows XP Tablet PC Edition. With a Tablet PC, you can write directly on the screen by using a tablet pen and use the pen to perform mouse functions. Also known as a tablet computer.), you can insert a voice comment or a handwritten comment.

Type a comment

1. Select the text or item that you want to comment on, or click at the end of the text.
2. On the Review tab, in the Comments group, click New Comment.
3. Type the comment text in the comment balloon or in the Reviewing Pane.

To respond to a comment, click its balloon, and then click New Comment in the Comments group. Type your response in the new comment balloon.

Insert a voice comment

If your computer is a Tablet PC, you can record voice comments. Voice comments are added as sound objects inside comment balloons.

To,

The General Manager
Mahanagar Telephones Nigam Limited
Khurshid Lal Bhawan
New Delhi - 110 001

Ref: Telephone No. 4611098

Sir

Comment [m1]: This is a comment

I am in receipt of bill for the above telephone number dated Rs. 4,678.90. This bill is to be paid by 21.10.2010. While go that I have been charged at two accounts for the calls which me. These entries are:

Called id	Duration
0017249873769	120
0013245934234	60

As you can notice that both these entries pertain to Internati phone does not have this facility, these calls could not have

I hope that you would look into and send me the revised bill, payment in time.

Hoping for an early action,

Thanking you,

Yours faithfully,

Before you can add a voice comment for the first time, you need to add the Insert Voice command to the Quick Access Toolbar.

1. Click the Microsoft Office Button , and then click Word Options.
2. Click Customize.
3. In the list under Choose commands from, select All Commands.
4. In the list of commands, click Insert Voice, and then click Add.

To add a voice comment to your document, do the following:

1. On the Quick Access Toolbar, click Insert Voice .
2. In the dialog box that opens, click the start button and record the voice comment.
3. When you finish recording the comment, press the stop button and close the dialog box.
4. If Microsoft Office Word displays a message asking whether you want to update the sound object, click Yes.

To hear the recorded comment, right-click the comment balloon, point to Sound Recorder Document Object, and then click Play.

For additional information about recording and editing a sound object, see the documentation for your sound card and microphone.

Insert a handwritten comment

If your computer is a Tablet PC, you can make handwritten comments in your document. The ink is added and displayed inside comment balloons.

1. On the Review tab, in the Comments group, click New Comment.
2. Write the comment in the comment bubble.

Delete a comment

- To quickly delete a single comment, right-click the comment, and then click Delete Comment.
- To quickly delete all comments in a document, click a comment in the document. On the Review tab, in the Comments group, click the arrow below Delete, and then click Delete All Comments in Document.

Delete comments from a specific reviewer

1. On the Review tab, in the Tracking group, click the arrow next to Show Markup.
2. To clear the check boxes for all reviewers, point to Reviewers, and then click All Reviewers.
3. Click the arrow next to Show Markup again, point to Reviewers, and then click the name of the reviewer whose comments you want to delete.
4. In the Comments group, click the arrow below Delete , and then click Delete All Comments Shown.

This procedure deletes all comments from the reviewer that you selected, including comments throughout the document.

You can also review and delete comments by using the Reviewing Pane. To show or hide the Reviewing Pane, click Reviewing Pane in the Tracking group. To move the Reviewing Pane to the bottom of your screen, click the arrow next to Reviewing Pane, and then click Reviewing Pane Horizontal.

Change a comment

If comments aren't visible on the screen, click Show Markup in the Tracking group on the Review tab.

1. Click inside the balloon for the comment that you want to edit.

2. Make the changes that you want.

Notes

- If the balloons are hidden or if only part of the comment is displayed, you can change the comment in the Reviewing Pane. To show the Reviewing Pane, in the Tracking group, click Reviewing Pane. To make the reviewing pane run across the bottom of your screen rather than down the side of your screen, click the arrow next to Reviewing Pane, and then click Reviewing Pane Horizontal.
- To respond to a comment, click its balloon, and then click New Comment in the Comments group. Type your response in the new comment balloon.

Add or change the name used in comments

1. On the Review tab, in the Tracking group, click the arrow next to Track Changes, and then click Change User Name.
2. Click Personalize.
3. Under Personalize your copy of Office, change the name or initials that you want to use in your own comments.

Notes

- The name and initials that you type are used by all Microsoft Office programs. Any changes that you make to these settings affect other Office programs.
- When you make a change to the name or initials that you want to use for your own comments, only comments that you make after the change are affected. Comments that are already in the document before you change the name or initials are not updated.

Drop Cap

It is a way of emphasizing the text with the first letter being made big enough to run into 2-3 lines. Word also allows you to do so. This command is available under the **Drop Cap** under the **Insert Tab**.

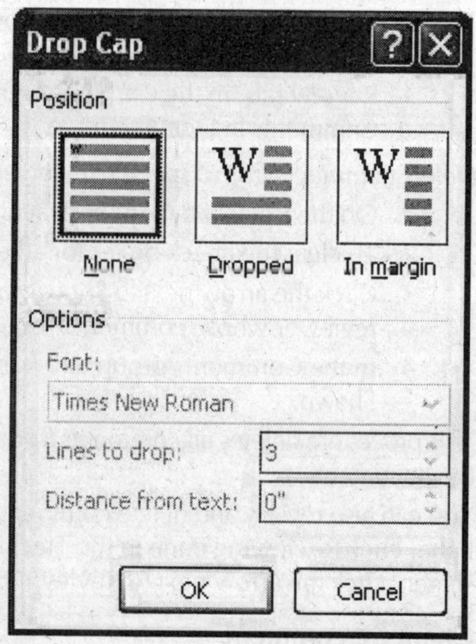

Envelopes and Labels

It is not that Word has options only for the documents. It also has features for printing envelopes and labels. Access Envelopes and Labels from the Mailing tab and do as mentioned next.

Create and print a sheet of different labels

This information applies to creating sheet of labels that are not identical. For example, you can create a sheet of nametags where each tag is personalized with an individual's name.

Create labels

1. Start Word.

   A blank document opens by default. Leave it open. If you close it, the commands in the next step are not available.
2. On the Mailings tab, in the Create group, click Labels.
3. Leave the Address box blank.
4. To select the label type and other options, click Options.

5. In the Label Options dialog box, make your choices, and then click OK.
   1. The type of printer that you are using to print labels
   2. The supplier that produced your label sheets
   3. The number that corresponds to the product number listed on your package of label sheets

   The product number for my label sheets doesn't match any of the choices in the Label Options dialog box

   You can still print your labels. You just have to do some customizing.

   1. Measure the labels on the sheet that you have, and note the measurements and how many labels fit on a single sheet.

      Measure the labels carefully. The actual label size might be smaller than the size that is indicated by the label manufacturer. For example, a 1-by-2-inch label might actually be 15/16-inch high and 1 15/16-inches wide.
   2. In the Product number list, click a label type that is similar in size to your labels.

      If you don't see the label type that you want in the Product number list, you may be able to use another of the listed labels, or you can create a new label size.
   3. Click Details, and then compare the label dimensions and the number of labels per sheet (for labels printed on laser and ink-jet printers) or the number of columns on the label form (for labels printed on dot-matrix printers).

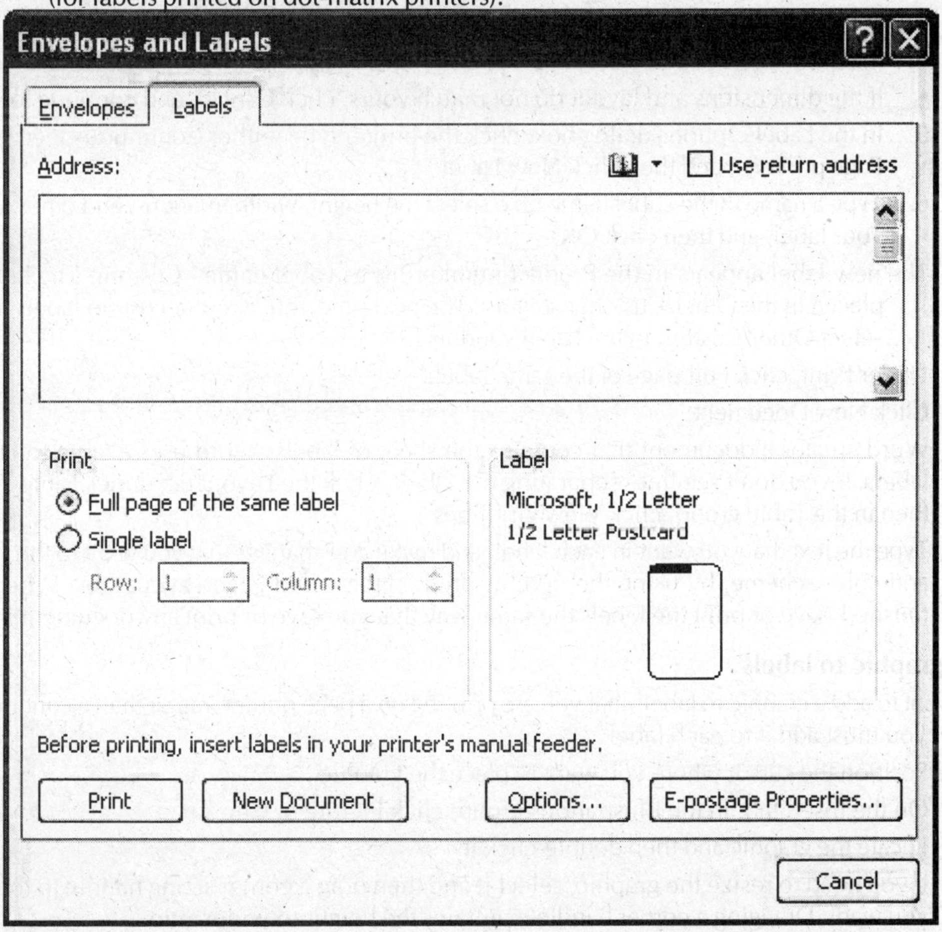

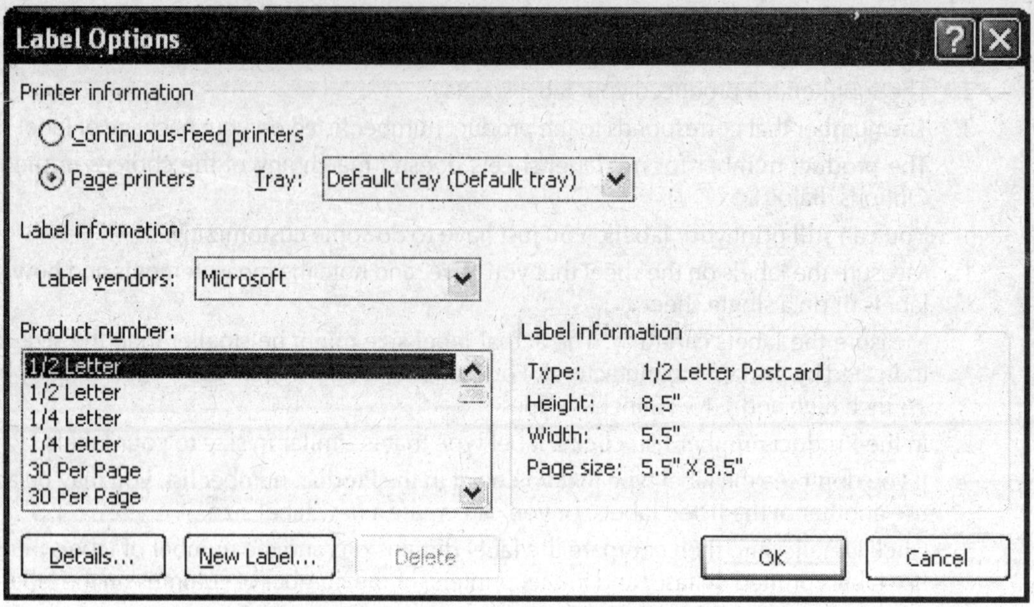

4. Do one of the following:
   - If the dimensions and label layout match those of your labels, use the selected label.
   - If the dimensions and layout do not match yours, click Cancel, and continue to step 5.
5. In the Label Options dialog box, click the printer type (either Continuous-feed printers or Page printers), and then click New Label.
6. Type a name in the Label name box, select the height, width, margins, and other options for your label, and then click OK.

   The new label appears in the Product number list as Label name - Custom. The label is also placed in the Other/Custom category. The next time you use your custom labels, be sure to select Other/Custom in the Label vendors list.

6. Under Print, click Full page of the same label.
7. Click New Document.
8. Word creates a document that contains the sheet of labels. Word uses a table to lay out the labels. If you don't see lines separating the labels, click the Layout tab under Table Tools, and then in the Table group, click View Gridlines.
9. Type the text that you want in each label, and make any changes that you want to the formatting and color scheme, by using the options on the Home and Page Layout tabs. When you are finished, save or print the labels the same way that you save or print any document in Word.

Add a graphic to labels

If you want to add a graphic to labels that you are printing on a page printer (rather than a continuous-feed printer), you must add it to each label:

1. Position the cursor where you want to place the graphic.
2. On the Insert tab, in the Illustrations group, click Picture or Clip Art.
3. Locate the graphic and then double-click it.
4. If you need to resize the graphic, select it and then drag a corner sizing handle to the size that you want. Dragging a corner handle maintains the height-to-width ratio.

5. If the graphic does not align with the label text, right-click the graphic and do the following:
   1. Point to Text Wrapping, and then click More Layout Options.
   2. Click the Text Wrapping tab, and under Wrapping style, click Square.
   3. Click the Picture Position tab, and under Horizontal, click Alignment, and then click the alignment that you want: Left, Centered, or Right.
   4. Click OK.

      If you want to use the same picture for each label, you can adjust the size and placement in the first label, and then copy the picture and paste it into your other labels.
   5. The image in this article was excerpted from Training on Microsoft Office Online.

Create and print a single envelope

If you want to include your return address on the envelope, you can set this up before you start working on the envelope.

When you have set up your envelope the way you want, you can print it, as well as save it so that you can reuse it.

Set up a return address

1. Start Word.

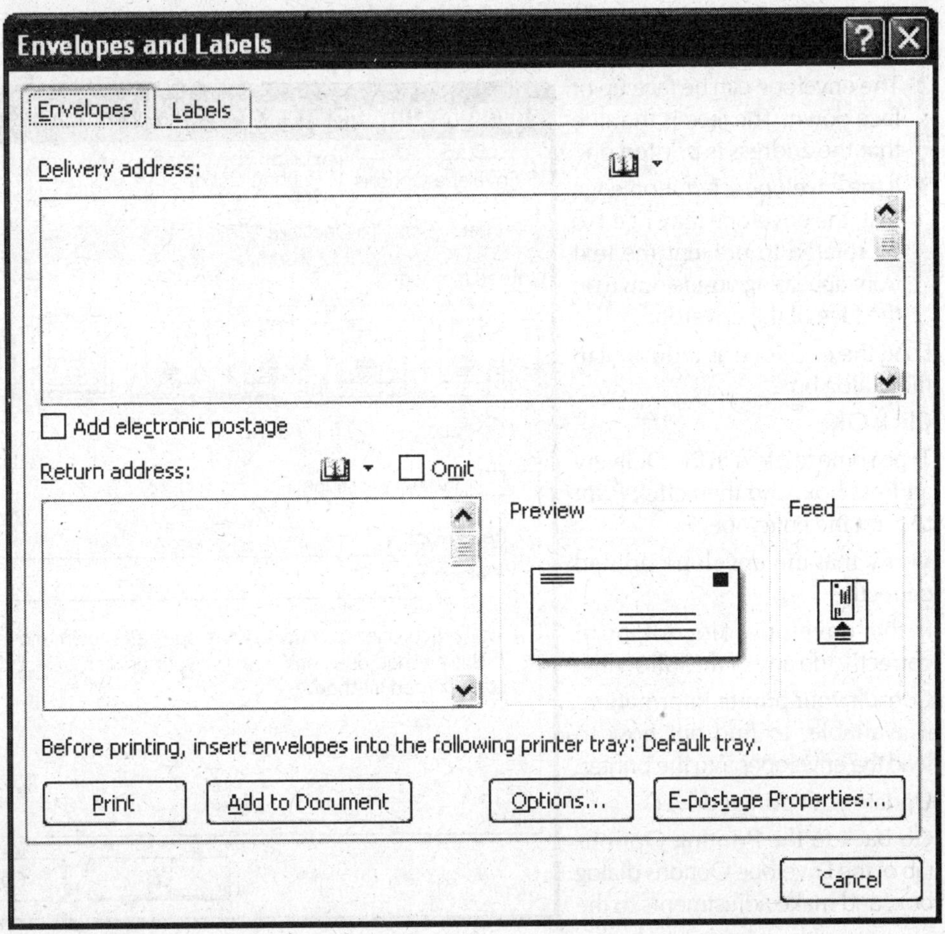

2. Click the Microsoft Office Button , and then click Word Options.
3. Click Advanced.
4. Scroll down, and under General, type your return address in the Mailing address box.

   Word stores the address so that you can use it whenever you want to insert your return address in an envelope, label, or other document.
5. Click OK.

Verify printing options

Before you run a batch of envelopes through your printer, you can verify that the printer options are set up correctly.

1. On the Mailings tab, in the Create group, click Envelopes.
2. Click Options, and then click the Envelope Options tab.
3. In the Envelope size box, click the choice that matches the size of your envelope. If none of the choices matches your envelope size, scroll to the bottom of the list, click Custom size, and then type the dimensions of your envelope in the Width and Height boxes.
4. Click the Printing Options tab.

   The printer driver tells Word which way the envelope should be loaded into the printer, and this information is displayed in the Printing Options tab of the Envelope Options dialog box.
   1. The feed method determines the position of the envelope (right, middle, left) and whether the long or short edge is being fed into the printer.
   2. The envelope can be face up or face down. The face is the side that the address is printed on.
   3. If the envelope is fed short edge first, the envelope may need to be rotated to prevent the text from appearing upside down on the face of the envelope.

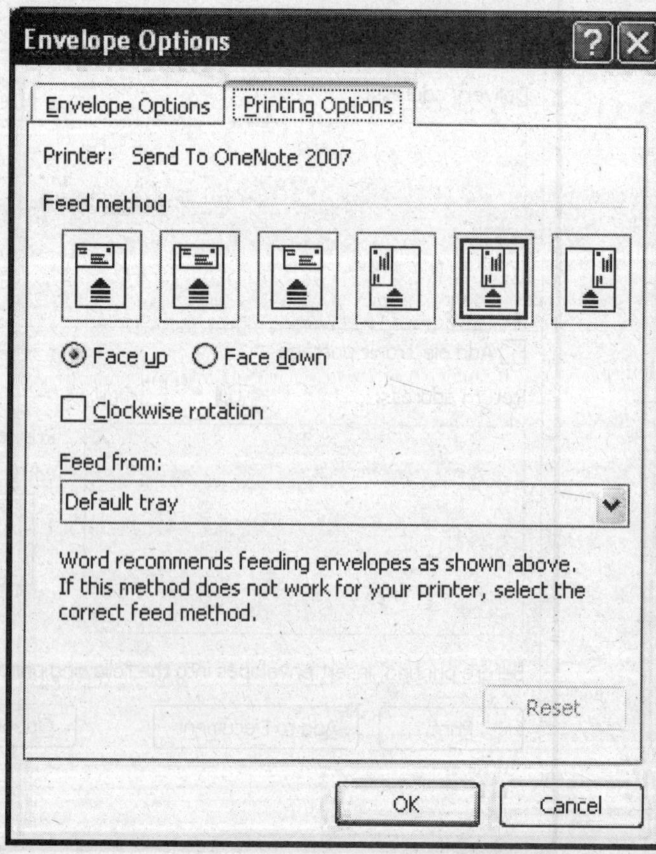

5. Load the envelope as indicated in the dialog box.
6. Click OK.
7. Type some test text in the Delivery address box, and then click Print to print the envelope.
8. Verify that the envelope printed correctly.
9. If the envelope did not print correctly, do any of the following:

- Consult your printer information, if available, to find out how to load the envelopes into the printer.
- Update your printer driver.
- Go back to the Printing Options tab of the Envelope Options dialog box, and make adjustments to the

printing options. Print the envelope again. Repeat this process until you discover a configuration of printing options that yields the results that you want.

Create and print or save an envelope

1. On the Mailings tab, in the Create group, click Envelopes.
2. In the Delivery address box, type the mailing address.

   If you want to use an address in the electronic address book installed on your computer, click Insert Address .

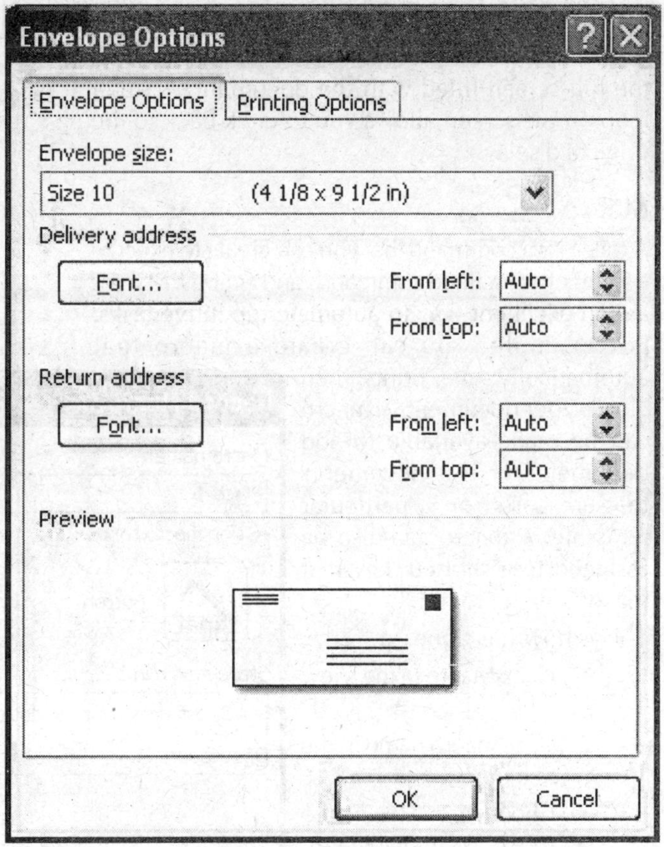

3. If you want to format the text, select the text, right-click the selected text, and then click Font on the shortcut menu.
4. In the Return address box, type the return address or use the preconfigured one.
5. If you want to use an address in the electronic address book installed on your computer, click Insert Address

   If you want to keep the return address for future use, but you don't want to include it on the current envelope, select the Omit check box.
6. If you have access to electronic postage, for example if you purchased it from a service on the World Wide Web (World Wide Web (WWW): The multimedia branch of the Internet that presents not only text, but also graphics, sound, and video. On the Web, users can easily jump from item to item, page to page, or site to site by using hyperlinks.), you can add it to your envelope.
   1. Select the Add electronic postage check box.

      If you do not have an electronic postage program installed, Microsoft Word prompts you to install one and offers to connect to the Microsoft Office Online Web site. There you can get more information and links to other sites that offer electronic postage.
   2. To set options for the electronic postage programs that are installed on your computer, click E-postage Properties.
7. Do one of the following:

- If you want to print the envelope without saving it for reuse, insert an envelope in the printer as shown in the Feed box, and then click Print.
- If you want to save the envelope for reuse, click Add to Document, and then click the Microsoft Office Button, click Save As, and type a name for the document.

Word adds the envelope to the current document as Page 1. If you want, you can use the rest of the document for typing correspondence that will automatically be stored with the envelope.

To print the envelope, insert an envelope in the printer as shown in the Feed box on the Printing Options tab in the Envelope Options dialog box, click Add to Document, and then click Print.

If you want to print the envelope without printing the rest of the document, enter Page 1 in the Print dialog box. In the Page range section of the Print dialog box, click Pages, and then type 1 in the Pages box.

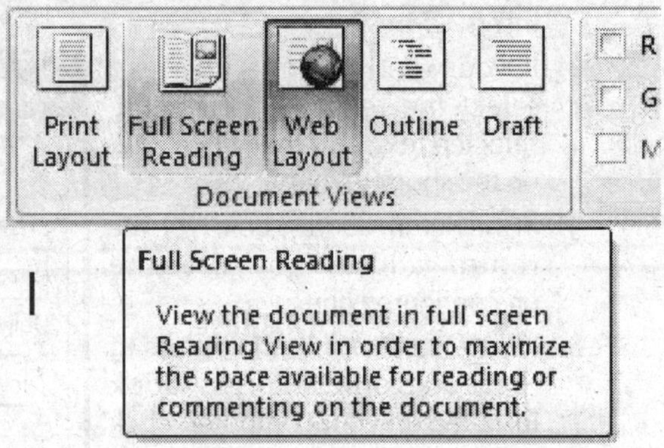

Full Screen

Available under the View menu, this command makes the full screen filled with the document. A small icon on the screen allows you to click back to the original display.

Macro

A macro is a command that you can create to execute a series of predefined commands and actions. Macros are an excellent way to automate repetitive tasks. For example, you can create a macro that automatically save, prints, then closes your document. A macro can be made available to add documents or just documents that are based on a particular template. A macro can also be assigned to a shortcut key that makes it easier to run.

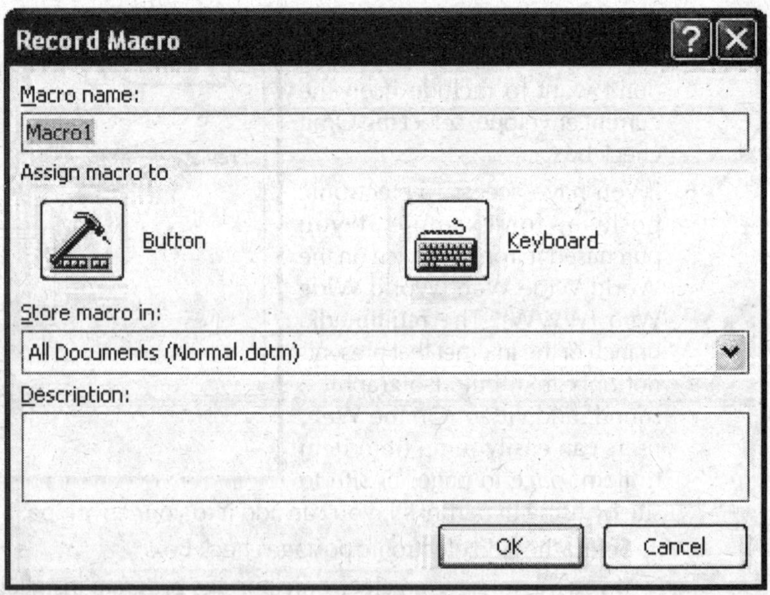

This is how it is done.

1. Click Macro in the View tab.
2. Type macro name in the text box.
3. Choose to run the macro from: Toolbar, Menu, Keyboard.
4. Make macro available to one of the desired template.

The Record macro dialog box closes and the macro toolbar displays.

Paragraph

This command is used to set the setting for a paragraph. As you can see from the figure shown next, you can set spacing before and after the paragraph. You can set the Alignment of the paragraph. You can also set the left and right paragraph spacing.

Using the Line and Page Breaks panel you can set the various options of line and page breaks.

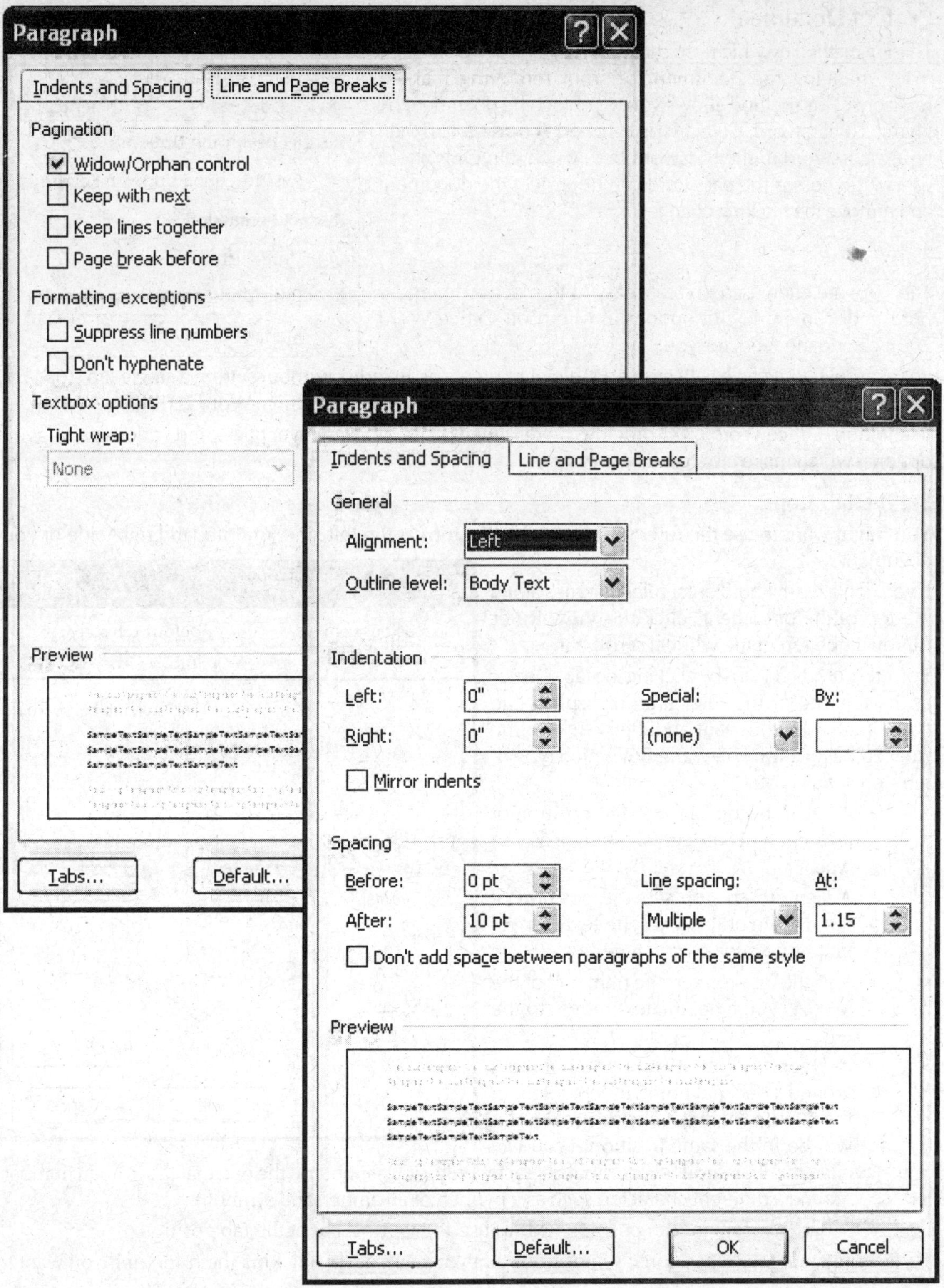
Paragraph
Indents and Spacing
Line and Page Breaks
Pagination
Widow/Orphan control
Keep with next
Keep lines together
Page break before
Formatting exceptions
Suppress line numbers
Don't hyphenate
Textbox options
Tight wrap:
None
Preview
Tabs...
Default...
Paragraph
Indents and Spacing
Line and Page Breaks
General
Alignment:
Left
Outline level:
Body Text
Indentation
Left:
0"
Right:
0"
Special:
(none)
By:
Mirror indents
Spacing
Before:
0 pt
After:
10 pt
Line spacing:
Multiple
At:
1.15
Don't add space between paragraphs of the same style
Preview
Tabs...
Default...
OK
Cancel

Protect Document

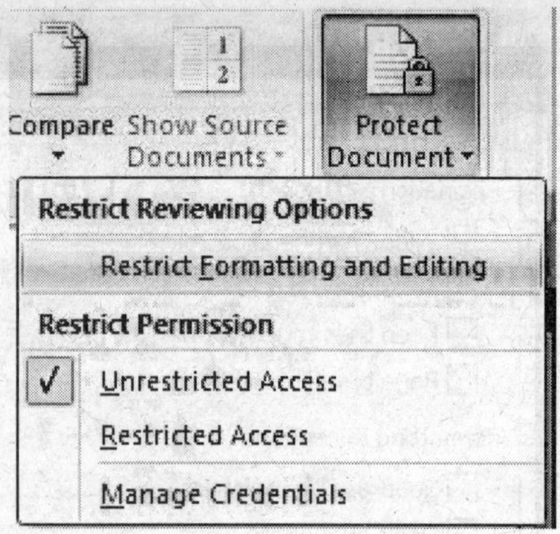

This is a method by which you can prevent unauthorized persons from changing the document or from removing marked revisions. This method allows you to protect the document by giving it a password. Select **Restricted Access** and then type a password in the Password box. Click Ok. Only those users who posses the password can unprotect the document and remove the tracking changes.

Tabs

Tab stops are often used to create easy-to-format documents — but the document layout options in Microsoft Office Word 2013 can do the work for you.

For example, you can easily create a table of contents or an index without setting a single tab stop. You can also use the predesigned table and header and footer options in Office Word 2013.

In addition, Office Word 2013 provides predesigned pages, such as cover pages and various page layout options, which make tab stops unnecessary.

Set the tab stops

You might want to use the ruler to set manual tab stops at the left side, middle, and right side of your document.

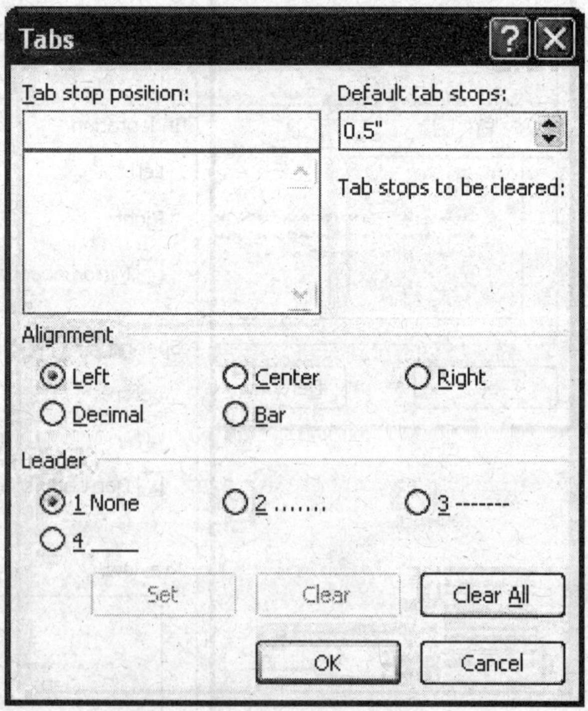

If you don't see the horizontal ruler that runs along the top of the document, click the View Ruler button at the top of the vertical scroll bar.

You can quickly set tabs by clicking the tab selector at the left end of the ruler until it displays the type of tab that you want and then clicking the ruler at the location you want. But which type of tab stop should you use?

- A Left Tab stop sets the start position of text that will then run to the right as you type.
- A Center Tab stop sets the position of the middle of the text. The text centers on this position as you type.
- A Right Tab stop sets the right end of the text. As you type, the text moves to the left.
- A Decimal Tab stop aligns numbers around a decimal point. Independent of the number of digits, the decimal point will be in the same position. (You can align numbers around a decimal character only; you cannot use the decimal tab to align numbers around a different character, such as a hyphen or an ampersand symbol.)
- A Bar Tab stop doesn't position text. It inserts a vertical bar at the tab position.

If you want your tab stops at precise positions that you can't get by clicking the ruler, or if you want to insert a specific character (leader) before the tab, you can use the Tabs dialog box. To display this dialog box, double-click any tab stop on the ruler.

About using the horizontal ruler to set tab stops

- By default, there are no tab stops on the ruler when you open a new blank document.
- The final two options on the tab selector are actually for indents. You can click these and then click the ruler to position the indents, rather than sliding the indent markers along the ruler. Click First Line Indent , and then click the upper half of the horizontal ruler where you want the first line of a paragraph to begin. Click Hanging Indent , and then click the lower half of the horizontal ruler where you want the second and all following lines of a paragraph to begin.
- When you set a bar tab stop, a vertical bar line appears where you set the tab stop (you don't need to press the TAB key). A bar tab is similar to strikethrough formatting, but it runs vertically through your paragraph at the location of the bar tab stop. Like other types of tabs, you can set a bar tab stop before or after you type the text of your paragraph.
- You can remove a tab stop by dragging it (up or down) off the ruler. When you release the mouse button, the tab stop disappears.
- You can also drag existing tab stops left or right along the ruler to a different position.
- When multiple paragraphs are selected, only the tabs from the first paragraph show on the ruler.

Portions of this article were excerpted from Training on Microsoft Office Online.

Change the spacing between the default tab stops

If you set manual tab stops, the default tab stops are interrupted by the manual tab stops that you set. Manual tab stops that are set on the ruler override the default tab stop settings.

1. On the Page Layout tab, click the Paragraph Dialog Box Launcher.
2. In the Paragraph dialog box, click Tabs.
3. In the Default tab stops box, enter the amount of spacing that you want between the default tab stops.

When you press the TAB key, your tab will stop across the page at the distance that you specified.

Word Count

Sometimes it is required to know the number of words typed in a particular document. It is usually required when you are given an assignment to write an article of a fixed number of words, maybe 200 or 400. So after typing each line you may like to know of how many words the file has become.

Count the number of words in a document

Some of the content in this topic may not be applicable to some languages.

Microsoft Office Word 2013 counts the number of words in a document while you type. Office Word 2013 can also count the following:

- Pages
- Paragraphs
- Lines
- Characters, either including or excluding the spaces

Although the footnotes and text in text boxes aren't automatically counted, you can set up Office Word 2013 to count them.

Count the words as you type

When you type in a document, Office Word 2013 automatically counts the number of pages and words in your document and displays them on the status bar at the bottom of the workspace .

Count the words in a selection or selections

You can count the number of words in a selection or selections, rather than all of the words in a document. The selections don't need to be next to each other for you to count them.

- Select the text that you want to count.

  The status bar displays the number of words in the selection. For example, 100/1440 means that the section accounts for 100 words of the total number of words in the document, 1,440.

  To select sections of text that aren't next to each other, select the first section, and then hold down CTRL and select additional sections.

Include footnotes and endnotes in the word count

1. On the Review tab, in the Proofing group, click Word Count.
2. In the Word Count dialog box, select the Include textboxes, footnotes and endnotes check box.

Count the words in a text box

- Select the text in the text box.

  The status bar displays the number of words in the text box. For example, 100/1440 means that the text box contains 100 words of the total number of words in the document, 1,440.
- To count the words in multiple text boxes, press and hold CTRL while you select the text in each text box that you want to count. The word count automatically adds the total number of selected words in the text boxes.

View the number of pages, characters, paragraphs, and lines

You can view the number of pages, paragraphs, and lines in your document, as well as the number of characters, either including or excluding spaces.

- On the Review tab, in the Proofing group, click Word Count.

Zoom

This command allows you to see the document either in an enlarged form, i.e., 200% or in a smaller form maybe 75%.

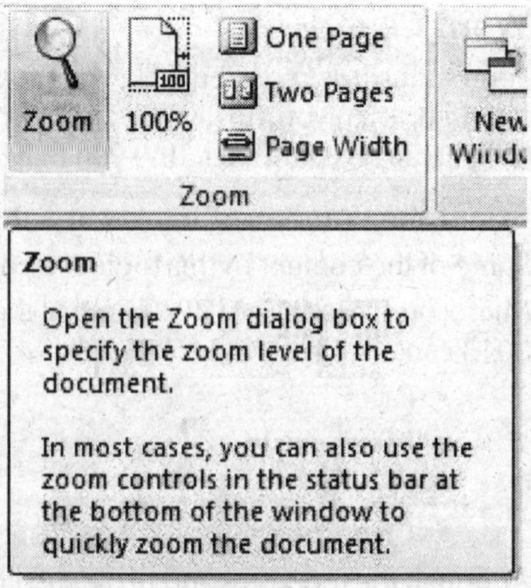

Hyperlinks

You can assign a hyperlink to a block of text or to a picture in a Word document. The hyperlink connects the text or picture to a target location. The target location can be a Web page, an Office document or other file or a folder which can be located on a disk, network drive or Internet document or within another file it or can be an e-mail address. Clicking the hyperlink displays the target location or sends a message to the target e-mail address.

Create a hyperlink

Microsoft Office Word creates a hyperlink for you when you press ENTER or the SPACEBAR after you type the address of an existing Web page, such as www.contoso.com.

Create a customized hyperlink to a document, file, or Web page

1. Select the text or picture that you want to display as the hyperlink.
2. On the Insert tab, in the Links group, click Hyperlink .
   You can also right-click the text or picture and then click Hyperlink on the shortcut menu.
3. Do one of the following:
   - To link to an existing file or Web page, click Existing File or Web Page under Link to, and then type the address that you want to link to in the Address box. If you don't know the address for a file, click the arrow in the Look in list, and then navigate to the file that you want.
   - To link to a file that you haven't created yet, click Create New Document under Link to, type the name of the new file in the Name of new document box, and then, under When to edit, click Edit the new document later or Edit the new document now.

   To customize the ScreenTip that appears when you rest the pointer over the hyperlink, click ScreenTip and then type the text that you want. If you don't specify a tip, Word uses the path or address of the file as the tip.

Create a hyperlink to a blank e-mail message

1. Select the text or picture that you want to display as the hyperlink.
2. On the Insert tab, in the Links group, click Hyperlink .
   You can also right-click the text or picture and then click Hyperlink on the shortcut menu.
3. Under Link to, click E-mail Address.
4. Either type the e-mail address that you want in the E-mail address box, or select an e-mail address in the Recently used e-mail addresses list.
5. In the Subject box, type the subject of the e-mail message.

Notes

- Some Web browsers and e-mail programs might not recognize the subject line.

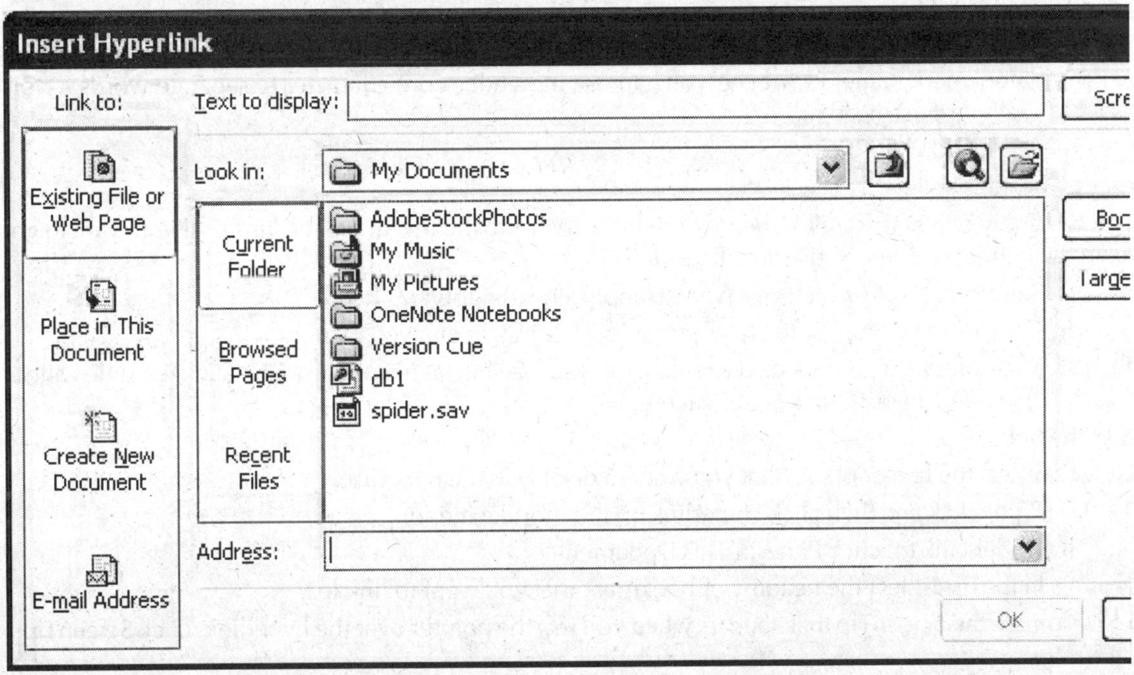

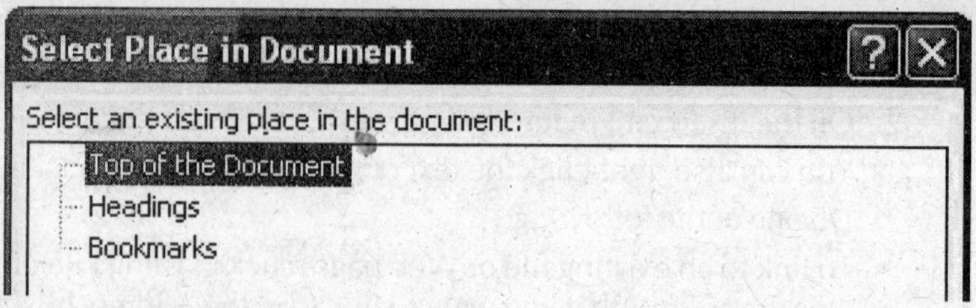

- To customize the ScreenTip that appears when you rest the pointer over the hyperlink, click ScreenTip and then type the text that you want. If you don't specify a tip, Word uses "mailto" followed by the e-mail address and the subject line as the tip. You can also create a hyperlink to a blank e-mail message by typing the address in the document. For example, type someone@example.com, and Word creates the hyperlink for you, unless you turned off automatic formatting of hyperlinks.

Create a hyperlink to a location in the current document or Web page

To link to a location in a document or Web page that you created in Word, you must mark the hyperlink location or destination and then add the link to it.

Mark the hyperlink location

You can mark the hyperlink location by using either a bookmark (bookmark: A location or selection of text in a file that you name for reference purposes. Bookmarks identify a location within your file that you can later refer or link to.) or a heading style (heading style: Formatting applied to a heading. Microsoft Word has nine different built-in styles: Heading 1 through Heading 9.) in Word.

Insert a bookmark

1. In the current document, do the following:
2. Select the text or item to which you want to assign a bookmark, or click where you want to insert a bookmark.
3. On the Insert tab, in the Links group, click Bookmark.
4. Under Bookmark name, type a name.
5. Bookmark names must begin with a letter and can contain numbers. You can't include spaces in a bookmark name. However, you can use the underscore character to separate words — for example, First_heading.
6. Click Add.

Apply a heading style

You can apply one of the built-in heading styles in Word to the text at the location that you want to go to. In the current document, do the following:

1. Select the text to which you want to apply a heading style.
2. On the Home tab, in the Styles group, click the style that you want.
3. For example, if you selected text that you want to style as a main heading, click the style called Heading 1 in the Quick Styles gallery.

Add the link

1. Select the text or object that you want to display as the hyperlink.
2. Right-click and then click Hyperlink on the shortcut menu.
3. Under Link to, click Place in This Document.
4. In the list, select the heading or bookmark that you want to link to.

To customize the ScreenTip that appears when you rest the pointer over the hyperlink, click ScreenTip, and then type the text that you want. If you don't specify a tip, Word uses "Current document" as the tip for links to headings. For links to bookmarks, Word uses the bookmark name.

Create a hyperlink to a specific location in another document or Web page

To link to a location in a document or Web page that you created in Word, you must mark the hyperlink location, or destination, and then add the link to it.

Mark the hyperlink location

1. Insert a bookmark in the destination file or Web page.
2. Open the file that you want to link from, and select the text or object you want to display as the hyperlink.
3. Right-click and then click Hyperlink on the shortcut menu.
4. Under Link to, click Existing File or Web Page.
5. In the Look in box, click the down arrow, and navigate to and select the file that you want to link to.
6. Click Bookmark, select the bookmark that you want, and then click OK.

   To customize the ScreenTip that appears when you rest the pointer over the hyperlink, click ScreenTip and then type the text that you want. If you don't specify a tip, Word uses the path to the file, including the bookmark name, as the tip.

Add the link

1. Select the text or object that you want to display as the hyperlink.
2. Right-click and then click Hyperlink on the shortcut menu.
3. Under Link to, click Place in This Document.
4. In the list, select the heading or bookmark that you want to link to.

   To customize the ScreenTip that appears when you rest the pointer over the hyperlink, click ScreenTip and then type the text that you want. If you don't specify a tip, Word uses "Current document" as the tip for links to headings. For links to bookmarks, Word uses the bookmark name.

   From Word documents, you can create links to specific locations in files that are saved in the Microsoft Office Excel (.xls) file format or the Microsoft Office PowerPoint (.ppt) file format. To link to a specific location in an Excel workbook, create a defined name in the workbook, and then at the end of the file name in the hyperlink, type # (number sign) followed by the defined name. To link to a specific slide in a PowerPoint presentation, type # followed by the slide number after the file name.

Quickly create a hyperlink to another file

You can create a hyperlink quickly without having to use the Insert Hyperlink dialog box by dragging selected text or pictures from a Word document or by dragging a Web address or hyperlink from some Web browsers. You can also copy a selected cell or range in Microsoft Office Excel. For example, you may want to create a hyperlink to a longer explanation in another document or to a news story on a Web page. The text that you copy must come from a file that has already been saved. You cannot drag drawing objects, such as Shapes, to create hyperlinks. To create a hyperlink for a drawing object, select the object, right-click, and then click Hyperlink on the shortcut menu.

Create a hyperlink by dragging content from another Word document

1. Save the file that you want to link to. This is the destination document.
2. Open the document where you want to add a hyperlink.

3. Open the destination document and select the text, graphic, or other item you want to go to.
4. For example, you might want to select the first few words of a section of a document that you want to link to.
5. Right-click the selected item, drag it to the task bar and rest over the icon of the document to which you want to add a hyperlink.
6. Release the right mouse button where you want the hyperlink to appear on the page, and then click Create Hyperlink Here .

   The text, graphic, or other item that you selected is the link to the destination document.

Create a hyperlink by dragging from a Web page

1. Open the document where you want to add a hyperlink.
2. Open a Web page and right-click the item that you want to link to on the Web page.
3. Drag the item to the task bar and rest over the document icon to which you want to add a hyperlink.
4. Release the right mouse button where you want the hyperlink to appear on the page, and then click Create Hyperlink Here .

Create a hyperlink by copying and pasting from an Excel worksheet

1. Open the Excel worksheet that you want to link to, and select a cell or range of cells to link to.
2. Right-click and then click Copy on the shortcut menu.
3. Open the Word document where you want to add a hyperlink.
4. On the Home tab, in the Clipboard group, click the Paste arrow, and then click Paste as Hyperlink.

Turn on automatic hyperlinks

1. To turn on automatic hyperlinks after you have turned them off, do the following:
2. Click the Microsoft Office Button , and then click Word Options.
3. Click Proofing.
4. Click AutoCorrect Options, and then click the AutoFormat As You Type tab.
5. Select the Internet and network paths with hyperlinks check box.

Turn off automatic hyperlinks

1. To turn off automatic hyperlinks, do one of the following.
2. Turn off the automatic hyperlink recognition feature
3. Click the Microsoft Office Button , and then click Word Options.
4. Click Proofing.
5. Click AutoCorrect Options, and then click the AutoFormat As You Type tab.
6. Clear the Internet and network paths with hyperlinks check box.

Delete an individual hyperlink

- Press CTRL+Z. You must press CTRL+Z immediately after you type the address, or URL, to delete a hyperlink from a typed URL. If you press CTRL+Z a second time, the typed URL is deleted.

CHAPTER 10

Creating Lists in Microsoft Word 2013

Introduction

Bulleted and numbered lists can be used in your documents to outline, arrange and emphasize text. In this lesson, you will learn how to modify existing bullets, insert new bulleted and numbered lists, select symbols as bullets, and format multilevel lists.

To Create a Bulleted List:

Select the text you wish to format as a list.

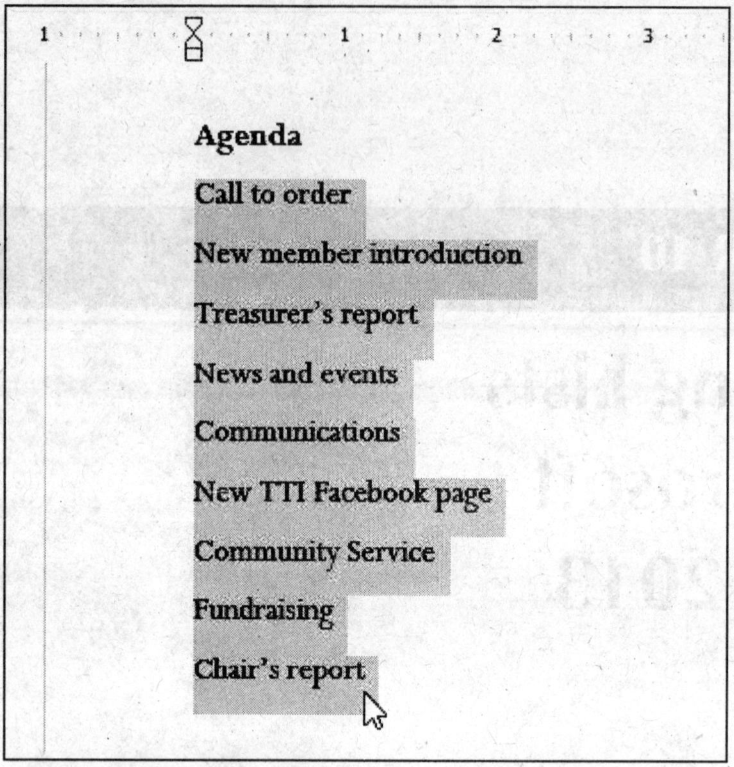

Selecting text to format

On the Home tab, click the drop-down arrow next to the Bullets command. A menu of bullet styles will appear.

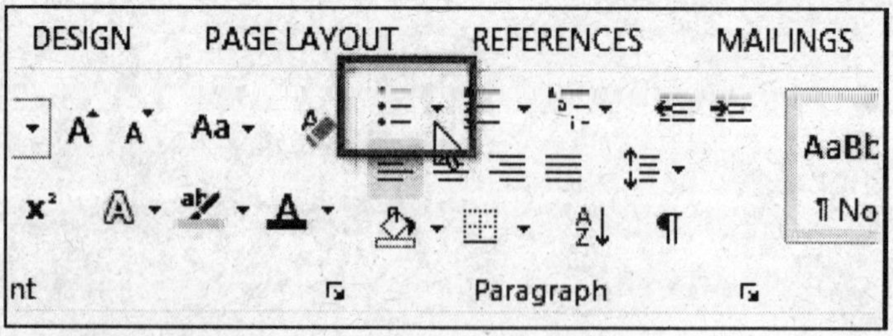

Clicking the Bullets drop-down arrow

Move the mouse over the various bullet styles. A live preview of the bullet style will appear in the document. Select the bullet style you wish to use.

The text will format as a bulleted list.

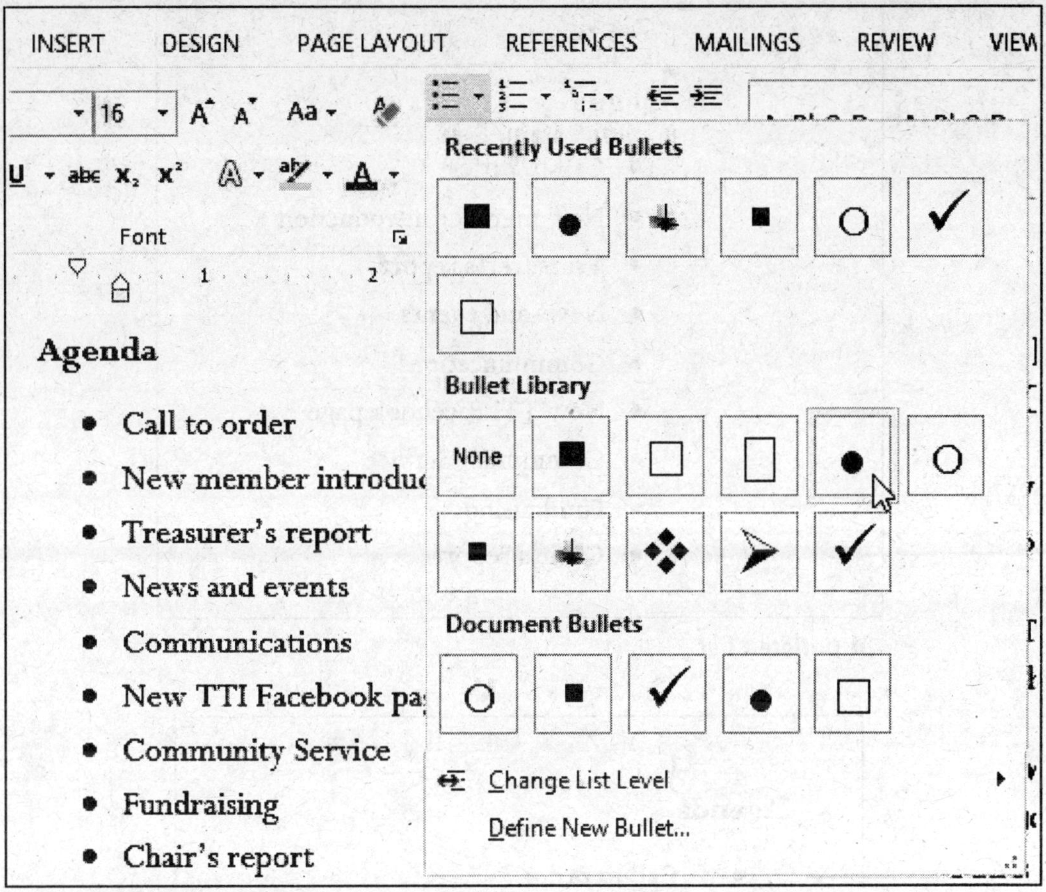

Selecting a bullet style

Options for Working with Lists

- To remove numbers or bullets from a list, select the list and click the Bulleted or Numbered list shortcut button.
- When you're editing a list, you can press Enter to start a new line, and the new line will automatically have a bullet or number. When you've reached the end of your list, press Enter twice to return to "normal" formatting.
- By dragging the indent markers on the Ruler, you can customize the indenting of your list and the distance between the text and the bullet or number.

To Create a Numbered List:

When you need to organize text into a numbered list, Word offers several numbering options. You can format your list with numbers, letters, or Roman Numerals.

Select the text you wish to format as a list.

Selecting text to format

- On the Home tab, click the drop-down arrow next to the Numbering command. A menu of numbering styles will appear.

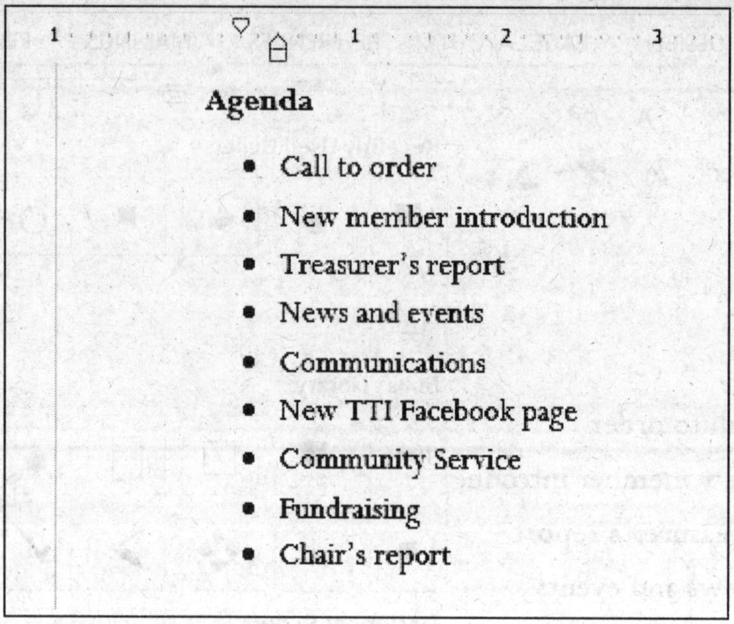

A bulleted list

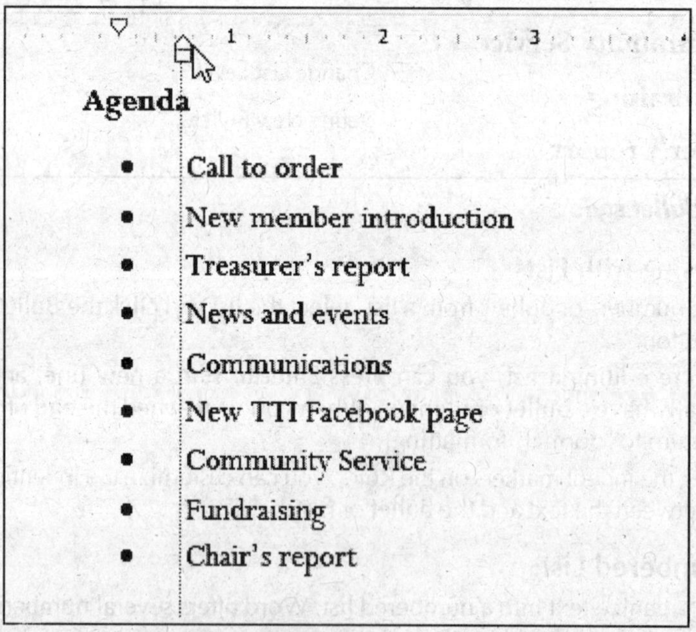

Customizing the indentation

Move the mouse over the various numbering styles. A live preview of the numbering style will appear in the document. Select the numbering style you wish to use.

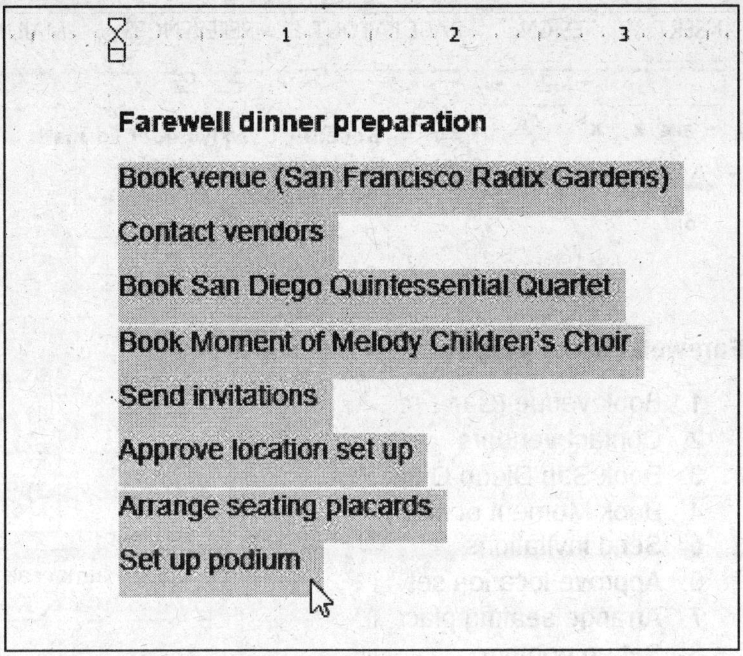

Selecting text to format

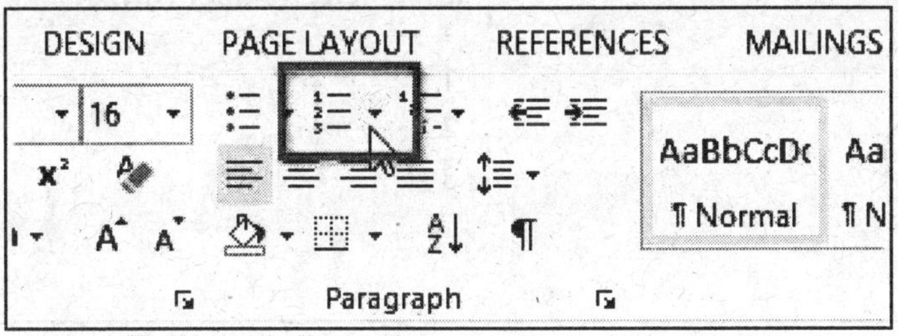

The number command

The text will format as a numbered list.

To Restart a Numbered List:

- If you want to restart the numbering of a list, Word has a Restart at 1 option. It can be applied to numeric and alphabetical lists.
- Right-click on the list item that you would like to restart the numbering for, and then select Restart at 1 from the menu that appears.

Restarting a list

The list numbering will restart.

Customizing Bullets

Customizing the look of the bullets in your list can help you emphasize certain list items or personalize the design of your list. Word allows you to format bullets in a variety of ways. You can use symbols, different colors, or even upload a picture as a bullet.

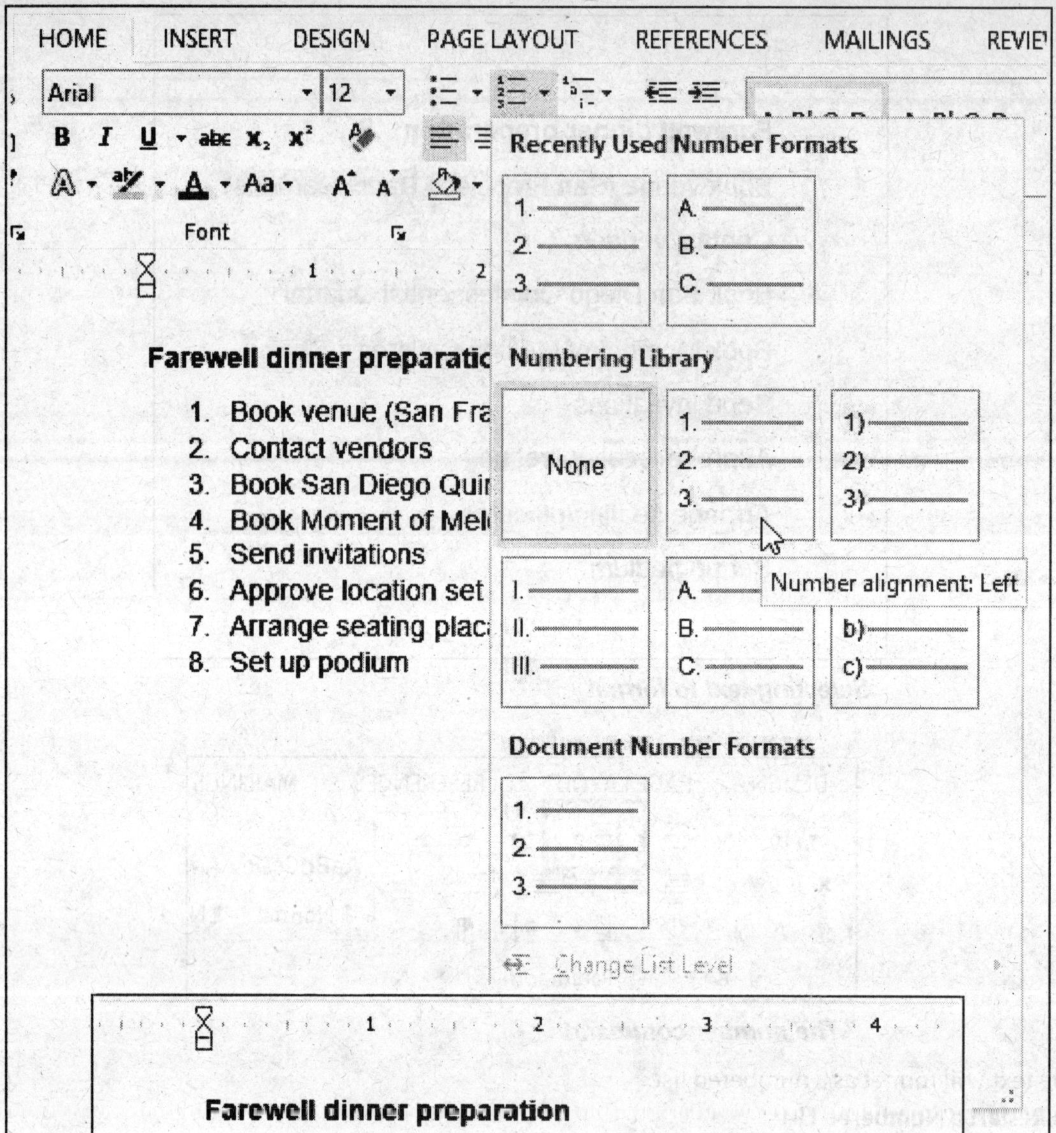

Viewi

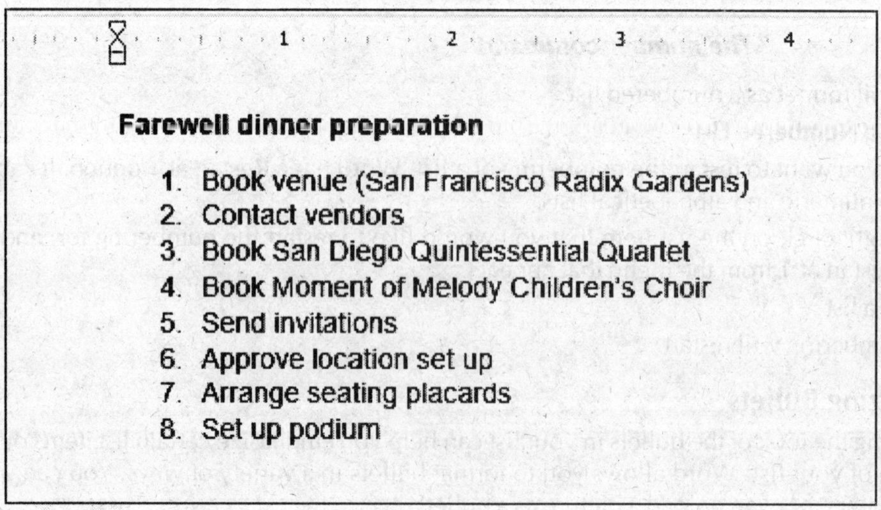

The formatted list

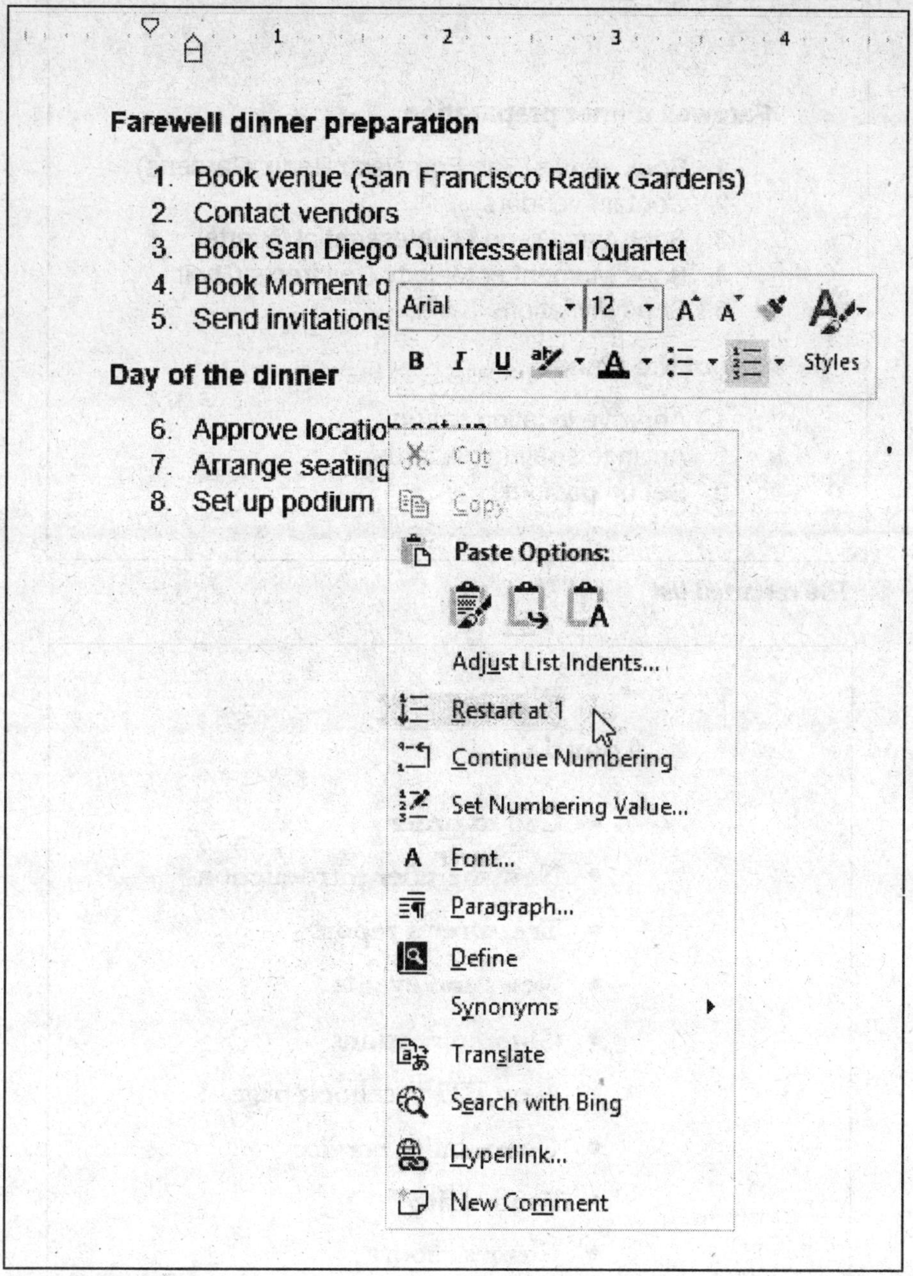

Restarting a list

To Use a Symbol as a Bullet:

Select an existing list that you wish to format.

On the Home tab, click the drop-down arrow next to the Bullets command. Select Define New Bullet... from the drop-down menu.

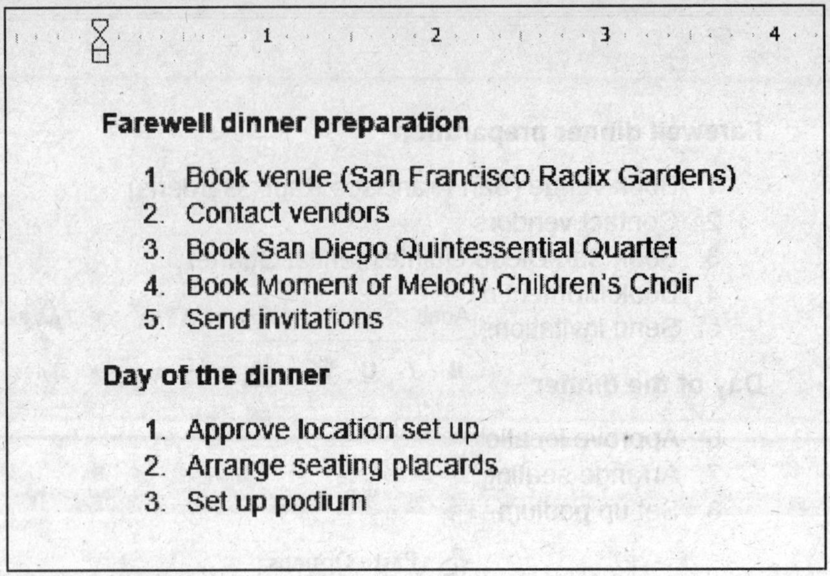

The restarted list

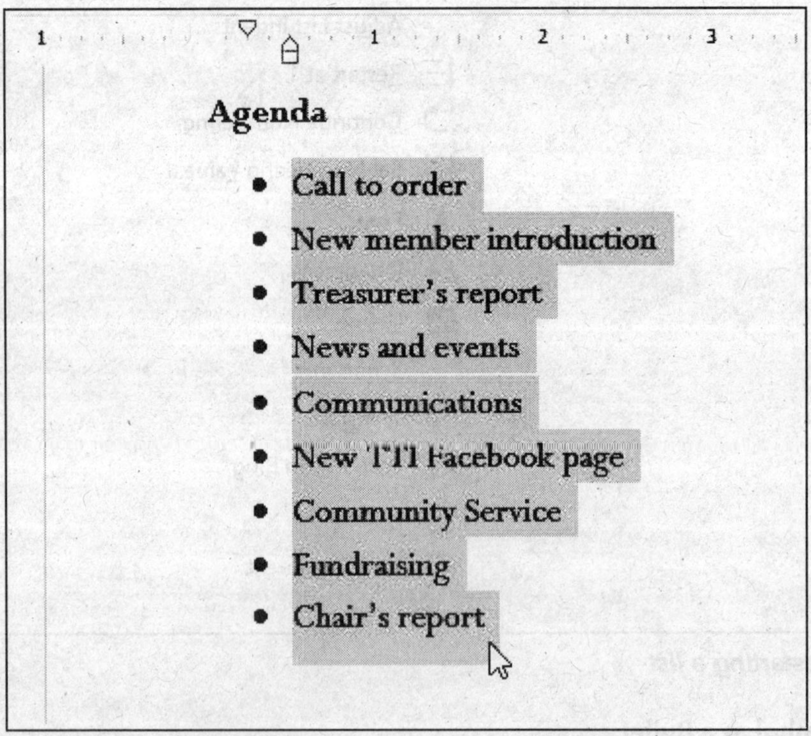

Selecting an existing list

The Define New Bullet dialog box will appear. Click the Symbol... button. The Symbol dialog box will appear.

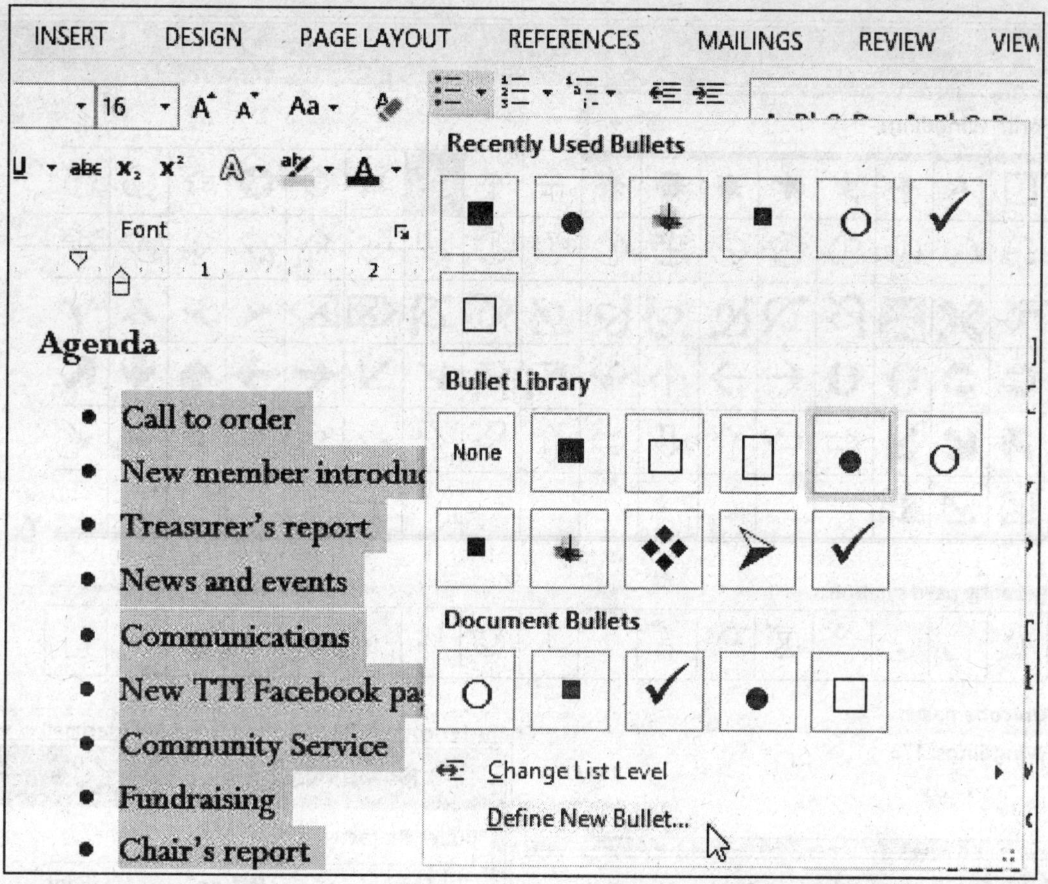

Defining a new bullet

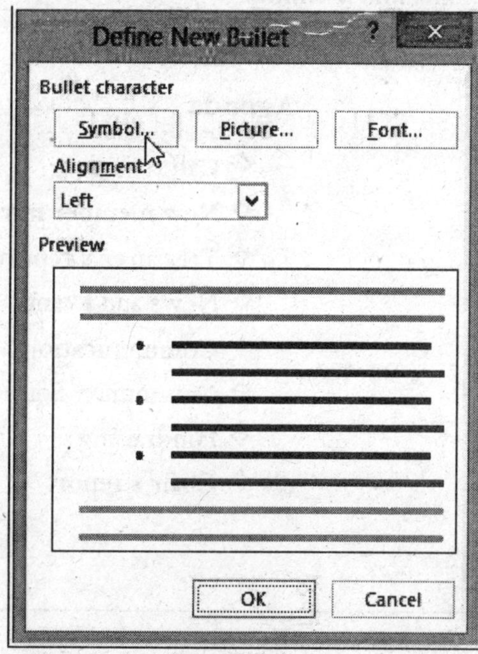

Clicking the Symbol button

Click the Font drop-down box and select a font. The Wingdings and Symbol fonts are good choices as they have a large number of useful symbols.

Select the desired symbol and click OK.

The symbol will appear in the Preview section of the Define New Bullet dialog box. Click OK.

The symbol will appear in the list.

To Change the Bullet Color:

Select an existing list that you wish to format.

On the Home tab, click the drop-down arrow next to the Bullets command. Select Define New Bullet... from the drop-down menu.

The Define New Bullet dialog box will appear. Click the Font button.

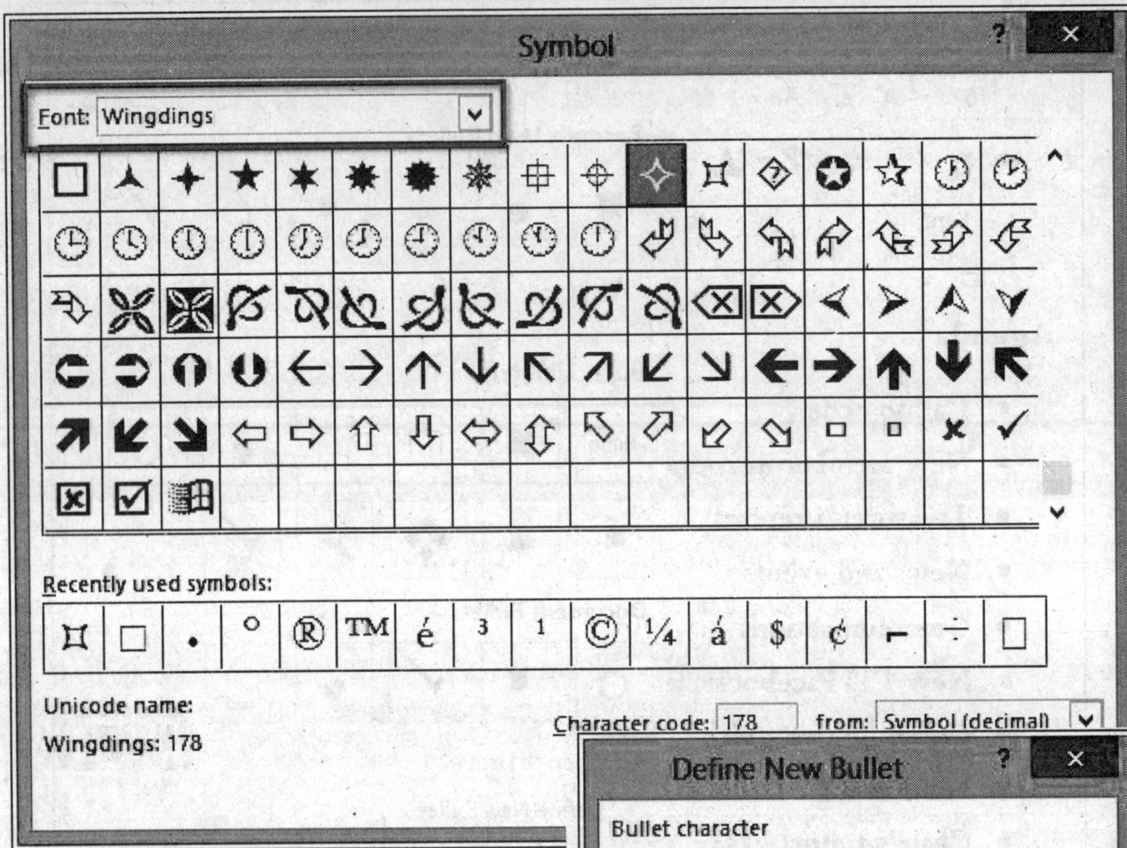

Selecting a symbol

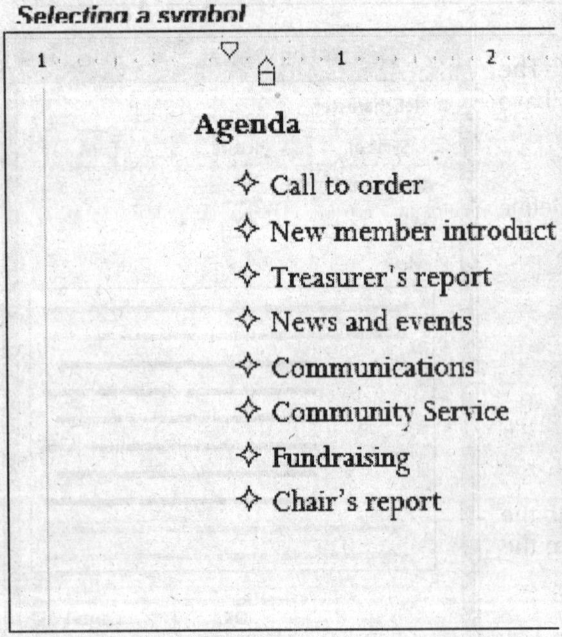

The formatted list

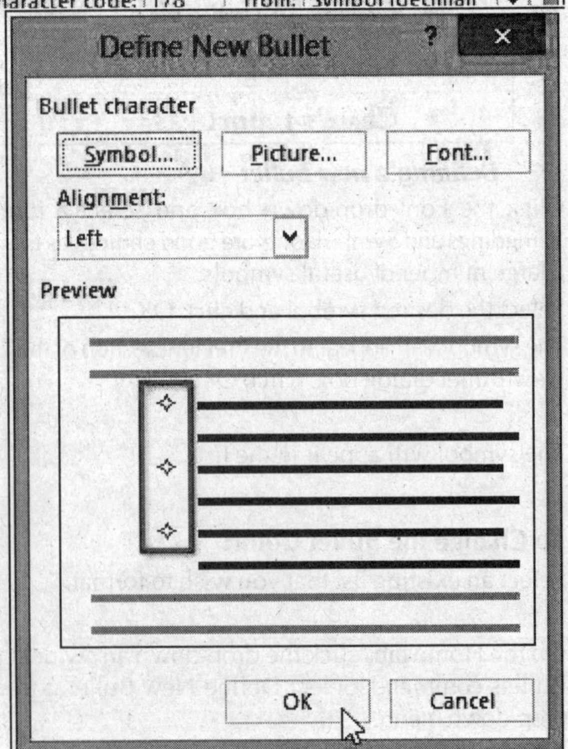

Preview of the new symbol

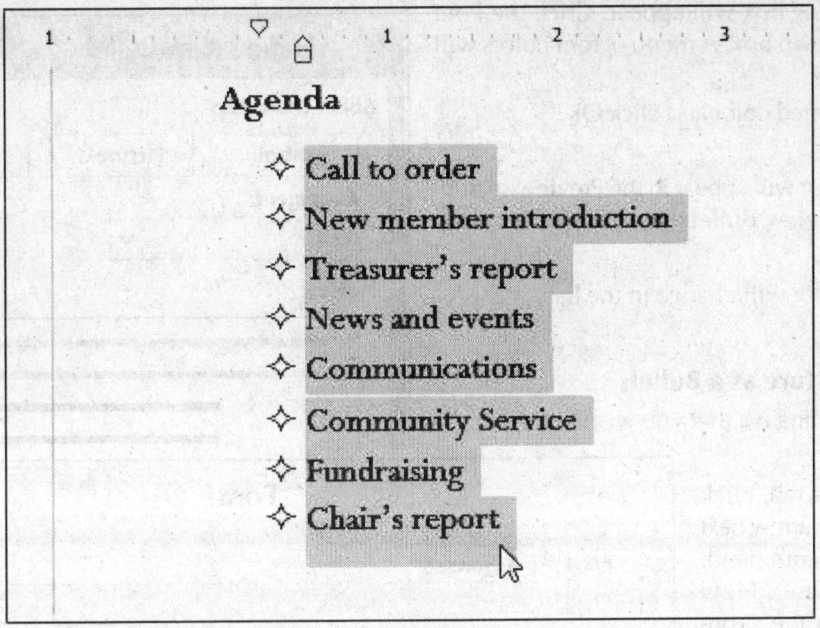

Selecting a list to format

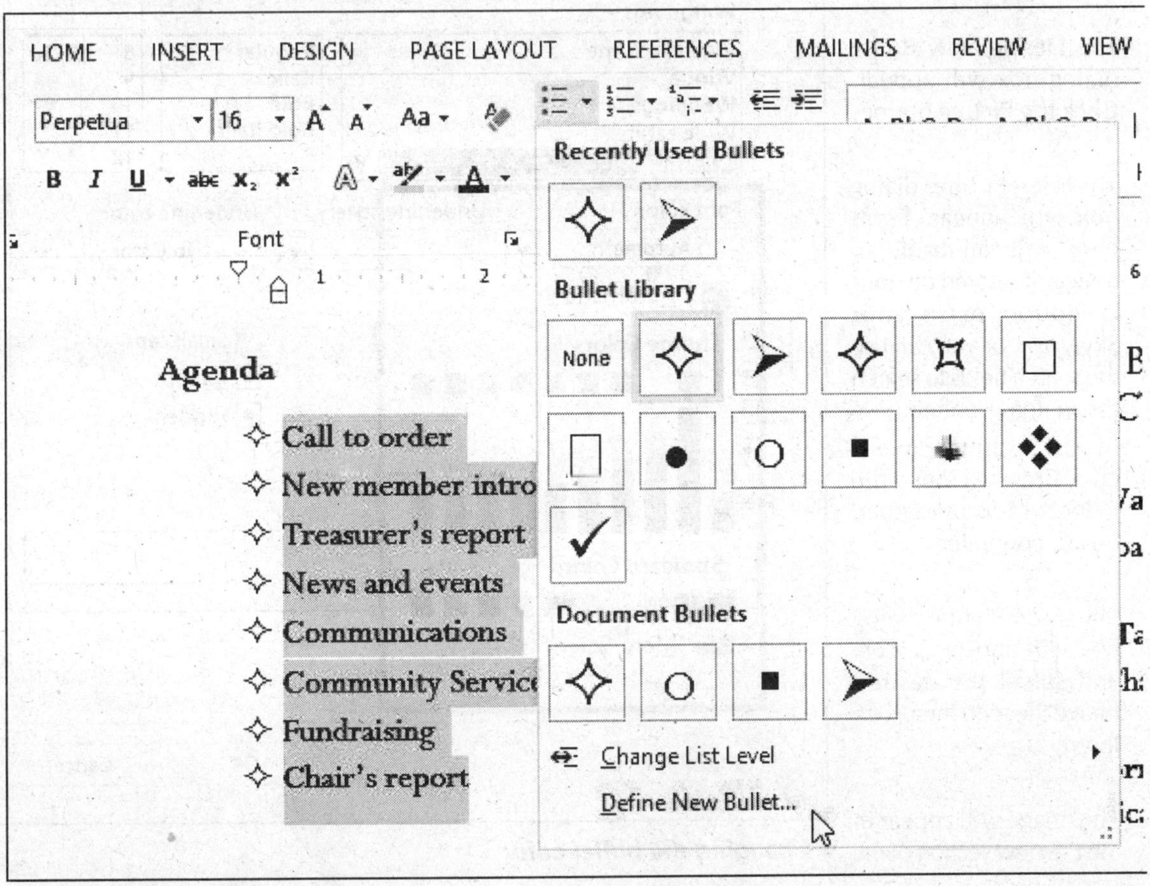

Selecting Define New Bullet...

The Font dialog box will appear. Click the Font Color drop-down box. A menu of font colors will appear.

Select the desired color and click OK.

The bullet color will appear in the Preview section of the Define New Bullet dialog box. Click OK.

The bullet color will change in the list.

To Use a Picture as a Bullet:

Select an existing list that you wish to format.

On the Home tab, click the drop-down arrow next to the Bullets command. Select Define New Bullet... from the drop-down menu.

The Define New Bullet dialog box will appear. Click the Picture button.

The Insert Pictures dialog box will appear. From here, you can locate an image file stored on your computer or in your SkyDrive, or you can use the search fields to search for an image online.

In our example, we'll click Browse From a file to locate a picture stored on our computer.

The Insert Picture dialog box will appear. Locate and select the desired image file, and then click Insert.

The image will appear in the Preview section of the

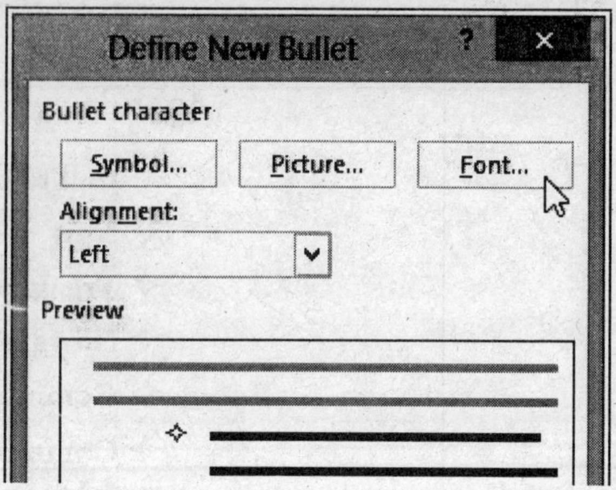

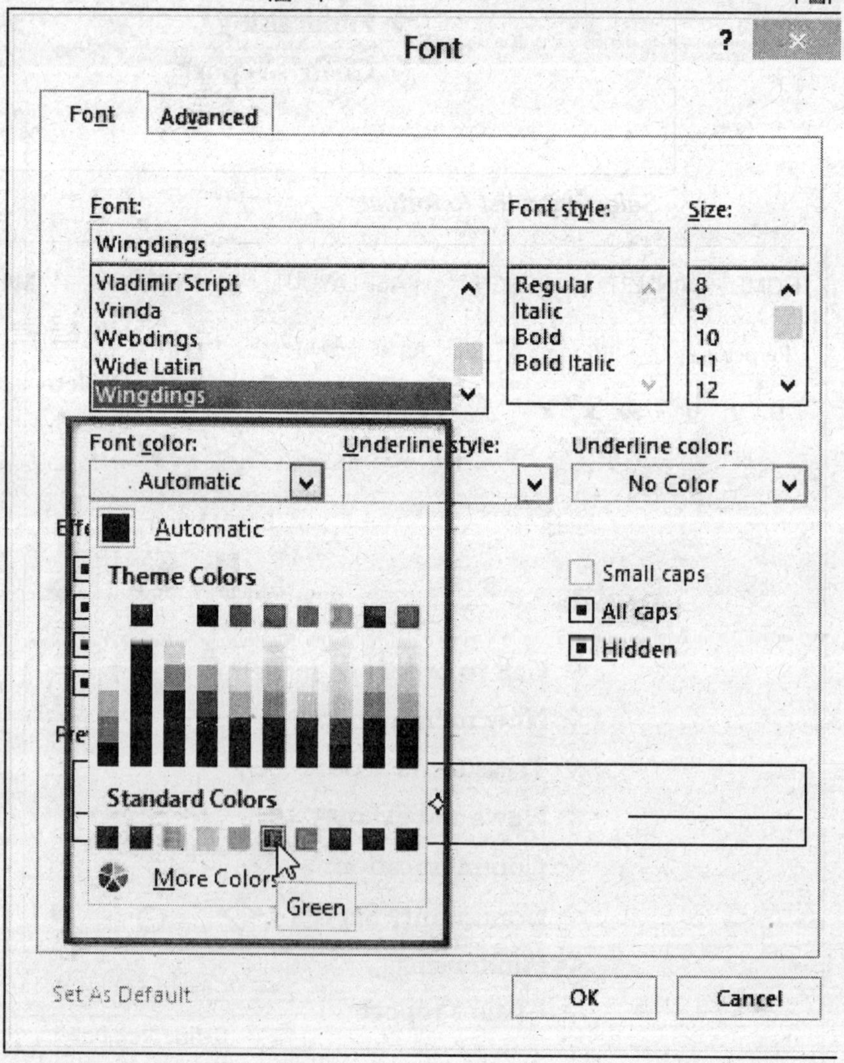

Changing the bullet color

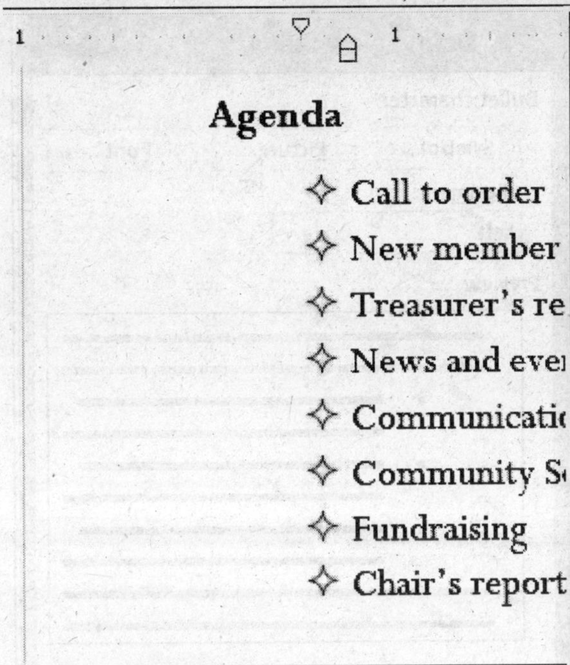

The new bullet color

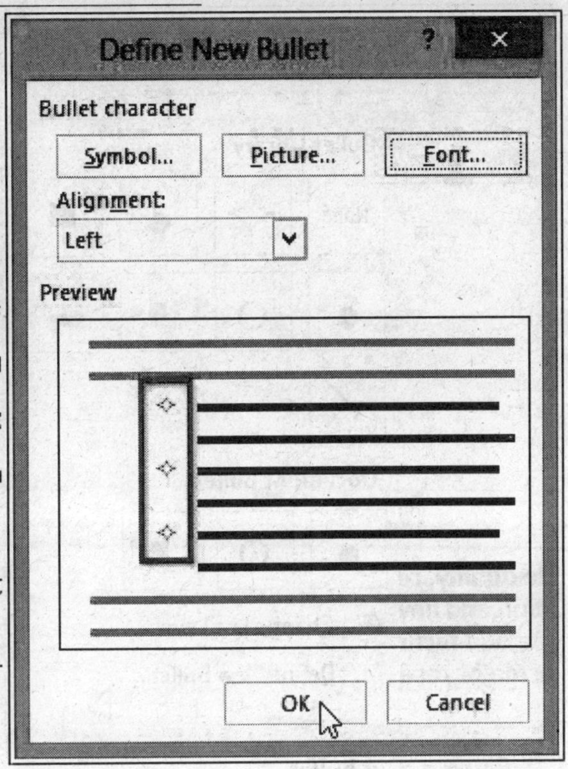

Clicking OK

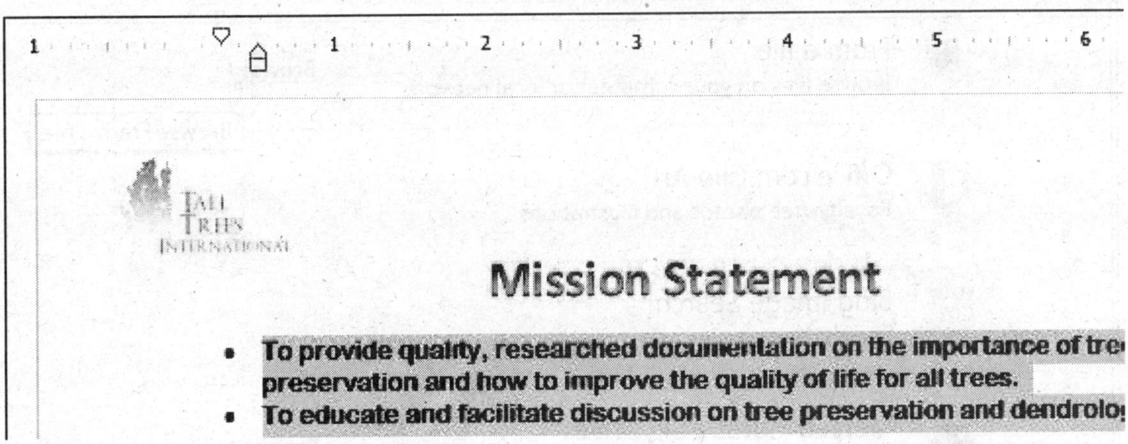

Define New Bullet dialog box. Click OK.

The image will appear in the list.

Not all pictures work well as bullets. Generally, it's best to use a simple graphic that has a white (or transparent) background. This ensures that the bullet will have a recognizable shape.

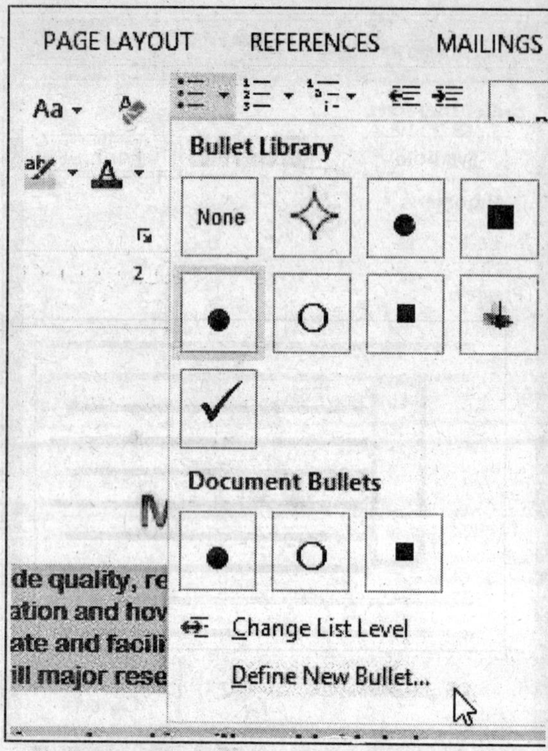

Defining a new bullet

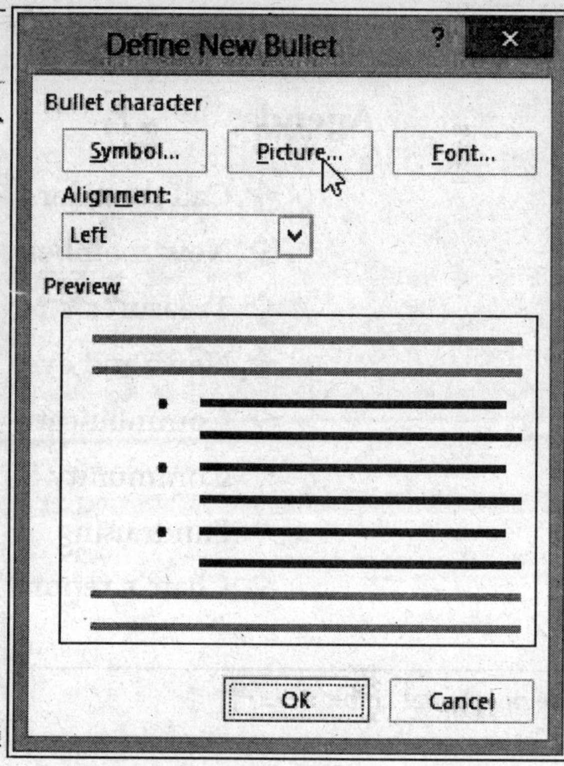

Clicking the Picture button

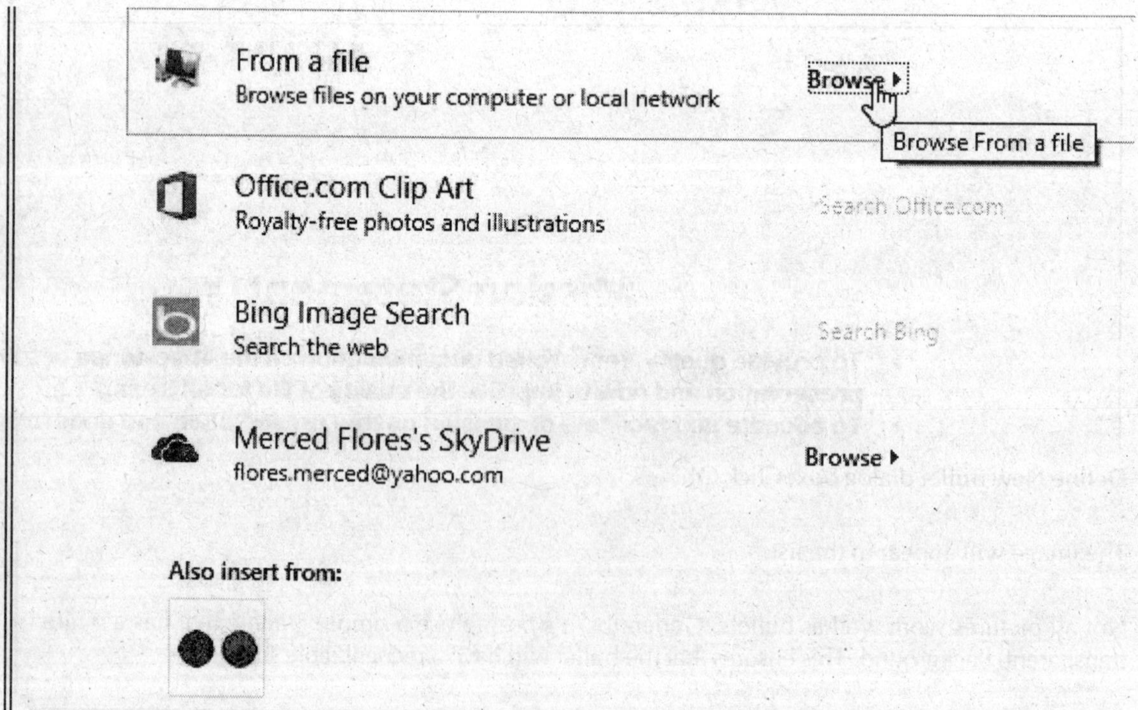

Clicking Browse From a file

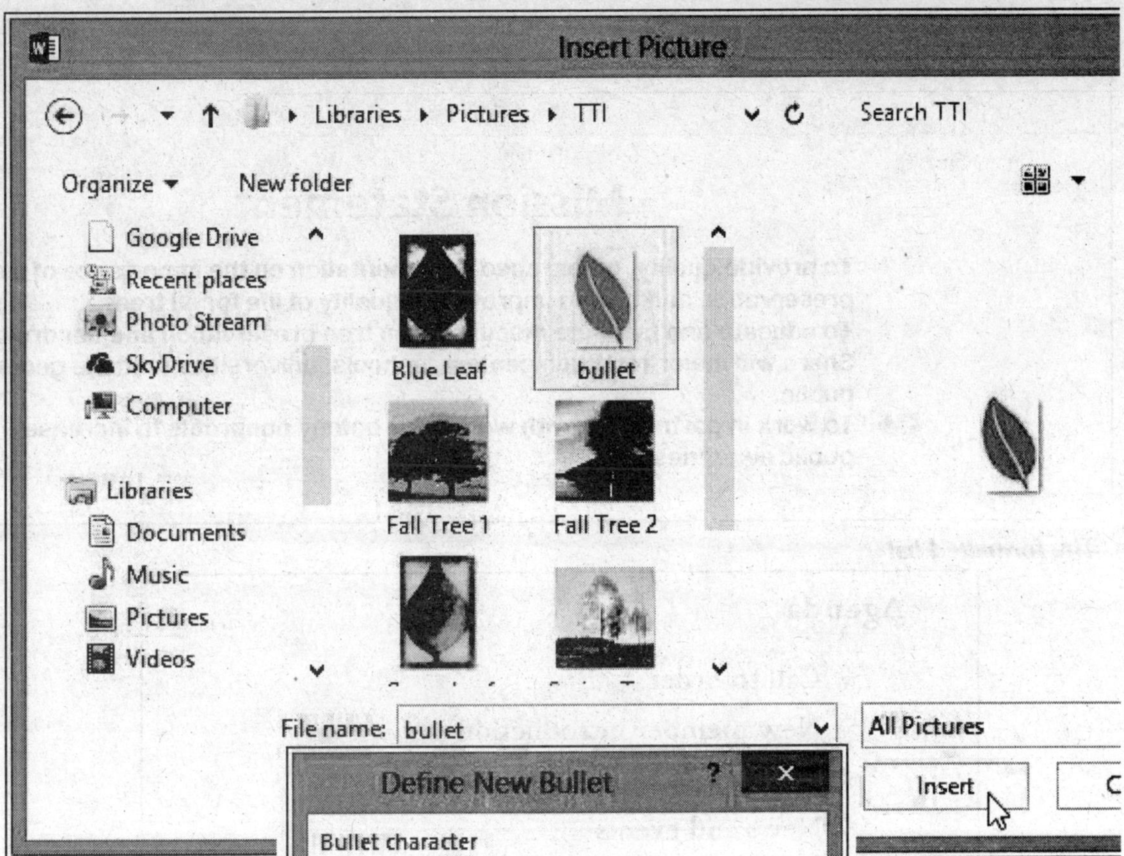

Inserting a picture

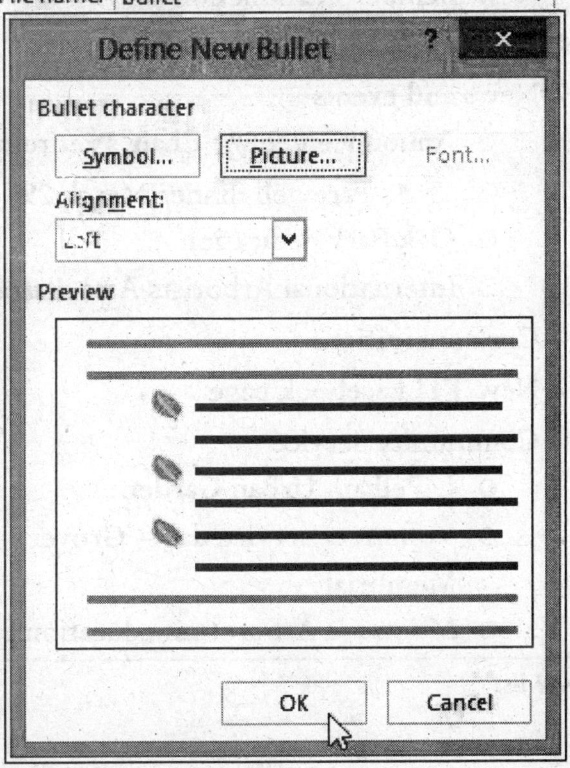

Preview of the picture

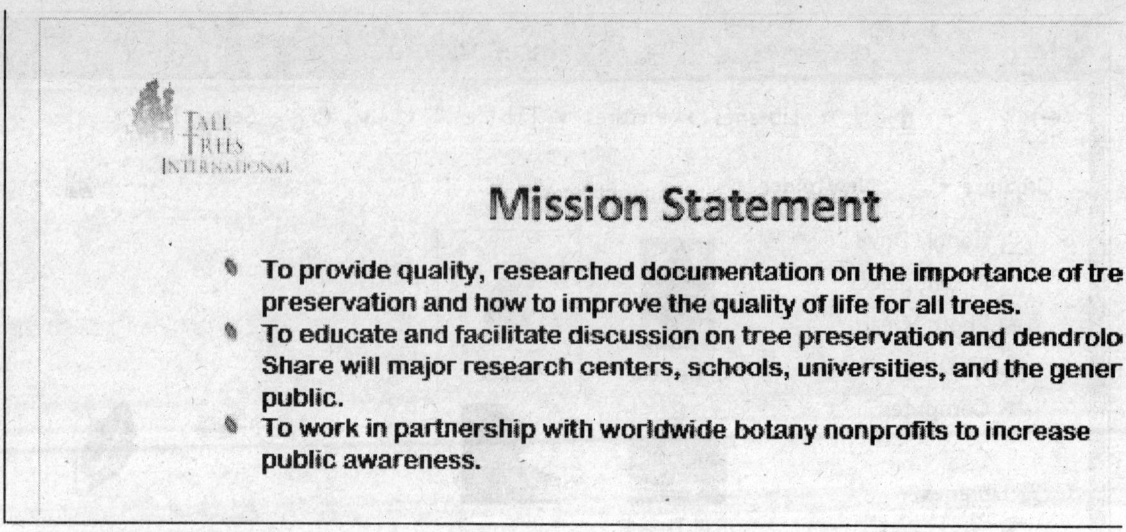
Tall Trees International

Mission Statement

- To provide quality, researched documentation on the importance of tre
preservation and how to improve the quality of life for all trees.
- To educate and facilitate discussion on tree preservation and dendrolo
Share will major research centers, schools, universities, and the gener
public.
- To work in partnership with worldwide botany nonprofits to increase public awareness.

The formatted list

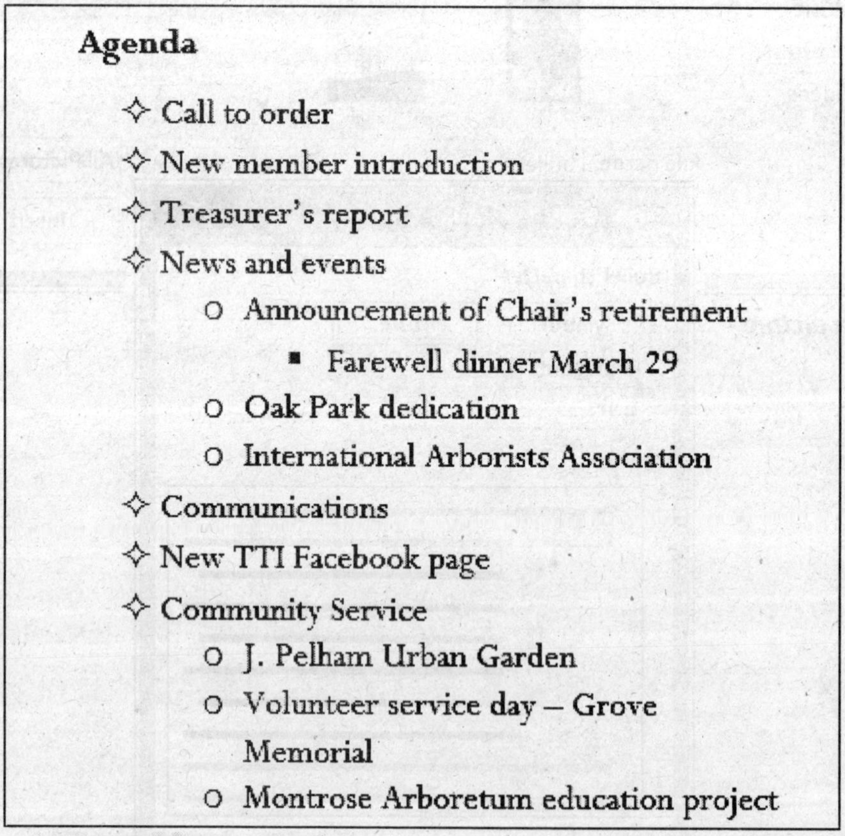
Agenda

- Call to order
- New member introduction
- Treasurer's report
- News and events
  - Announcement of Chair's retirement
    - Farewell dinner March 29
  - Oak Park dedication
  - International Arborists Association
- Communications
- New TTI Facebook page
- Community Service
  - J. Pelham Urban Garden
  - Volunteer service day – Grove Memorial
  - Montrose Arboretum education project

A multilevel list

Multilevel Lists

Multilevel lists allow you to create an outline with multiple levels. Any bulleted or numbered list can be turned into a multilevel list by using the Tab key.

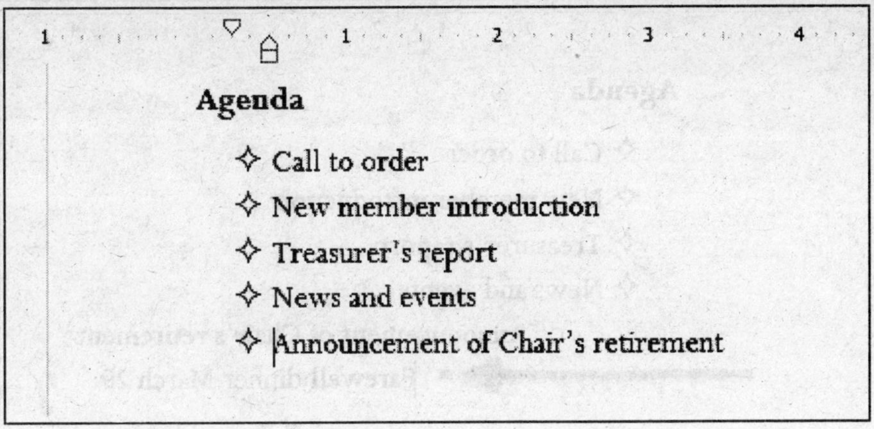

Placing the insertion point

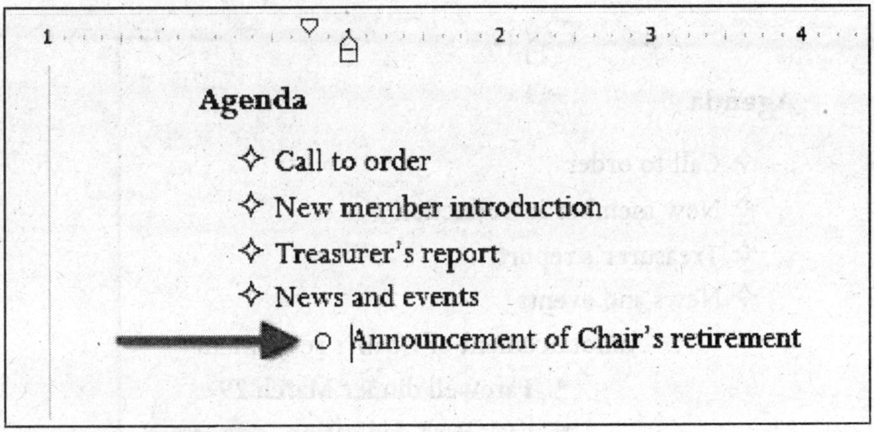

Increasing the indent level

To Create a Multilevel List:

Place the insertion point at the beginning of the line you wish to move.

Press the Tab key to increase the indent level of the line. The line will move to the right.

To Increase or Decrease an Indent Level:

You can make adjustments to the organization of a multilevel list by increasing or decreasing the indent levels. There are several ways to change the indent level:

To increase the indent by more than one level, place the insertion point at the beginning of the line and press the Tab key until the desired level is reached.

To decrease the indent level, place the insertion point at the beginning of the line, then hold the Shift key and press the Tab key.

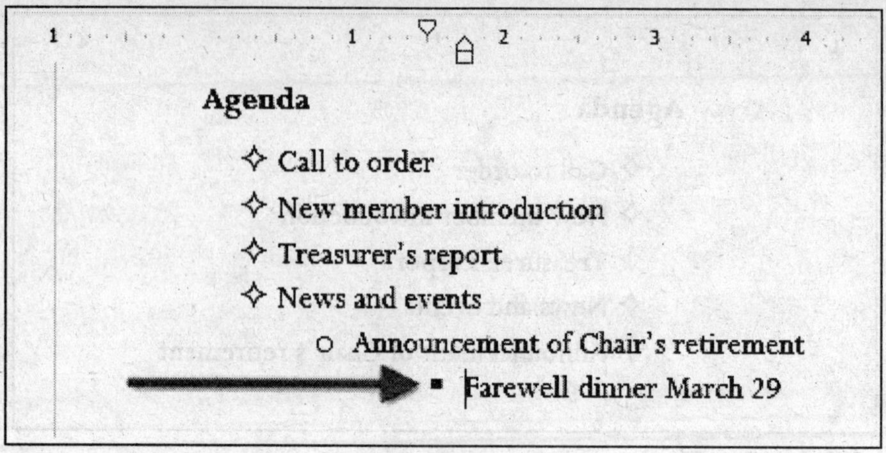

Increasing the indent level more than once

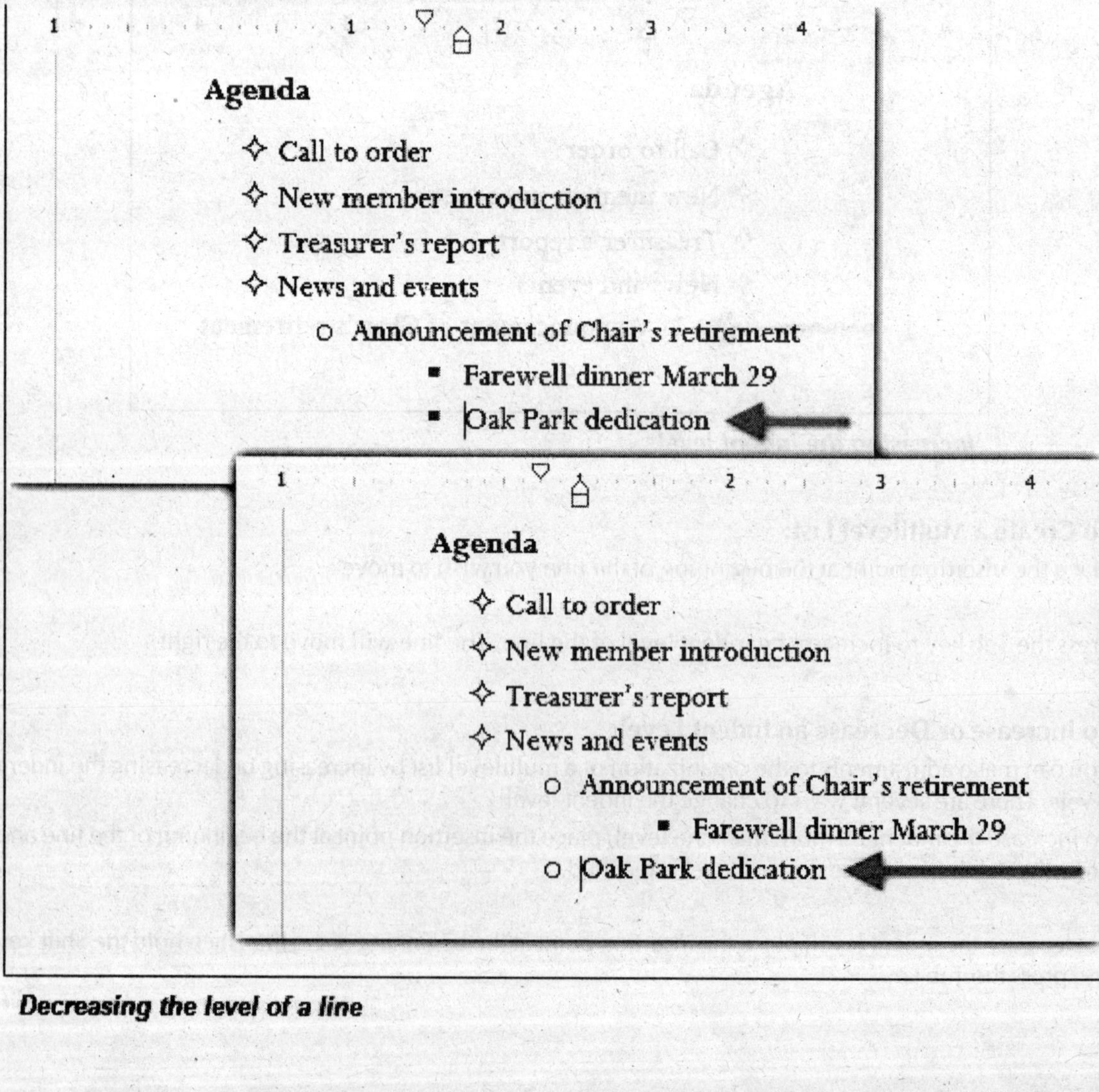

Decreasing the level of a line

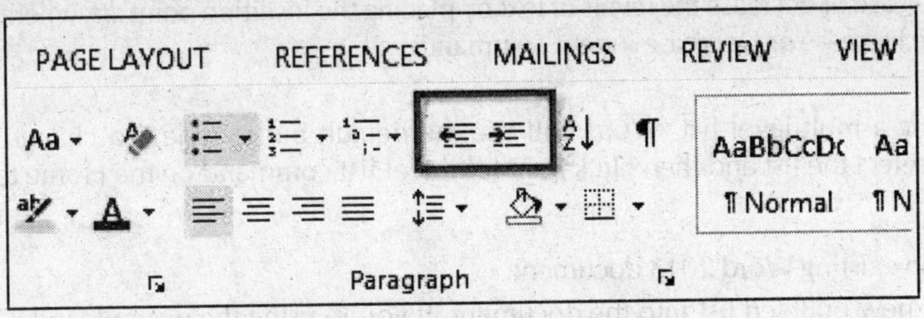

The Increase and Decrease indent commands

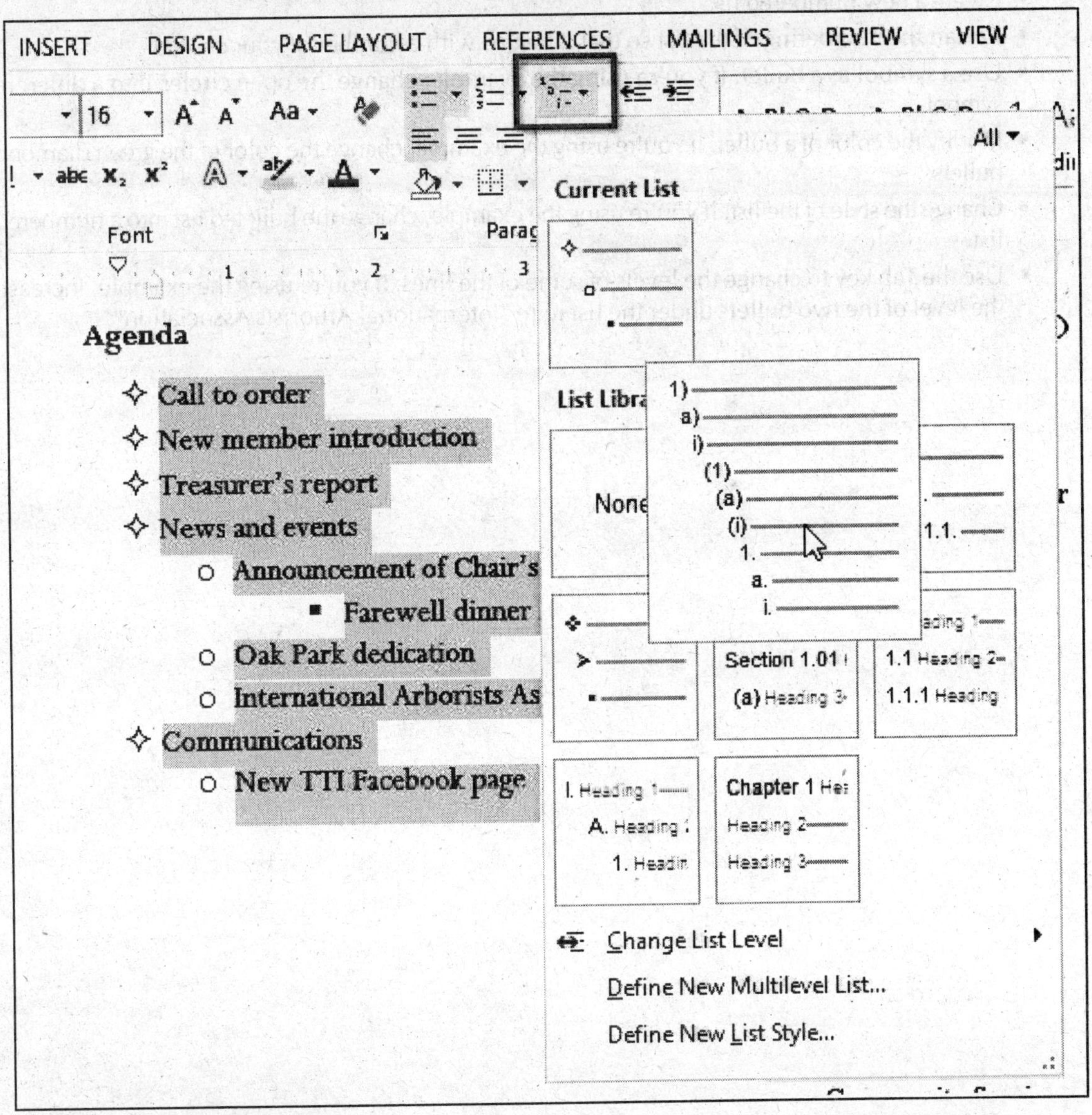

Formatting a multilevel list

You can also increase or decrease the levels of text by placing the insertion point anywhere in the line and then clicking the Increase or Decrease indent commands.

When formatting a multilevel list, Word will use the default bullet style. To change the style of a multilevel list, select the list and then click the Multilevel list command on the Home tab.

For Practice

- Open an existing Word 2013 document.
- Insert a new bulleted list into the document. If you're using the example, add "Fundraising", "Chair's Report", and "Other business" to the bottom of the list.
- Create a new numbered list.
- Restart the numbering of the list so that it begins with a number of your choice.
- Use a symbol as a bullet. If you're using the example, change the open circles into a different symbol.
- Modify the color of a bullet. If you're using the example, change the color of the green diamond bullets.
- Change the style of the list. If you're using the example, change the bulleted list into a numbered list.
- Use the Tab key to change the levels of some of the lines. If you're using the example, increase the level of the two bullets under the list item "International Arborists Association".

CHAPTER 11

Keyboard Shortcuts of Microsoft Word 2013

Introduction

Shortcut keys are key combinations that start commands. For example, you can press CTRL + O to open a file and CTRL + S to save a file, which is the same result as choosing Open and Save from the File menu.

Keyboard shortcuts for Microsoft Office Word

For keyboard shortcuts in which you press two or more keys simultaneously, the keys to press are separated by a plus sign (+) in Microsoft Office Word. For keyboard shortcuts in which you press one key immediately followed by another key, the keys to press are separated by a comma (,).

Microsoft Office basics

To do this	Press
Switch to the next window.	ALT+TAB
Switch to the previous window.	ALT+SHIFT+TAB
Close the active window.	CTRL+W or CTRL+F4
Restore the size of the active window after you maximize it.ALT+F5	
Move to a task pane from another pane in the program window (clockwise direction). You may need to press F6 more than once.	F6
Move to a task pane from another pane in the program window (counterclockwise direction).	SHIFT+F6
When more than one window is open, switch to the next window.	CTRL+F6
Switch to the previous window.	CTRL+SHIFT+F6
Maximize or restore a selected window.	CTRL+F10
Copy a picture of the screen to the Clipboard.	PRINT SCREEN
Copy a picture of the selected window to the Clipboard.	ALT+PRINT SCREEN

To do this	Press
Move from an open dialog box back to the document, for dialog boxes such as Find and Replace that support this behavior.	ALT+F6
Move to the next option or option group.	TAB
Move to the previous option or option group.	SHIFT+TAB
Switch to the next tab in a dialog box.	CTRL+TAB
Switch to the previous tab in a dialog box.	CTRL+SHIFT+TAB
Move between options in an open drop-down list, or between options in a group of options.	Arrow keys
Perform the action assigned to the selected button; select or clear the selected check box.	SPACEBAR
Select an option; select or clear a check box.	ALT+ the letter underlined in an option
Open a selected drop-down list.	ALT+DOWN ARROW
Select an option from a drop-down list.	First letter of an option in a drop-down list
Close a selected drop-down list; cancel a command and close a dialog box.	ESC
Run the selected command.	ENTER

An edit box is a blank in which you type or paste an entry, such as your user name or the path to a folder.

To do this	Press
Move to the beginning of the entry.	HOME
Move to the end of the entry.	END
Move one character to the left or right.	LEFT ARROW or RIGHT ARROW
Move one word to the left.	CTRL+LEFT ARROW
Move one word to the right.	CTRL+RIGHT ARROW

Select or unselect one character to the left.	SHIFT + LEFT ARROW
Select or unselect one character to the right.	SHIFT + RIGHT ARROW
Select or unselect one word to the left.	CTRL + SHIFT + LEFT ARROW
Select or unselect one word to the right.	CTRL + SHIFT + RIGHT ARROW
Select from the insertion point to the beginning of the entry.	SHIFT + HOME
Select from the insertion point to the end of the entry.	SHIFT + END

Use the Open and Save As dialog boxes

To do this	**Press**
Display the Open dialog box.	CTRL + F12 or CTRL + O
Display the Save As dialog box.	F12
Go to the previous folder.	ALT + 1
Up One Level button: Open the folder one level above the open folder.	ALT + 2
Delete button: Delete the selected folder or file.	DELETE
Create New Folder button: Create a new folder.	ALT + 4
Views button: Switch among available folder views.	ALT + 5
Display a shortcut menu for a selected item such as a folder or file.	SHIFT + F10
Move between options or areas in the dialog box.	TAB
Open the Look in list.	F4 or ALT + I
Update the file list.	F5

Undo and redo actions

To do this	**Press**
Cancel an action.	ESC
Undo an action.	CTRL + Z
Redo or repeat an action.	CTRL + Y

Access and use task panes and galleries

To do this	**Press**
Move to a task pane from another pane in the program window. (You may need to press F6 more than once.)	F6
When a menu is active, move to a task pane. (You may need to press CTRL + TAB more than once.)	CTRL + TAB
When a task pane is active, select the next or previous option in the task pane.	TAB or SHIFT + TAB
Display the full set of commands on the task pane menu.	CTRL + SPACEBAR
Perform the action assigned to the selected button.	SPACEBAR or ENTER
Open a drop-down menu for the selected gallery item.	SHIFT + F10
Select the first or last item in a gallery.	HOME or END
Scroll up or down in the selected gallery list.	PAGE UP or PAGE DOWN

Close a task pane

Press F6 to move to the task pane, if necessary.	Press CTRL + SPACEBAR.
Use the arrow keys to select Close, and then press ENTER.	

Access and use smart tags

To do this	Press
Display the shortcut menu for the selected item.	SHIFT+F10
Display the menu or message for a smart tag or for the AutoCorrect Options button or the Paste options button . If more than one smart tag is present, switch to the next smart tag and display its menu or message.	ALT+SHIFT+F10
Select the next item on a smart tag menu.	DOWN ARROW
Select the previous item on a smart tag menu.	UP ARROW
Perform the action for the selected item on a smart tag menu.	ENTER
Close the smart tag menu or message.	ESC

If you have access to the World Wide Web, you can download Microsoft Office Sounds from the Microsoft Office Online Web site. After you install the sound files, do the following in Microsoft Office Access 2013, Microsoft Office Excel 2013, Microsoft Office PowerPoint 2013, or Microsoft Office Word 2013:

Press ALT+F to open the menu under the Microsoft Office Button , and then press I to open Program Options.

Press A to select Advanced, and then press TAB to move to the Advanced Options for working with Program.

Press ALT+S twice to move to the Provide feedback with soundcheck box, which is under General, and then press SPACEBAR.

Press TAB repeatedly to select OK, and then press ENTER.

When you select or clear this check box, the setting affects all Office programs that support sound.

Navigating the Ribbon user interface

Access any command with a few keystrokes

Access keys provide a way to quickly use a command by pressing a few keys, no matter where you are in the program. Every command in Office Word 2013 can be accessed by using an access key. You can get to most commands by using two to five keystrokes. To use an access key:

Press ALT.

The KeyTips are displayed over each feature that is available in the current view.

Change the keyboard focus without using the mouse

Another way to use the keyboard to work with Ribbon programs is to move the focus among the tabs and commands until you find the feature that you want to use. The following table lists some ways to move the keyboard focus without using the mouse.

To do this	**Press**
Select the active tab of the Ribbon and activate the access keys.	ALT or F10. Press either of these keys again to move back to the document and cancel the access keys.
Move to another tab of the Ribbon.	F10 to select the active tab, and then LEFT ARROW or RIGHT ARROW
Hide or show the Ribbon.	CTRL+F1
Display the shortcut menu for the selected command.	SHIFT+F10

Move the focus to select each of the following areas of the window:

- Active tab of the Ribbon

- Any open task panes
- Toolbar at the bottom of the window
- Your document

Move the focus to each command on the Ribbon, forward or backward, respectively.	TAB or SHIFT+TAB
Move down, up, left, or right, respectively, among the items on the Ribbon.	DOWN ARROW, UP ARROW, LEFT ARROW, or RIGHT ARROW
Activate the selected command or control on the Ribbon.	SPACEBAR or ENTER
Open the selected menu or gallery on the Ribbon.	SPACEBAR or ENTER
Activate a command or control on the Ribbon so you can modify a value.	ENTER
Finish modifying a value in a control on the Ribbon, and move focus back to the document.	ENTER
Get help on the selected command or control on the Ribbon. (If no Help topic is associated with the selected command, a general Help topic about the program is shown instead.)	F1

Quick reference for Microsoft Office Word

Common tasks in Microsoft Office Word

To do this	Press
Create a nonbreaking space.	CTRL+SHIFT+SPACEBAR
Create a nonbreaking hyphen.	CTRL+HYPHEN
Make letters bold.	CTRL+B
Make letters italic.	CTRL+I
Make letters underline.	CTRL+U
Decrease font size one value.	CTRL+SHIFT+<
Increase font size one value.	CTRL+SHIFT+>
Decrease font size 1 point.	CTRL+[
Increase font size 1 point.	CTRL+]
Remove paragraph or character formatting.	CTRL+SPACEBAR
Copy the selected text or object.	CTRL+C
Cut the selected text or object.	CTRL+X
Paste text or an object.	CTRL+V
Paste special	CTRL+ALT+V
Paste formatting only	CTRL+SHIFT+V
Undo the last action.	CTRL+Z
Redo the last action.	CTRL+Y
Open the Word Count dialog box.	CTRL+SHIFT+G

Working with documents and Web pages

Create, view, and save documents

To do this	Press
Create a new document of the same type as the current or most recent document.	CTRL+N

Open a document.	CTRL+O
Close a document.	CTRL+W
Split the document window.	ALT+CTRL+S
Remove the document window split.	ALT+SHIFT+C
Save a document.	CTRL+S

Find, replace, and browse through text

To do this	Press
Find text, formatting, and special items.	CTRL+F
Repeat find (after closing Find and Replace window).	ALT+CTRL+Y
Replace text, specific formatting, and special items.	CTRL+H
Go to a page, bookmark, footnote, table, comment, graphic, or other location.	CTRL+G
Switch between the last four places that you have edited.	ALT+CTRL+Z
Open a list of browse options. Press the arrow keys to select an option, and then press ENTER to browse through a document by using the selected option.	ALT+CTRL+HOME
Move to the previous edit location.	CTRL+PAGE UP
Move to the next edit location.	CTRL+PAGE DOWN

Switch to another view

To do this	Press
Switch to Print Layout view.	ALT+CTRL+P
Switch to Outline view.	ALT+CTRL+O
Switch to Draft view.	ALT+CTRL+N

Outline view

To do this	Press
Promote a paragraph.	ALT+SHIFT+LEFT ARROW
Demote a paragraph.	ALT+SHIFT+RIGHT ARROW
Demote to body text.	CTRL+SHIFT+N
Move selected paragraphs up.	ALT+SHIFT+UP ARROW
Move selected paragraphs down.	ALT+SHIFT+DOWN ARROW
Expand text under a heading.	ALT+SHIFT+PLUS SIGN
Collapse text under a heading.	ALT+SHIFT+MINUS SIGN
Expand or collapse all text or headings.	ALT+SHIFT+A
Hide or display character formatting.	The slash (/) key on the numeric keypad
Show the first line of body text or all body text.	ALT+SHIFT+L
Show all headings with the Heading 1 style.	ALT+SHIFT+1
Show all headings up to Heading n.	ALT+SHIFT+n
Insert a tab character.	CTRL+TAB

Print and preview documents

To do this	Press
Print a document.	CTRL+P
Switch in or out of print preview.	ALT+CTRL+I

Move around the preview page when zoomed in.	Arrow keys
Move by one preview page when zoomed out.	PAGE UP or PAGE DOWN
Move to the first preview page when zoomed out.	CTRL+HOME
Move to the last preview page when zoomed out.	CTRL+END

Review documents

To do this	Press
Insert a comment.	ALT+CTRL+M
Turn change tracking on or off.	CTRL+SHIFT+E
Close the Reviewing Pane if it is open.	ALT+SHIFT+C

Full Screen Reading view

Some screen readers may not be compatible with Full Screen Reading view.

To do this	Press
Go to beginning of document.	HOME
Go to end of document.	END
Go to page n.	n, ENTER
Exit reading layout view.	ESC

References, footnotes, and endnotes

To do this	Press
Mark a table of contents entry.	ALT+SHIFT+O
Mark a table of authorities entry (citation).	ALT+SHIFT+I
Mark an index entry.	ALT+SHIFT+X
Insert a footnote.	ALT+CTRL+F
Insert an endnote.	ALT+CTRL+D

Work with Web pages

To do this	Press
Insert a hyperlink.	CTRL+K
Go back one page.	ALT+LEFT ARROW
Go forward one page.	ALT+RIGHT ARROW
Refresh.	F9

Edit and move text and graphics

Delete text and graphics

To do this	Press
Delete one character to the left.	BACKSPACE
Delete one word to the left.	CTRL+BACKSPACE
Delete one character to the right.	DELETE
Delete one word to the right.	CTRL+DELETE
Cut selected text to the Office Clipboard.	CTRL+X
Undo the last action.	CTRL+Z
Cut to the Spike.	CTRL+F3

Copy and move text and graphics

To do this	**Press**
Open the Office Clipboard	Press ALT+H to move to the Home tab, and then press F,O.
Copy selected text or graphics to the Office Clipboard.	CTRL+C
Cut selected text or graphics to the Office Clipboard.	CTRL+X
Paste the most recent addition to the Office Clipboard.	CTRL+V
Move text or graphics once.	F2 (then move the cursor and press ENTER)
Copy text or graphics once.	SHIFT+F2 (then move the cursor and press ENTER)
When text or an object is selected, open the Create New Building Block dialog box.	ALT+F3
When the building block — for example, a SmartArt graphic — is selected, display the shortcut menu that is associated with it.	SHIFT+F10
Cut to the Spike.	CTRL+F3
Paste the Spike contents.	CTRL+SHIFT+F3
Copy the header or footer used in the previous section of the document.	ALT+SHIFT+R

Insert special characters

To insert this	**Press**
A field	CTRL+F9
A line break	SHIFT+ENTER
A page break	CTRL+ENTER
A column break	CTRL+SHIFT+ENTER
An em dash	ALT+CTRL+MINUS SIGN
An en dash	CTRL+MINUS SIGN
An optional hyphen	CTRL+HYPHEN
A nonbreaking hyphen	CTRL+SHIFT+HYPHEN
A nonbreaking space	CTRL+SHIFT+SPACEBAR
The copyright symbol	ALT+CTRL+C
The registered trademark symbol	ALT+CTRL+R
The trademark symbol	ALT+CTRL+T
An ellipsis	ALT+CTRL+PERIOD
A single opening quotation mark	CTRL+'(single quotation mark), '(single quotation mark)
A single closing quotation mark	CTRL+' (single quotation mark), ' (single quotation mark)
Double opening quotation marks	CTRL+' (single quotation mark), SHIFT+' (single quotation mark)
Double closing quotation marks	CTRL+' (single quotation mark), SHIFT+' (single quotation mark)
An AutoText entry	ENTER (after you type the first few characters of the AutoText entry name and when the ScreenTip appears)

Insert characters by using character codes

To do this	Press
Insert the Unicode character for the specified Unicode (hexadecimal) character code. For example, to insert the euro currency symbol ( ), type 20AC, and then hold down ALT and press X.	The character code, ALT+X
Find out the Unicode character code for the selected character	ALT+X
Insert the ANSI character for the specified ANSI (decimal) character code. For example, to insert the euro currency symbol, hold down ALT and press 0128 on the numeric keypad.	ALT + the character code (on the numeric keypad)

Select text and graphics

Select text by holding down SHIFT and using the arrow keys to move the cursor.

Extend a selection

To do this	Press
Turn extend mode on.	F8
Select the nearest character.	F8, and then press LEFT ARROW or RIGHT ARROW
Increase the size of a selection.	F8 (press once to select a word, twice to select a sentence, and so on)
Reduce the size of a selection.	SHIFT+F8
Turn extend mode off.	ESC
Extend a selection one character to the right.	SHIFT+RIGHT ARROW
Extend a selection one character to the left.	SHIFT+LEFT ARROW
Extend a selection to the end of a word.	CTRL+SHIFT+RIGHT ARROW
Extend a selection to the beginning of a word.	CTRL+SHIFT+LEFT ARROW
Extend a selection to the end of a line.	SHIFT+END
Extend a selection to the beginning of a line.	SHIFT+HOME
Extend a selection one line down.	SHIFT+DOWN ARROW
Extend a selection one line up.	SHIFT+UP ARROW
Extend a selection to the end of a paragraph.	CTRL+SHIFT+DOWN ARROW
Extend a selection to the beginning of a paragraph.	CTRL+SHIFT+UP ARROW
Extend a selection one screen down.	SHIFT+PAGE DOWN
Extend a selection one screen up.	SHIFT+PAGE UP
Extend a selection to the beginning of a document.	CTRL+SHIFT+HOME
Extend a selection to the end of a document.	CTRL+SHIFT+END
Extend a selection to the end of a window.	ALT+CTRL+SHIFT+PAGE DOWN
Extend a selection to include the entire document.	CTRL+A
Select a vertical block of text.	CTRL+SHIFT+F8, and then use the arrow keys; press ESC to cancel selection mode
Extend a selection to a specific location in a document.	F8+arrow keys; press ESC to cancel selection mode

Select text and graphics in a table

To do this	**Press**
Select the next cell's contents.	TAB
Select the preceding cell's contents.	SHIFT+TAB

Extend a selection to adjacent cells.

Hold down SHIFT and press an arrow key repeatedly Select a column.

Use the arrow keys to move to the column's top or bottom cell, and then do one of the following:

- Press SHIFT+ALT+PAGE DOWN to select the column from top to bottom.
- Press SHIFT+ALT+PAGE UP to select the column from bottom to top.

Extend a selection (or block).

CTRL+SHIFT+F8, and then use the arrow keys; press ESC to cancel selection mode

Select an entire table. ALT+5 on the numeric keypad (with NUM LOCK off)

Select an entire table.	ALT+5 on the numeric keypad (with NUM LOCK off)

Move through your document

To move	**Press**
One character to the left	LEFT ARROW
One character to the right	RIGHT ARROW
One word to the left	CTRL+LEFT ARROW
One word to the right	CTRL+RIGHT ARROW
One paragraph up	CTRL+UP ARROW
One paragraph down	CTRL+DOWN ARROW
One cell to the left (in a table)	SHIFT+TAB
One cell to the right (in a table)	TAB
Up one line	UP ARROW
Down one line	DOWN ARROW
To the end of a line	END
To the beginning of a line	HOME
To the top of the window	ALT+CTRL+PAGE UP
To the end of the window	ALT+CTRL+PAGE DOWN
Up one screen (scrolling)	PAGE UP
Down one screen (scrolling)	PAGE DOWN
To the top of the next page	CTRL+PAGE DOWN
To the top of the previous page	CTRL+PAGE UP
To the end of a document	CTRL+END
To the beginning of a document	CTRL+HOME
To a previous revision	SHIFT+F5
After opening a document, to the location you were working in when the document was last closed	SHIFT+F5

Move around in a table

To move	**Press**
To the next cell in a row	TAB
To the previous cell in a row	SHIFT+TAB

To the first cell in a row	ALT+HOME
To the last cell in a row	ALT+END
To the first cell in a column	ALT+PAGE UP
To the last cell in a column	ALT+PAGE DOWN
To the previous row	UP ARROW
To the next row	DOWN ARROW
One row up	ALT+SHIFT+UP ARROW
One row down	ALT+SHIFT+DOWN ARROW

Insert paragraphs and tab characters in a table

To insert	**Press**
New paragraphs in a cell	ENTER
Tab characters in a cell	CTRL+TAB

Character and paragraph formatting

Copy formatting

To do this	**Press**
Copy formatting from text.	CTRL+SHIFT+C
Apply copied formatting to text.	CTRL+SHIFT+V

Change or resize the font

The following keyboard shortcuts do not work in Full Screen Reading mode.

To do this	**Press**
Open the Font dialog box to change the font.	CTRL+SHIFT+F
Increase the font size.	CTRL+SHIFT+ >
Decrease the font size.	CTRL+SHIFT+ <
Increase the font size by 1 point.	CTRL+]
Decrease the font size by 1 point.	CTRL+[

Apply character formats

To do this	**Press**
Open the Font dialog box to change the formatting of characters.	CTRL+D
Change the case of letters.	SHIFT+F3
Format all letters as capitals.	CTRL+SHIFT+A
Apply bold formatting.	CTRL+B
Apply an underline.	CTRL+U
Underline words but not spaces.	CTRL+SHIFT+W
Double-underline text.	CTRL+SHIFT+D
Apply hidden text formatting.	CTRL+SHIFT+H
Apply italic formatting.	CTRL+I
Format letters as small capitals.	CTRL+SHIFT+K
Apply subscript formatting (automatic spacing).	CTRL+EQUAL SIGN
Apply superscript formatting (automatic spacing).	CTRL+SHIFT+PLUS SIGN
Remove manual character formatting.	CTRL+SPACEBAR

Change the selection to the Symbol font. CTRL + SHIFT + Q

View and copy text formats

To do this	Press
Display nonprinting characters.	CTRL + SHIFT + * (asterisk on numeric keypad does not work)
Review text formatting.	SHIFT + F1 (then click the text with the formatting you want to review)
Copy formats.	CTRL + SHIFT + C
Paste formats.	CTRL + SHIFT + V

Set the line spacing

To do this	Press
Single-space lines.	CTRL + 1
Double-space lines.	CTRL + 2
Set 1.5-line spacing.	CTRL + 5
Add or remove one line space preceding a paragraph.	CTRL + 0 (zero)

Align paragraphs

To do this	Press
Switch a paragraph between centered and left-aligned.	CTRL + E
Switch a paragraph between justified and left-aligned.	CTRL + J
Switch a paragraph between right-aligned and left-aligned.	CTRL + R
Left align a paragraph.	CTRL + L
Indent a paragraph from the left.	CTRL + M
Remove a paragraph indent from the left.	CTRL + SHIFT + M
Create a hanging indent.	CTRL + T
Reduce a hanging indent.	CTRL + SHIFT + T
Remove paragraph formatting.	CTRL + Q

Apply paragraph styles

To do this	Press
Open Apply Styles task pane.	CTRL + SHIFT + S
Open Styles task pane.	ALT + CTRL + SHIFT + S
Start AutoFormat.	ALT + CTRL + K
Apply the Normal style.	CTRL + SHIFT + N
Apply the Heading 1 style.	ALT + CTRL + 1
Apply the Heading 2 style.	ALT + CTRL + 2
Apply the Heading 3 style.	ALT + CTRL + 3

Close the Styles task pane

If the Styles task pane is not selected, press F6 to select it. Press CTRL + SPACEBAR.

Use the arrow keys to select Close, and then press ENTER.

Insert and edit objects

Insert an object

Press ALT, N, J, and then J to open the Object dialog box.

Do one of the following.

- Press DOWN ARROW to select an object type, and then press ENTER to create an object.
- Press CTRL+TAB to switch to the Create from File tab, and then type the file name of the object that you want to insert or browse to the file.

Edit an object

With the cursor positioned to the left of the object in your document, select the object by pressing SHIFT+RIGHT ARROW.

Press SHIFT+F10.

Press the TAB key to get to Object name Object, press ENTER, and then press ENTER again.

Insert SmartArt graphics

Press and release ALT, N, and then M to select SmartArt.

Press the arrow keys to select the type of graphic that you want.

Press TAB, and then press the arrow keys to select the graphic that you want to insert.

Press ENTER.

Insert WordArt

Press and release ALT, N, and then W to select WordArt.

Press the arrow keys to select the WordArt style that you want, and then press ENTER.

Type the text that you want.

Press TAB, and then press ENTER.

Mail merge and fields

Perform a mail merge

You must be on the Mailings tab to use these keyboard shortcuts.

To do this	Press
Preview a mail merge.	ALT+SHIFT+K
Merge a document.	ALT+SHIFT+N
Print the merged document.	ALT+SHIFT+M
Edit a mail-merge data document.	ALT+SHIFT+E
Insert a merge field.	ALT+SHIFT+F

Work with fields

To do this	Press
Insert a DATE field.	ALT+SHIFT+D
Insert a LISTNUM field.	ALT+CTRL+L
Insert a PAGE field.	ALT+SHIFT+P
Insert a TIME field.	ALT+SHIFT+T
Insert an empty field.	CTRL+F9
Update linked information in a Microsoft Office Word source document.	CTRL+SHIFT+F7
Update selected fields.	F9
Unlink a field.	CTRL+SHIFT+F9
Switch between a selected field code and its result.	SHIFT+F9
Switch between all field codes and their results.	ALT+F9

Run GOTOBUTTON or MACROBUTTON from the field that displays the field results.	ALT+SHIFT+F9
Go to the next field.	F11
Go to the previous field.	SHIFT+F11
Lock a field.	CTRL+F11
Unlock a field.	CTRL+SHIFT+F11

Language bar

Handwriting recognition

To do this	Press
Switch between languages or keyboard layouts.	Left ALT+SHIFT
Display a list of correction alternatives.	+C
Turn handwriting on or off.	+H
Turn Japanese Input Method Editor (IME) on 101 keyboard on or off.	ALT+~
Turn Korean IME on 101 keyboard on or off.	Right ALT
Turn Chinese IME on 101 keyboard on or off.	CTRL+SPACEBAR

Tips

- You can choose the key combination for switching between languages or keyboard layouts in the Advanced Key Setting dialog box. To open the Advanced Key Setting dialog box, right-click the Language bar, and then click Settings. Under Preferences, click Key Settings.
- The Windows logo key is available on the bottom row of keys on most keyboards.

Function key reference

Function keys

To do this	Press
Get Help or visit Microsoft Office Online.	F1
Move text or graphics.	F2
Repeat the last action.	F4
Choose the Go To command (Home tab).	F5
Go to the next pane or frame.	F6
Choose the Spelling command (Review tab).	F7
Extend a selection.	F8
Update the selected fields.	F9
Show KeyTips.	F10
Go to the next field.	F11
Choose the Save As command (Microsoft Office Button).	F12

SHIFT+Function key

To do this	Press
Start context-sensitive Help or reveal formatting.	SHIFT+F1
Copy text.	SHIFT+F2
Change the case of letters.	SHIFT+F3
Repeat a Find or Go To action.	SHIFT+F4
Move to the last change.	SHIFT+F5

Go to the previous pane or frame (after pressing F6).	SHIFT+F6
Choose the Thesaurus command (Review tab, Proofing group).	SHIFT+F7
Shrink a selection.	SHIFT+F8
Switch between a field code and its result.	SHIFT+F9
Display a shortcut menu.	SHIFT+F10
Go to the previous field.	SHIFT+F11
Choose the Save command (Microsoft Office Button).	SHIFT+F12

CTRL+Function key

To do this	**Press**
Choose the Print Preview command (Microsoft Office Button).	CTRL+F2
Cut to the Spike.	CTRL+F3
Close the window.	CTRL+F4
Go to the next window.	CTRL+F6
Insert an empty field.	CTRL+F9
Maximize the document window.	CTRL+F10
Lock a field.	CTRL+F11
Choose the Open command (Microsoft Office Button).	CTRL+F12

CTRL+SHIFT+Function key

To do this	**Press**
Insert the contents of the Spike.	CTRL+SHIFT+F3
Edit a bookmark.	CTRL+SHIFT+F5
Go to the previous window.	CTRL+SHIFT+F6
Update linked information in an Office Word 2013 source document.	CTRL+SHIFT+F7
Extend a selection or block.	CTRL+SHIFT+F8, and then press an arrow key
Unlink a field.	CTRL+SHIFT+F9
Unlock a field.	CTRL+SHIFT+F11
Choose the Print command (Microsoft Office Button).	CTRL+SHIFT+F12

ALT+Function key

To do this	Press
Go to the next field.	ALT+F1
Create a new Building Block.	ALT+F3
Exit Office Word 2013.	ALT+F4
Restore the program window size.	ALT+F5
Move from an open dialog box back to the document, for dialog boxes such as Find and Replace that support this behavior.	ALT+F6
Find the next misspelling or grammatical error.	ALT+F7
Run a macro.	ALT+F8
Switch between all field codes and their results.	ALT+F9
Maximize the program window.	ALT+F10
Display Microsoft Visual Basic code.	ALT+F11

ALT+SHIFT+Function key

To do this	**Press**
Go to the previous field.	ALT+SHIFT+F1
Choose the Save command (Microsoft Office Button).	ALT+SHIFT+F2
Display the Research task pane.	ALT+SHIFT+F7
Run GOTOBUTTON or MACROBUTTON from the field that displays the field results.	ALT+SHIFT+F9
Display a menu or message for a smart tag.	ALT+SHIFT+F10

CTRL+ALT+Function key

To do this	**Press**
Display Microsoft System Information.	CTRL+ALT+F1
Choose the Open command (Microsoft Office Button).	CTRL+ALT+F2

CHAPTER 12

Questions

Introduction

Questions help you in revising the matter read in the various chapters.

Answer the Following Questions

Chapter 1 — Introduction to Microsoft Office 2013

1. Describe the various constituents of Microsoft Office 2013.
2. What's new in the newer version?
3. Describe how would you use the mouse?

Chapter 2 — Introduction to Microsoft Word 2013

1. Describe the various new commands of Word 2013.
2. Describe the commands under the various panels of Word 2013.

Chapter 3 — Working with a Document in Microsoft Word 2013

1. Describe the various alignments of the text in Word.
2. Describe what the red and green lines in the document signify and how you get rid of them.
3. How are Styles used? Describe.
4. Describe the process of putting Borders and Shades.
5. How do you close the Word document?
6. Describe the difference between Save and Save As commands.
7. Describe the various options of printing in Word.
8. How would you spell check the document?
9. How would you use Thesaurus?
10. What are fonts? How are they applied?
11. How would you see the preview of the document before printing?
12. What all editing tools you can use in Word?
13. Describe the working of AutoCorrect command.
14. What does the command AutoFormat do? Explain.
15. Explain how would you find a word and replace it with another in Word 2013.
16. Describe the method of putting page numbers in a Word document.
17. Describe how Header and Footer are put in the Word document.
18. What are Endnotes and Footnotes? Explain.
19. Describe how does it help by using the Split command.
20. What do you mean by tiling of the document? Explain.

Chapter 4 — Customizing Word 2013

1. Describe the various options of the following in the Options menu:

View	Save
Edit	Spell Checking and Grammar

2. Describe the various options of Page Setup.

Chapter 5 — MailMerge in Word 2013

1. Describe the process of mail merging in Word 2013.

Chapter 6 — Working with Longer Documents in Word 2013

1. What is Table of Contents? How is it created in Word?
2. Describe the method of creating index in Word.
3. What is a bookmark? How it is created in Word?
4. How would you see the thumbnail to see pages?

Chapter 7 — Working with Tables in Microsoft Word 2013

1. Describe the proces of creating a Table.
2. How would you enter the data in the table? Explain.
3. How would you insert a row or a column?
4. Describe how would you total a column in a table.
5. How would you apply Borders and Shades to a table in Word 2013?
6. Describe the method of converting Text to a Table.
7. How would you sort the data in a table in Word 2013?
8. What are nesting tables? How do you create them in Word 2013?

Chapter 8 — Working with Graphics and Charts in Word 2013

1. Describe the method of inserting graphics into the word document.
2. How can the inserted graphics in Word be cropped?
3. Describe how would you wrap the text around the graphics?
4. Descibe the working of WordArt program.
5. Which program is used for creating charts in Word 2013?
6. Descibe the process of creating a chart.
7. How would you create a chart form a table? Describe.
8. What options do you have for modifying a chart in Word 2013?

Chapter 9 — Additional Commands of Word 2013

1. Describe how would you insert a page break in a Word document in Word.
2. What all you can change by using the Change Case command?
3. Describe how would you put bullets and numbers in a word docuemtn using the Bullets and Numbering commands in Word.
4. Describe how would you create a newspaper like columnar text in Word.
5. Describe the process of putting a comment in the Word document in Word.

6. Is it possible to see the full screen of the word document? If yes, how?
7. Describe the various options of paragraph spacing and alignment in Word.
8. Describe how would you protect your document?
9. Is it possible to count the number of words in a word document? How?
10. What are Hyperlinks? How are they created in Word?

Chapter 10 — Creating Lists in Word 2013

1. How would you create a bulleted list?
2. What is the method of creating a numbered list?
3. Describe the method of Customizing Bullets
4. How are Multilevel lists created?